PLACE IN RETURN BOX to remove this checkout from your record.
TO AVOID FINES return on or before date due.
MAY BE RECALLED with earlier due date if requested.

DATE DUE	DATE DUE	DATE DUE
030501 JUN 8 2001	AUG 1 4 2012 07 29 14	
AUG 03 2001		
AUG 0 4 2002		
FEB 25 2003 0 2 4 08		
JUL 1 8 2011 05 02 11 JAN 0 4 2016		

1/98   c:/CIRC/DateDue.p65-p.14

THE PROBLEM OF CONTEXT

Methodology and History in Anthropology

General Editor: David Parkin, Director of the Institute of Social and Cultural Anthropology, University of Oxford

THE PROBLEM OF CONTEXT

Edited by Roy Dilley

Berghahn Books
New York • Oxford

First published in 1999 by

Berghahn Books

Editorial Offices:
55 John Street, 3rd Floor, New York, NY 10038, USA
3 NewTec Place, Magdalen Road, Oxford OX4 1RE, UK

Library of Congress Cataloging-in-Publication Data

The problem of context / edited by Roy Dilley.
    p.   cm. – (Methodology and history in anthropology ; v. 4)
Includes bibliographical references and index.
ISBN 1-57181-700-X (hardback)
ISBN 1-57181-773-5 (paperback)
    1. Ethnology – Philosophy. 2. Ethnology – Methodology.
3. Context (Linguistics). 4. Cultural relativism. I. Dilley, Roy.
II. Series.
GN345.P75 1999   99-35007
306'.01 – dc21   CIP

British Library Cataloguing in Publication Data

A catalogue record for this book is available from the British Library.

Printed in the United States on acid-free paper.

20014545

———

CONTENTS

NOTES ON CONTRIBUTORS

ROY DILLEY is Senior Lecturer in Social Anthropology at the University of St Andrews. He has a range of publications relating to his fieldwork in Senegal and in Northern Ireland. He has interests in language and cultural discourse, and is editor of *Contesting Markets: Analyses of Ideology, Discourse and Practice* (1992).

JOHANNES FABIAN holds the Chair of Cultural Anthropology at the University of Amsterdam. He has published widely within anthropology, and his most recent books include *Remembering the Present: Painting and Popular History in Zaire* (1996), and *Moments of Freedom: Anthropology and Popular Culture* (1998).

PENELOPE HARVEY is Senior Lecturer in Social Anthropology at the University of Manchester. She has worked in the Peruvian Andes and at Expo '92 in Seville, and is author of *Hybrids of Modernity: Anthropology, the Nation-State and the Universal Exhibition* (1996). She is also completing a book on politics and bilingualism in Peru.

SÁNDOR HERVEY was Reader in Linguistics in the Department of Social Anthropology at the University of St Andrews. His main publications include *Semiotic Perspectives* (1982), and more recently a series of texts in collaboration with others: *Thinking Translation* (1992) and companion volumes for German and Spanish translation in 1995.

MARK HOBART is Senior Lecturer in Social Anthropology at the School of Oriental and African Studies, London. Since 1970 he has conducted a total of seven years fieldwork in Bali. He has interests in philosophical issues in anthropology and, increasingly, in mass media in Asia. He is also Head of the Media Research Group at SOAS.

LADISLAV HOLY was Professor in Social Anthropology at the University of St Andrews. During his career he carried out extensive fieldwork in the Czech Republic, Sudan and Zambia. His major publications include *Actions, Norms and Representations* (1983), *Kinship, Honour and Solidarity* (1989), *Religion and Custom in a Muslim Society* (1991), and *The Little Czech and the Great Czech Nation* (1996).

BRIAN MORRIS teaches Anthropology at Goldsmiths College, University of London. He has published books and articles on a wide range of topics and issues, and his latest work includes *Ecology and Anarchism* (1996), *Chewa Medical Botany* (1996), and *The Power of Animals* (1998).

RUTH PRINCE is a Research Associate, Department of Social Anthropology, University of St Andrews. She has conducted fieldwork in Glastonbury, England and is co-author (with David Riches) of *The New Age in Glastonbury: the Construction of a Religious Movement* (forthcoming).

NIGEL RAPPORT is Professor of Anthropological and Philosophical Studies at the University of St Andrews. He has conducted fieldwork in England, Newfoundland and Israel, and has authored a number of books including *The Prose and the Passion: Anthropology, Literature and the Writing of E. M. Forster* (1994), and *Transcendent Individual: Essays Towards a Literary and Liberal Anthropology* (1997).

DAVID RICHES is Senior Lecturer in Social Anthropology at the University of St Andrews. He has conducted fieldwork among the Inuit of Canada, and is author of *Northern Nomadic Hunter-Gatherers* (1982). He is also editor of *Anthropology of Violence* (1986), and co-author (with Ruth Prince) of *The New Age in Glastonbury: the Construction of a Religious Movement* (forthcoming).

ELŻBIETA TABAKOWSKA is Professor of Linguistics at the Institute of English, Jagiellonian University of Kraków. A praticising translator and specialist in cognitive linguistics, she has published widely, including *Cognitive Linguistics and Poetics of Translation* (1993).

PREFACE

This book arises from the sixth conference or workshop in Social Anthropology organised at the University of St Andrews. The previous meetings in this series, all of which were conceived by members of the St Andrews Department, have each generated important contributions to social anthropological theory and practice with respect to such topics as comparison, power and knowledge, violence, traditions of ethnographic writing, and the free market. The sixth workshop on the theme of interpretation and context took place in January 1994, involving a group of around 20 scholars from a number of different academic disciplines and from institutions within and outwith Britain. The disciplines represented were Social Anthropology, Linguistics and Philosophy, each of which addresses the question of context in one form or another. Social Anthropology and Linguistics share a series of common concerns about context, and indeed each has drawn on the other in the development of the concept. Contextualism in Philosophy is frequently discussed as an issue connected with relativism, another issue of relevance to Social Anthropology.

This resulting thematic volume collects together those papers of immediate anthropological interest, with the aim of presenting a focused set of chapters that touches on issues common to both anthropology and linguistics. The selection was made with a view to enabling the volume to achieve a greater coherence and integrity, reflecting the developments of, and influences on, the idea of context within a broad domain of anthropological interest. Interpretative anthropology is one of the main exponents of contextualism in social anthropology, and it is this approach that forms one of the main points of departure for this book.

Stress on context in interpretation is a distinguishing feature of social anthropology. Phenomena are illuminated by appeal to their surroundings; but these surroundings themselves are selected and interpreted in different ways. These differences are relevant to what is seen as problematic and to what counts as explanation. The apparently simple notion that it is contextualisation and the invocation of context that give form to our interpretations raises important questions about context definition.

Two key terms of social anthropological methodology are, therefore, mutually implicated in this investigation: interpretation and context. Each of these terms perhaps deserves a separate dedicated volume; indeed, an exhaustive discussion of either of them could well exceed the bounds of any one work. One way in which I have chosen to frame the problem of context and its related term 'interpretation' is to think of them both in terms of 'connection'. To interpret is to make a connection. Context too involves making connections and, by implication, disconnections. An object is set in context, connected by relevant relations to its surroundings. This book attempts to view kinds of connections analysts and others make in their interpretations and contextualisations.

This book points to the problem that the concept of context has received perhaps less attention than is due such a central, key concept in social anthropology. The chapters here address the way in which context is often treated as a 'given' or a self-evident construct, and they consider how analysts interpret contexts and then contextualise interpretations. The objective of the book overall is not to reiterate the view that interpretation is context-dependent, but to start from the recognition that context is itself problematic, and is the result of prior interpretation.

Some recent literature has suggested fertile lines of enquiry into context – Mark Hobart's body of work and Marilyn Strathern's contributions within social anthropology are particularly pertinent and suggestive here – and there have also been parallel developments in neighbouring disciplines. This volume aims to draw some of these developments together and to build upon them. It also attempts to achieve the synthesis of a dialogue that began with the St Andrews workshop. What is proposed is an investigation of the kinds of connection made by those claiming that particular types of context are relevant to their analyses. A sense of self-critical reflection by analysts on the problem of context was thus sought.

This reflection upon contexts is given an extra dimension by the participation in this dialogue of other members of disciplines. Different disciplines involved in the interpretation of phenomena construe contexts in different ways. These procedures are thrown into relief through a comparative inter-disciplinary perspective. Comparison can be achieved, moreover, not only by considering other disciplinary practices, but also by attending to the interpretative practices of people situated in different places and in different cultures. This volume asks how do these ways differ? What analytical and even political strategies are adopted in order to suggest that the relevant context is 'self-evident'?

Hermeneuts and philosophers have recently discussed transformations in the hermeneutic context, such as Gayle Ormiston and Alan Schrift's collection *Transforming the Hermeneutic Context*. What lessons, which might be pertinent to our own investigations, can be learned from their reflections? Similarly, the recent work by Duranti and Goodwin entitled *Rethinking Context* (CUP 1992) deals with problems of context in relation to linguistics, pragmatics, and the ethnography of speaking and performance. The concept of context has been progressively transformed through its movement back and forth between linguistics and social anthropology. What can be learned by social anthropologists from the present state of the exchange between these two neighbouring traditions? What the Duranti and Goodwin volume does not seek to address, however, is the problem of context in interpretative anthropology.

The problem of interpretation in social anthropology constitutes one of the central foci of this volume. Geertzian interpretive anthropology is one among a broad stream of interpretative approaches, and Geertz draws particularly heavily on literary and textual models. The kinds of connections suggested by such literary metaphors need close inspection, and this task brings us to consider forms of literary criticism and cultural studies which have focused on the subject of interpretative contexts.

This book is about the 'life of connections' - in the guise of interpretation and context - that are pertinent to forms of analysis within social anthropology. The Introduction plots the conditions for such a life of connections, and it traces some of the movements and transformations this life has undergone in the displacement of the problem of context from one discipline to another. Many of the chapters contained here focus on the performative character of the act of contextualising, the way in which people are caught or framed in the process of making or construing contexts, interpretations and meanings for themselves. Their 'contextualising moves', or the ways in which their subject matter is ordered, are examined below. Contextualising is a form of social action, and a very particular form too. It is first and foremost a discursive strategy, a mode of articulation that can be detailed within specific analyses and particular disciplines. This perspective, from the vantage point of discourse, entails at least a temporary epoché, a momentary suspense of judgement, a bracketing off or a withholding of assent or dissent with regard to the truth claims of any specific form of contextualisation. This suspension in the short term allows not only for the thorough examination of the discursive forms of contextualisation, but also for a view of contextualisation as a social practice and not as a transparent claim to truth.

The examination suggested here demands attention to two related problems of context. The first aspect takes context as part of a set of methodological and epistemological problems in social anthropology itself. Analysts claim to place phenomena in context; sometimes they are accused of taking things out of context. What is entailed in these analytical processes? How do we make the distinction between being in and out of context? In short, how have social anthropologists construed as relevant the contexts they deploy in their analyses?

This question is almost as large as the discipline itself. In order to limit it to a relatively manageable size, the book focuses primarily on interpretative approaches within social anthropology. The second aspect of the problem of context is to extend an examination of context construction to an appreciation of the acts of interpretation and contextualisation that those whom we study claim for themselves. The goal within interpretative anthropology has been to seek definitive native meanings for social practices, symbols, concepts and so on. In the process, however, it has perhaps for too long superimposed our own conceptions of what interpretation is about and what the appropriate contexts of native practice might be. It has thereby overlooked how contexts might be construed by local social agents with respect to the definitions, negotiations and contestations of meaning within situated contextualising practices. The present work does not suggest a short cut to definitive native meanings by some new magic which the anthropological contextualiser might weave with a superior wand of context. Instead, it suggests that they, like us, are involved at various times in the active pursuit of meanings and the drawing of relevant contexts for their explanations. The call is made here, then, for more attention to be paid to the contextualising practices and to the framing of significances relative to both our own analytical (and local) as well as their own local (and analytical) accounts of the world. These two related aspects to the problem of context can be subsumed under the gloss of the *knowledge of context*.

While knowledge of context implies a series of problems for consideration, the issue of *contexts of knowledge* gives onto another set of enquiries. Our own anthropological knowledge is obviously implicated in the construction of those contexts we regard as relevant to particular problems - these problems are themselves a function of our knowledge systems. The construction of contexts is therefore intimately connected with how we conceive of knowledge, and this fact must, therefore, have consequences for how we conceive of what contexts might or might not be appropriate for the analysis of other people's practices. If the idea holds that contextualising is a very specific form of social practice — as a discursive, expressive and performative type — then the kinds of knowledge claims behind this type of practice need inspecting. This is an enormous issue with far-reaching implications for social anthropology.

There is no unified voice with which all the contributors speak nor a single message that can be expressed as a concluding view. Each of the contributors, however, does share a commitment to regard the problem of context reflexively and to be alert to the processes by which their claims for interpretative contexts are made. The function of the Introduction that follows is to provide some kind of historical and 'transdisciplinary' context for the appreciation of the chapters that comprise this book. It also addresses the much-discussed crisis in social anthropology with a view to inspect the 'a-contextual' claims of some contemporary theorists.

The idea for this workshop emerged in early 1991 in discussion between Ladislav Holy and me during the course of a postgraduate forum in Saarbrücken, Germany. Confronted by the problem of explaining the hermeneutic circle to a group of postgraduate students, we chanced upon the idea of context as an appropriate issue for a contemporary re-examination in social anthropology. This historical context to the development of the idea for the workshop is pertinent in that the project was conceived as much by Ladislav Holy as by me. More poignantly, in the passage of time since the organisation of the workshop and the subsequent publication of this set of contributions, Ladislav Holy died. His death in April 1997 was a great loss not only to this project as originally conceived (and undoubtedly to the form of this present publication) but also to the wider community of social anthropology. In response, it was decided that this publication should stand in memory of, and as a testament to, his life-time's work. Indeed the problem of context is implicit in much of his writing, and it is made the explicit object of discussion in a number of parts of specific publications.[1] It is perhaps fitting, therefore, that this book on the problem of context should be dedicated to his life and work.

One further sad note is that Sándor Hervey, a much-appreciated colleague and friend in the St Andrews Social Anthropology Department, died suddenly in July 1997. His workshop paper, along with Ladislav's, is included in this volume as part of the continuing debate between linguists and social anthropologists about what context is all about. The Department at St Andrews has felt deeply both of these losses.

With this dedication in mind, two other anthropologists who are closely associated with social anthropology at St Andrews took up the invitation to submit papers not previously presented at the workshop for inclusion in this volume. I thank both David Riches and Nigel Rapport for their subsequent contributions. The absence of Johannes Fabian from the workshop proceedings was sorely felt, and I thank him for allowing his then unpublished paper to be circulated to all participants for discussion at our meeting.

As convenor of the workshop, I must thank warmly a number of organisations and people who lent all manner of help and assistance that secured the success of the meeting. First, invaluable financial support was provided by the following institutions: The Aristotelian Society, The British Academy, the Gibson-Sykora Fund, Mind, the Philosophical Quarterly, the Royal Anthropological Institute, and the John Wright Trust. Without their help in providing funds, the workshop would never have taken place. I thank them all for their generosity. To Peter Clark, John Haldane, Stephen Read, Roger Squires, and Leslie Stevenson — philosophers all from St Andrews — and to Pascal Engel, Timothy O'Hagan, Rik Pinxten, Tristan Platt, Narahari Rao, and Julia Tanney, I am extremely grateful for their guidance, support and valuable contributions to discussion. Richard Fardon and John Skorupski acted as rapporteurs at the workshop, and I thank them both for their efforts and dedication to the task.

Numerous members of staff and students gave unselfishly of their time and energy in contributing to aspects of the organisation of the workshop. I warmly acknowledge their support, and I would especially like to mention Bambi Ceuppens, Barry Reeves, Maggie Bolton, and the then Departmental Secretary, Mrs Pam Lee. Lastly, my appreciation and thanks are extended to Andrew Whitehouse who has assisted with the preparation of the manuscript for publication and in compiling an index.

Roy Dilley
St Andrews
October 1998

Note

1. *See* for example his *Comparative anthropology* (1987), *Kinship, honour and solidarity* (1989), 'Culture, cognition and practical interaction' (1990), *Religion and custom in a Muslim society* (1991), and *The little Czech and the great Czech nation* (1996); *see* also his collaborative work with M. Stuchlik: *The structure of folk models* (1981), and *Actions, norms and representations* (1983). Full bibliographic citations can be found in the references cited to the Introduction.

THE PROBLEM OF CONTEXT

Roy Dilley

Why Context?[1]

Context is one of the central concepts of social anthropology. It is one of the distinctive features of the discipline and it is relied upon as an indispensable part of anthropological method. Despite the importance of context to social anthropology – and the fact that it has been so central for so long – it is surprising to find how little attention has been given to the topic over the history of the discipline. Of late, a number of key articles and chapters have emerged which have begun to address this central issue of methodological and theoretical importance.[2] This collection of essays is an attempt to draw together some of these recent threads of discussion and to synthesise some of these developments into a single volume.

Ever since Malinowski, anthropologists have chanted the mantra of 'placing social and cultural phenomena in context', an analytical strategy adopted to throw light on, and indeed make some sort of authentic sense of, ethnographic material. This process has had an all too self-evident ring to it; it is a process that has been seen as unproblematic. We should appeal, conventional wisdom has it, to features and characteristics surrounding a phenomenon in order to illuminate it and to understand or give sense to it. The idea is that anthropologists who interpret social and cultural phenomena do so with reference, therefore, to something called 'context'. This apparently simple notion that it is contextualisation that gives form to our interpretations raises important questions about what a context is, how it is defined and selected, and by whom. An implicit parallel can be seen here with linguistics and philosophy, some branches of which have argued that the meaning of a word is determined by the words and sentences that surround it, and vice versa. Context has been treated accordingly, as self-evident, as a given attribute in the world, something that is stable, clear and sufficient, and not requiring any qualification of its own. Fabian refers in his chapter to the 'positivity of context'.[3]

The essays in this volume do not simply reiterate the view that interpretation is context-dependent; but they start from the recognition that context is itself problematic, indeed the result of prior interpretation. Hobart discusses what he calls 'pre-interpretation', as well as 'post-interpretation' of phenomena. Context is, therefore, part of the problem of the way in which anthropologists interpret the rules of interpretation (see Parkin 1995). One of the difficulties in handling a topic such as context is that it is linked in our conception of things to other equally problematic analytical concepts such as 'meaning' and 'interpretation'. Hobart (1982) has tackled a number of important concerns surrounding the conception of 'meaning' in social anthropology, and in this volume he turns his attention to the question of interpretation itself.[4]

If there is a problem in delimiting the extent of the domain indicated by 'context', one possible line of approach is to think of context in terms of 'connection'. The act of interpreting has been described as the act of creating connections; that to interpret is to make a connection (Ormiston and Schrift 1990). Context too involves making connections and, by implication, disconnections. A phenomenon is connected to its surroundings: contexts are sets of connections construed as relevant to someone, to something or to a particular problem, and this process yields an explanation, a sense, an interpretation for the object so connected. The context or frame also creates a disjunction between the object of interest and its surroundings on the one hand, and those features which are excluded and deemed as irrelevant on the other. Another means of fixing a stable foothold on the problem of context is to frame context as an object of investigation, the subject of analysis itself – making context into an 'analysand', to use Hervey's term. This is one of the major themes of the volume: contributors have taken Wittgenstein's advice – himself a great contextualising philosopher in his later work – and have not sought to 'ask for the meaning' of context, but have sought instead to 'ask for the use' of the concept.

The purpose of this collection is to review the problem of context from a number of perspectives within social anthropology, not to suggest another meaning or definition for the appropriate or relevant context for the discipline in the late 1990s. The volume draws together some of the important recent contributions to debates about context, not only in social anthropology but in neighbouring disciplines too. It aims to push these debates further, and to highlight their relevance for anthropological analysis in itself.

Scharfstein, a philosopher, gives the following definition of context, which can be used as a point of departure rather than as one of fixity or conclusion. Context is 'that which environs the object of interest and helps by its relevance to explain it' (1989: 1). Worthy as this is, it leaves as much unsaid as it does clarify: for how is relevance to be formulated and what constitutes an explanation? Fardon (1985) has pointed out, for instance, that our sense of relevance is linked to our theoretical stance towards the world. Over the history of social anthropology, different features or characteristics have been conceived to be relevant or to surround (and be connected with) a phenomenon. These differences are referred to as theoretical shifts in the discipline (from function to meaning; from structure to process), and each movement appeals to a new sense or definition of context, namely of that which environs our object of study and how it is relevant to it. These shifts in the definition of what comprises relevant contexts is one way of thinking about paradigm shifts in the discipline. Holy describes this process and specifically what was entailed in the shift from structural-functionalism to semantic and interpretative approaches in an earlier stage of social anthropological theory. He tries to alert us to something Scharfstein observes: 'we are much more aware of contexts in practice than in theory' (1989: 3), and this is certainly the case for anthropological theory and practice. The paradigm shifts Holy discusses might be seen as new ways of making connections by means of a new context where once only disconnection and disjunction were perceived.

The importance of context as an analytical device is highlighted with regard to perspectives in social anthropology that emphasise the analogy depicting society or culture as a text. One of the most transparent exemplars of this approach is Geertz's interpretive anthropology, a methodology that explicitly develops the textual paradigm (1973). Context is, then, a device in this perspective by means of which anthropologists are able to reveal hidden meanings and deeper understandings, or to forward certain kinds of interpretation and particular forms of explanation. I will in due course below attempt a brief review of some of the key formulations of context in social anthropology, and particularly the way in which our subject has drawn on and been influenced by developments in neighbouring disciplines, such as philosophy, linguistics and literary studies. The problem of context should be a 'transdisciplinary enterprise' (Strathern 1987: 268) with regard to the contributions each discipline can make to the problem, and the way each thereby can become conscious of its own practices.

I will now, however, turn to consider the word 'context' itself, as well as other terms and phrases that are deployed in a similar manner

to context. These terms and phrases suggest parallel or complementary images to that of context.

On the Word 'Context'

The etymology of the word 'context' suggests a derivation from the
Latin verb *texere*, 'to weave'. The related Latin verb *contexere* carries the
meaning of 'to weave together', 'to interweave', 'to join together' or 'to
compose' (*The Shorter Oxford English Dictionary*).[5] Obsolete meanings of
the word, therefore, range from 'the weaving together of words and
sentences, and literary composition'; to 'the connection or coherence
between parts of a discourse'. More contemporary meanings suggest
'the parts which immediately precede or follow a particular passage or
text and determine its meaning'. Also, figurative uses refer to 'moral
context', 'the context of a building', and so on; or they suggest a type of
connection or relationship of a general kind as in 'the circumstances
relevant to something under consideration' or 'in this connection'.

The history of usage of 'context' suggests a shift in reference of the
term from the act of composing meaningful stretches of language
either as speech or writing (as in 'to contex [sic] a history', OED) to the
conditions of understanding a stretch of language and of the possibility of determining its meaning. It initially denoted the act of composition, of bringing together parts of language into meaningful
utterances or written texts. It later took on the sense of the conditions
under which meaning is attributed to a stretch of language, and
indeed how those conditions give sense to it. From describing the act of
conjoining, the term then comes to designate the conditions shaping
that which has been conjoined. A similar sense of involution in the
concept of context in social anthropology will be seen below. The idea
of culture has become the primary context for many social anthropologists. The conception of culture, however, has been transformed from
an idea that comprises what people say, do and think to the context for
the interpretation of what people say, do and think.

The figurative senses of the term develop the notion of the environing and surrounding conditions of a specified object or phenomenon.
These conditions can again be seen either in terms of a descriptive
composition of elements – such as between a building and its physical
location – or as a set of determinations of the meaning of the object
under consideration. At its most broad, the figurative sense of context
implies a generalised set of connections thought in some way or other
to be construed as relevant to the object or event under discussion.
Connections imply disconnections; that while some things are connected via context to the object under study, others are by implication

unconnected or disconnected. Indeed, some contexts might be regarded as relevant, others might be irrelevant. If things can be 'placed in context', they must by implication be found 'out of context' (see Strathern 1987 and Fardon 1995). What is left out of account, seen as irrelevant or disconnected can be, in other definitions of relevance or context, brought into the picture.

The contemporary broadening of the figurative sense of context links its usage to other kinds of metaphorical figure. Context as that which environs an object suggests a range of synonyms such as environment, milieu, setting and background (see Scharfstein 1989). Each of these re-figurings of context brings with it its own associations. Many of the images that such synonyms formulate are of a spatial or geographical kind. The spatial and, moreover, pictorial image is highlighted in the concept of 'frame' developed by Bateson (1973) and Goffman (1974); or again in the image of figure and ground from Gestalt theory. Here is suggested the image of an object of aesthetic appreciation contained within fixed boundaries or lines of demarcation of a frame or field of vision. The effect that boundaries can have in figure-ground configurations is profound, such that the same outline can be perceived as different alternating shapes as the figure alternates in our perception with the ground. The frame is, therefore, as much part of the ambiguous figure as what it contains. Moreover, the Gestalt analogy returns us again to the idea of context as a process or set of relations, and not as a thing in itself.

Transdisciplinary Perspectives on the Problem of Context

In the following pages I review the problem of context from different disciplinary view points. This review is intended to be neither comprehensive nor exhaustive. The purpose of moving between one discipline and another is illustrative, and I offer three reasons for it: first, to give a sense of the way in which other disciplines have construed the problem of context; second, to gain a sense of the way the problem of context in social anthropology has informed, and in turn has been informed by, the treatment of the problem elsewhere; third, to give a context to the chapters which comprise this collection. This contextualisation embraces too the historical developments and critiques of the idea within social anthropology as a whole.

Below, I look at context from a number of different disciplinary perspectives: first, from selected philosophical stances, and in particular the connection between contextualism and relativism; second, from a hermeneutical perspective; third, context in linguistics; fourth, context as seen from structuralism, post-structuralism and literary theory. I then endeavour in the subsequent sections to re-trace my steps to examine the way in which the concept of context developed in social anthropology, with reference to this earlier discussion. Against this backdrop of earlier commentary, I hope to show the borrowings and exchanges of ideas between disciplines, and the mutual influences in the intellectual developments of context as it shifts from one body of knowledge to another. Moreover, one can detect a sense of how the taken-for-granted nature of contexts of one period or academic discipline become the objects of study during a later period or with respect to other disciplinary practices.

Some Philosophical Perspectives on Contextualism[6]

Scharfstein states that 'the problem of context is too difficult for philosophers or anyone else to solve' (1989: 4). Not an optimistic start, one might observe, especially for anthropologists unfortunately classed under the catch-all category of 'anyone else'. The problem as he sees it is that it 'lays an intellectual burden on us that we cannot evade but that can become so heavy that it destroys the understanding it is meant to further' (1989: xi). While not perhaps being able to solve the problem, one can at least alert its users to its potential effects and addictive qualities. Moreover, the solving of high-order philosophical problems is not anthropology's forte (nor is it mine). What is, however, is social anthropology's focus on the study of use and the deployment of concepts as part of social practice, indeed as part of a discursive exchange or form of articulation.

Gellner discusses the 'unresolved dilemma', still present in social anthropology today, between 'a relativistic-functionalist view and the absolutist claims of enlightened reason' (1970: 31). This contrast between the relativising contextualist and the universalising absolutist is significant, although not wholly for the reasons Gellner gives. Asad criticises Gellner for treating these two 'concepts' out of context, without reference to the institutional structure and politics that accompany them; he has depoliticised them (1986: 148).[7] Claims for contextualism or for universalism are, therefore, an aspect of social practice, and involve questions of agency – as I will discuss later. Context as a concept, it would seem, is often invoked as part of an analytical strategy which stands in opposition to universalist, formalist or other generalising tendencies.[8] These approaches tend not to emphasise local, unique particularities but instead highlight more global principles of broad application and generality. Strathern points out one example of this shift in her discussion of Frazer's generalising evolutionism giving way to Malinowski's situated social analyses (1987). (I will return later to the subject of Malinowski, the father of context in British social anthropology.) Malinowski's insistence on the contemporary social context or situation for the proper understanding of phenomena led to a paradigm shift in the discipline. A similar shift took place in the United States, where Franz Boas led the challenge against comparable late nineteenth-century and early twentieth-century evolutionary theories that were universalistic in their application. He set in train a form of cultural relativism that his students, Melville Herskovits, Ruth Benedict and others, developed (*see* Scharfstein 1989: ch. 1).

Scharfstein highlights this connection between contextualism and other forms of relativism: 'Dependence on context is a kind of limited relativism, and that relativism, looked at philosophically, is hard to limit' (1989: 59). Where someone is invoking context, it would seem, someone else is proposing universals, essences, formal principles of general applicability and the like. Scharfstein makes a similar case, proposing that as two forms of philosophising, contextualism as a type of relativism is never far apart from universalism. He argues (universally?) that relativism and 'absolutism' are 'equally essential and mutually necessary', in that concepts that appear to be 'absolute' depend on relative notions for conceptual contrast in terms of their meaning as 'absolutes', and likewise, relative concepts depend on 'absolute' ones for their sense (1989: 131).

The dilemma of context for Scharfstein is that persistent contextualism leads to extreme relativity, which in his view is insupportable as a philosophical position. He states: 'the attempt to be thorough in understanding context leads to a total contextualisation, in which everything becomes the context of everything else. Such a contextualisation is equivalent to total relativity' (1989: xii-xiii). This is what he refers to as the difficulty in limiting context once it is admitted into an analysis, and is similar to what Culler, a literary critic, has called the 'unboundedness of context' (1983).

Scharfstein traces the philosophical implications of his statement, and especially the consequences of an extreme contextualist position. Not only is an extreme relativism the result, but also an extreme individualism:

> By attaching things more firmly to their contexts ... we increase our recognition of their individuality and make them more nearly unique. At the extreme limit of distinction by means of context, things should become utterly unique. (1989: 60)

Or again:

> ... the emphasis on context tends to make every event and individual essentially different from every other.... [This] leads to the essentially beguiling notion that everyone and everything is an absolute individual. (1989: xiii)

It would seem that if we press to the limits of context we pass through a sort of involution – perhaps an implosion of context – and re-appear in a world of 'absolutes' or essences. This is reminiscent of Ardener's idea of parameter collapse or 'twist', an epistemological implosion where the parameters of a problem are turned inside out (1989: 150). According to this view, that which provided the 'shell' or context collapses, so that now the context becomes the new problem and the old problem or contents become the new 'shell' or context. This kind of 'twist' occurs in anthropology with what I refer to later as the development of a new individualistic 'self-essentialism'. With this transformation we witness a collapse of parameters: where the individual was once put into cultural or historical context for the purpose of interpretation, now cultural contexts become a function of an essential individual, the source of all interpretation. This line of argument is developed by Rapport and to some extent by Prince and Riches. It is a view challenged here by Hobart and Morris (*see* also Morris 1991), among others.

Wittgenstein

The work of Wittgenstein on language, developed in its two stages from the *Tractatus Logico-Philosophicus* (1922) to *Philosophical Investigations* (1958), embodies the two tendencies outlined above – the formal and abstracted versus the contextual and relational.[9] The first work develops the idea of language as a formal system in an abstract account focusing on factual statements and discourse. It proposes a version of correspondence theory in which language can be linked through its reference to the external world. The second work is more concerned with language use, presenting language as part of human life. Language is now seen as a form of action that is multiple, variegated and multifaceted, such that the same utterance when uttered as parts of different types of activity and in different situations can come to have quite different meanings. A form of contextualism is therefore involved, and it can be compared to the abstract formalism of the earlier work. This contextualism encompasses the language games in which humans engage: the way two people come to an agreement about the meaning of a word when they see that they agree in their applications of it. Contact and social exchange between the two parties maintains the meaning of the word in the public life they live together, namely a 'form of life'. Language, language users and the social world of exchange and interaction are all bound up in the contexts of language games and forms of life. It is with respect to this later work that he gave his oft-quoted advice: 'don't ask for meaning, ask for the use'.

Wittgenstein's contextual theory of language is regarded by philosophers as a version of relativism, which posits a multiplicity of language games and cultural forms of life, each with its own criteria for what counts as valid and meaningful (Honderich 1995: 758). Social anthropology with its claims for the relevance of context must be seen in this respect as embodying a form of relativism.

Dilemmas and Relativisms

The dilemma of context, which Scharfstein points to, can also be read as the dilemma of social anthropology caught between the Scylla of contextual relativism and the Charybdis of 'extreme sameness and objectivity'. The intellectual dilemma at the heart of the discipline involves one in which anthropologists have conventionally claimed priority for one of two mutually opposed analytical possibilities: first, that it should explore the essential unity of human beings (the 'psychic unity of mankind', or the embodiment of universal mind or meaning-making or rational calculation); second, it should explore the uniqueness of each culture and society in its own terms, leading to a kind of relativism (*see* Herzfeld 1987: 13). The mutual necessity and implication of relativism and universalism creates a theoretical dialectic that is the motor of disciplinary debate. (See for example the motion debated at one of the early GDAT meetings as to whether social anthropology is a generalising science, Ingold [1996].) While pointing out the dilemmas associated with context, Scharfstein does nonetheless argue for the impossibility of absolute truth; indeed, he suggests that since no external source of adjudication can be brought in to give one vision priority over the other, he personally finds a greater sense of adventure and exhilaration in the pursuit of contextualism (1989: 192). This is reminiscent of Hobart's dictum that 'anthropology is our one chance of escaping the sheer tedium of our own thought' (1982: 58). What needs to be emphasised is that, from our own philosophical background, contextualism and its contraries are linked in a discourse of mutual implication, such that to propose one presupposes the other. It is an empirical question open to investigation whether they are or are not linked in other philosophical traditions.

Hobart examines the problem of context in relation to competing philosophical stances about the nature of truth and meaning (1985: 36). A contrast is drawn between correspondence or referential theories of language and meaning, and coherence theories. The former suggest that the meaning of language inheres in its reference to the world, and 'it presupposes the existence of an essence in things, events or states' (1986a: 16), such that truth comprises a correspondence between language and facts. The second, coherence theory suggests that truth or falsity inheres in whether a statement coheres or not within a system of other statements; that is, the meaning of language is suggested with reference not to the world but to other things which have been said or expressed.[10] Coherence theory, Hobart argues,

underwrites many brands of contextualism (1985 and 1986a).
Where correspondence theory searches for essences of meaning, contextualism he points out implies a focus on relationships. This contrast
of contextualism with essentialism is elaborated upon in Hobart's
1986b chapter,[11] where he concludes that these two strategies are
only two of four 'commonly used ways of structuring and interpreting
material' (1986b: 150). Moreover, the two modes of analysis are
mutually implicated parts of a range of political strategies used by
Balinese to make sense of the world. Here again, contextualism is one
discursive option among many. And moreover, contextualism can be
seen as merely one form of what he calls a 'contextualising move', a
strategy or practice of an agent who seeks to structure material in a
particular way (1985: 49).

I retain this idea as a fundamentally important concept in the
analysis of context. Indeed, it could be suggested that any claim to
impose order upon the world, either in the form of contextualism, universalism, absolutism or whatever, is a contextualising move seeking
to structure and give some kind of meaning to things. Furthermore,
any agent who makes such a claim can be situated in time and in
space, relative to other social agents and other discourses. All contextualising moves can be situated, therefore, in terms of their agents of
expression.[12] I turn my attention now to some of the contextualising
moves that philosophers make.

Relativism, unlike context, has inspired a great deal of philosophical discussion, Scharfstein points out (1989: 4), and this leads anthropologists into the choppy waters of high-order philosophical debate. A
claim for contextualism has, perhaps, a less provocative ring to it than
relativism, for even the arch contextualist Geertz falls short of endors-
ing unhesitatingly a full-blown relativist stance, but instead attacks its
contrary – anti-relativism.[13] It is perhaps timely to dust off the term
and specify what it commits one to in its various forms.[14]

Epistemological relativism in its full-bloodied form eschews the very
idea of an uninterrupted reality that is independent of us or of some
scheme of understanding.[15] At the level of a type of 'true-for-me' relativism, this has in the opinion of some commentators 'so little to recommend it that its popularity ... is truly astonishing' (Honderich
1995: 757). Extreme epistemological relativism has to confront the
problem, moreover, of the status of relativism as truth. In a less
extreme form 'the rhetoric of relativism draws our attention for a need
for a conceptual framework to interpret reality', without necessarily
denying that there is a reality to be understood (ibid.). Ethical relativism commits one to less, since it argues that moral and ethical codes
are related to the practices and norms accepted by a social group in a
specific place and time, and a vast body of anthropological evidence

supports such a view of cultural diversity. The question of 'incommensurability' arises, the complete absence of common concepts or perspectives, as the limiting condition of this position. (*See* Overing 1985 for a discussion of possible 'bridgeheads'.)

Hollis and Lukes raise the problem of what relativism is supposed to be relative to; relativism is 'relative to what?', they ask (1982: 11). They provide five answers with reference to the problem of the relativity of belief, and these answers turn out to be something very similar to the contexts anthropologists routinely deploy. They are: (1) the natural environment; (2) human equipment with which we perceive or reflect – our psychological or cognitive make-up; (3) social context; (4) language; and (5) a form-of-life, an 'all-embracing context'. Framing anthropological analyses in terms of a natural environment gives all manner of cultural ecological and materialist explanations, whereas those cast in terms of human psychological equipment suggest versions of cognitive anthropology. The contexts of the social and cultural, of language and of forms of life – conceived as all-embracing historical, discursive or ideological forms – are well known to anthropologists. A relativism that is specified becomes simply a particular form of contextualism, with which we are familiar. Relativism specified is contextualism particularised.

Anti-contextualists of whatever hue must face, however, the problem of the way philosophies and in particular philosophers are situated in social worlds of practice. All universal claims are made by persons who are situated in time and in space, and whose claims are made in a particular language. Their claims do not float 'free of the educational and institutional patterns of the day' (Rorty quoted in Hollis and Lukes [1982: 5]). Collingwood too in *An Essay on Philosophical Method* requires philosophy to account for itself and to scrutinise philosophical thought 'as a special kind of fact' (1933: 4) such that the activity of philosophising is to be seen as 'a datum to philosophy' (ibid: 174). The philosopher, he argues, works within particular contexts made up of 'his own experiences and that of other people' (ibid: 164), and that we should read his or her work like that of a poet, to see it as an 'expression of an individual experience, something which the writer has actually lived through' (ibid: 215). The anti-contextualist vision tries to cut itself free from such chains of context; but their claims can never be so divorced from experience, practice and the history and sociology of knowledge.

Anthropology is caught on the horns of a dilemma, impaled on the horn of contextualism and on the horn of universalism or essentialism – which mirrors Scharfstein's dilemma of context. This view is also perceived by Herzfeld gazing at *Anthropology through the looking glass* (1987), a discipline positing an essential unity of humanity as well as the uniqueness of each culture. What has been considered to be the essential unity of humankind (from psychic unity to meaning-making, from rational calculation to rational intellection) has changed radically in the course of the history of social anthropology. Anthropology's universalisms seem particular to its historical context. Anthropology retains, however, a methodological relativism, or what Jackson calls 'practical relativism'. This involves a 'suspension of inquiry into the divine or objective truth of particular customs' (1996: 10), and instead explores them as an aspect of lived human experience. This idea draws on a modified version of Husserl's concept of epoché, a suspense of judgement, a withholding of assent or dissent, a kind of scepticism regarding the world. In this sense, the word is stripped of its phenomenological associations with a transcendental ego and the primacy of perceptual consciousness, and instead becomes a practical attitude adopted in the face of fieldwork encounters.

The Directions of Contextualising Moves

The idea of the suspension of judgement, a rhetorical stance in the face of proclaimed certainties, is the spirit that needs to be adopted in considering the issue of contextualising moves undertaken in the course of analysis. It is not the results of any particular analysis that are important for the moment, nor its claims to truth or certainty. Instead, it is the directions of the contextualising moves that an analysis makes that is now the focus.

A distinction can be made between the directions that specific contextualising moves take an analysis. We have seen, following Hobart that, for example, theories of meaning involve either a relation between language and the world or a relation between types of statement, utterance, expression and so on. In this latter, meaning refers to how a statement coheres with other statements or expressions. One form of contextualising, in the broadest sense of the term, creates an *external context*, a connection between one domain of phenomena (language) and another (the world). The other form of contextualising creates an *internal context*, whereby a connection is made not with things outside of the object of enquiry, but internal to it, such that meaning involves the internal connections within language. These terms have been coined by numerous commentators at various times (*see* for example Hobart 1982, Hervey) and they form an important way of thinking about how contextualising moves are directed.[16] Indeed, the distinction plays an important role in many of the chapters which follow.

Another way philosophers talk about meaning, for example, is as a function of the relation between language and the mind. This possibility opens up a third direction for the analytical movement of contextualising. This is referred to as 'psychologism', and it involves a shift in attention in the study of meaning from the relationship between signs and the things they signify in the world towards a focus on the minds of sign-users and their intentions as inner states.[17] The mind, it could be suggested, becomes a particular kind of context that environs the object of study (here, meaning), and can be referred to as *psychological* or *mental* context.[18]

Rapport in chapter 8 holds in an analytical relationship the workings of the human mind and the world, such that the encounter between the two results in the creation of 'existential contexts', contexts of a 'personal provenance'. His analysis is founded initially upon work by Bertrand Russell, a contextualist in one strand of his writings with reference to 'incomplete symbols', but a 'cognitivist' in another which tackled the problem of knowledge of the external world in terms of a theory of 'logical atomism'.[19] Interested in the point of contact between mind and matter, Russell sets in motion a series of doubts about how we know about things that purport to live outside our minds. Russell's phenomenalism proposes, then a sceptical relationship between the contents of the mind, sense-data, and the doubted external objects of the world. This view of 'mind as context' was developed in a more extreme version by eighteenth-century philosopher Berkeley, who argued against Locke's championing of the achievements of seventeenth-century science, which posited an external world with a system of bodies. Berkeley argued that an observer can only be aware of his or her own ideas, and thus can never make contact with anything outside his or her own mind. Mind, in this most extreme form of idealism, therefore, is the only 'context' for explanation. Moreover, it is an approach that is disengaged from the world of social practice and human interaction and, as the basis for a discipline engaged in empirical participatory fieldwork, it might be seen to have little to recommend it.

This kind of analytical movement as a form of extreme contextualisation, which is highlighted by Scharfstein (1989) and discussed above, has its own failings in making every thing unique and everyone an 'absolute individual' (1989: xiii). Berkeley takes us through the 'implosion of contextualisation' where in its extreme form contextualism eventually gives on to a form of universalism or absolutism, in this case in the shape of the human mind. Rapport, in his analysis, however, draws back from taking us through that particular involution and points to another direction, to the external contexts of English dales' life in Wanet, which are the result, he would argue, of an overlap between individuals' existential contexts.

This discussion has suggested that a distinction might usefully be made between the kind of directions undertaken during the contextualising moves made by analysts. These moves involve the systematic ordering and structuring of material in the search for an interpretation or explanation. Contexts can be *external* by pointing to a different domain of phenomena or order of existence to the one under study, or they can be *internal* in the sense of being contained within a closed system of like entities (*see* Hervey). A third kind of direction is developed which points towards cognitive, psychological and mental domains (*see* Rapport and Tabakowska). Contextualising is an act of making connections, but the direction in which those connections are made are often quite specific. They might give on to, for example, a discrete external world, or on to an inner domain of 'the mind'. (It is possible to envisage as well different directions for contextualisation within different metaphysical systems and other philosophical traditions. Indeed, the spatial metaphors of inside and outside might not be pertinent to other systems of knowledge.) Connections made with one domain imply a series of disconnections with another: contexts not only include certain phenomena as relevant, they exclude others as marginal or put them out of the picture altogether.

I have not only reviewed in the above some of the philosophical implications of anthropological contextualism, but also looked at some of its alternatives or opposing views. These alternative perspectives must also been seen as types of contextualising that have their own particular direction or trajectory, and their practitioners can be situated once, following Collingwood's advice, philosophy is regarded as a special kind of fact and as a form of social action. I now turn to a particular branch of philosophical endeavour, hermeneutics.

Context in Hermeneutics

Hermeneutics, interpretation or the art of interpretation, emerged as an important perspective during the Reformation which demanded precise procedures for the accurate interpretation of the Bible. A philosophical tradition that runs from the Protestant theologian Schleiermacher through Dilthey to its more contemporary exponents Heidegger, Gadamer and Ricoeur, hermeneutics is concerned with the interpretation of texts and human understanding (*see* Palmer 1969). Palmer talks of the 'double focus of hermeneutics', on the theory of understanding in a general sense on the one hand, and on the hermeneutical exegesis of linguistic texts on the other (1968: 67).

One issue that has remained central to the hermeneutic project is the concept of the 'hermeneutic circle', a relation of part to whole. Palmer gives the following definition:

> We understand the meaning of an individual word by seeing it in reference to the whole sentence; and reciprocally, the sentence's meaning as a whole is dependent on the meaning of the individual words. (1968: 87)

He then broadens its scope:

> By extension, an individual concept derives its meaning from the context or horizon within which it stands; yet the horizon is made up of the very elements to which it gives meaning. (1968: 87)

The hermeneutic circle points to the circularity of all human understanding and to the problems that arise in the process of interpretation.[20] Indeed, the theme of this present collection is to emphasise the fact that interpretation in context requires the pre-interpretation of the relevant context, that in turn informs the subsequent interpretation. This is a reworking of the idea of the hermeneutic circle. For Ricoeur, the problem is that to understand a text one must understand the context, and to understand the context one must first understand the text. Hobart's critique of Ricoeur is that his 'focus on text tends to de-centre context, and to encourage the search for something essential rather than a plurality of views' (1985: 44). Context descends in hermeneutic theory, he states, as 'the deus ex machina to resolve the seemingly intractable problems of meaning' (1982: 47, a point developed by Hervey with respect to context in linguistics). The effect of this ghost in the machine, Hervey proposes, is 'to explain the unexplained by the inexplicable'.

The hermeneutics of Heidegger lead us in a slightly different direction.[21] Context is not something that simply illuminates the text or vice versa. Heidegger develops a different sense of interpretation and hence of what is the relevant context for his analyses. He is concerned in *Being and Time* with 'the interpretation of the being who interprets texts and other artefacts' (Honderich 1995: 353). Understanding this sense of being (*Dasein*) is 'like interpreting a text' that has been 'overlaid by past misinterpretations' (ibid). On this reading of Heidegger's work the interpretation of texts does most certainly lead to the search for something essential. Words for Heidegger point to something beyond themselves: to Being, that is something to be considered in addition to the text, and which is indeed beyond it (ibid: 353-54). The hermeneutic circle in this account links text and being; the form of analytical contextualisation this achieves connects two forms of interpretation: the interpretation of being and the interpretation of text. Ormiston and Schrift conceive of Heidegger's version of context as a 'traditional' conception of the hermeneutic context that results in the articulation of universal principles and conditions of understanding (1990: 14). The post-Heideggerian hermeneutic context, they argue, no longer suggests unity, but instead 'displacement and fragmentation', which I will discuss later. Note only at this stage that Heidegger is 'engaged in the pursuit of the "primordial meaning" of hermeneutics, that is to say, as a way to present the meaning of the question of being' (Ormiston and Schrift 1990: 33). This view can be broadly linked to those which define relevant contexts in psychological, cognitive or existential terms. It also contrasts with the view of Derrida, in whose work texts refer to nothing outside of themselves but only to other texts. The transformations that have occurred within the hermeneutic context result in a set of consequences for social anthropology that are addressed below.

Another way of conceiving the contextual background that informs understanding in the hermeneutic circle is that a body of shared knowledge is implicated in some manner: 'comprehension can only come about through a tacit foreknowledge that alerts us to salient features of the text which would otherwise escape notice' (Honderich 1995: 353). This is a view alluded to in Holy and Stuchlik's work on native folk models, which embody the kind of common-sense knowledge necessary for any competent social interaction (*see* 1981 and 1983). Alternatively, such foreknowledge could be conceived as a body of intersubjective knowledge, what ethnomethodologists recognise as the means by which social actors negotiate and achieve a common context. Another rendering of foreknowledge is Kristeva's concept of 'intertextuality', defined as 'the sum of knowledge that makes it possible for texts to have meaning' (quoted in Culler 1981: 104). Intertextuality, Culler argues, replaces inter-subjectivity or an inter-subjective body of knowledge, a type of prior mutual knowledge which makes sense of something otherwise unknown and unrecognisable.

Another version of this context of foreknowledge is found in the concept of 'mutual knowledge', now an explicit rather than tacit form of knowledge: 'the successful interpretation of utterances [or even texts] in context presupposes a fund of shared or mutual knowledge among the participants in a discourse' (Smith 1982). Mutual knowledge, it is argued, is shared and is known to be shared. A similar problem, however, awaits mutual knowledge as has been faced by context itself: the problem of how to limit it. 'To establish mutual knowledge between A and B of proposition P, A has to know P, and know that B knows P, and that B knows that A knows P and so on ad infinitum' (Smith 1982: xii). Context suffers the problem of infinite regress of contextualising, contextualising contexts and so on.

Sperber and Wilson (1982) have challenged the identification of mutual knowledge with context, and have focused instead on the concept of relevance, which is conceived as the number of inferences that can be drawn by the hearer from a particular utterance. Relevance is something the speaker intends too. Mutual knowledge is not, then, a sufficient condition for constituting a context for Sperber and Wilson. Instead, in verbal communication it is the intention to be relevant on the part of the speaker and the imputation of relevance on the part of the hearer that allow meanings to be generated: 'it is relevance which is treated as a given, and context which is treated as a variable' Scharfstein states (1989: 189). Sperber's notion of relevance is closely linked to the philosopher Grice's view that meaning is connected to speaker's intention, or 'meaning as recognised intention' as Hobart puts it (1985: 42). The context for meaning thus becomes the psychological states of speakers who have particular intentions in mind.

To abandon all sense of a form of mutual or shared foreknowledge is to strain the conditions of possibility for any form of understanding. Critics of this theory of relevance argue that Sperber and Wilson themselves presuppose a kind of mutual foreknowledge about the concept of relevance and its calculation (*see* Smith 1982: 88-100). To approach a text, for example, without foreknowledge in the hope of gaining a sense of its meaning presupposes a knowledge of literacy and written texts, as well as, one trusts, the language in which the text is written. Foreknowledge, as Culler points out above, transforms something that is unknown and unrecognisable into a recognised thing that can be known.

The concept of relevance, however, in a modified form is an important one in that it makes the concept of context less positivistic. Seen not so much, following Sperber, in terms of a function of implicatures that can be derived from a given statement, relevance can be linked to the diverse purposes, interests, reasons and concerns of interpreters who invoke contexts as legitimising devices of the meanings they make. Indeed a relevant context for one interpreter might be irrelevant for another (*see* Hobart's discussion of Geertz and Boon), and what is seen as relevant is a function of social interaction and of the play of power (see Hobart 1986a).

The Linguistic Contexts of Speaking

The reliance on context as an analytic device in linguistics mirrors its usage in philosophy, namely that it sets up a counter movement to those theories and perspectives which view language as a formal system, or which develop context-free grammars or structures of meaning. Contextualist linguistics can be contrasted to theoretical linguistics whose highly abstracted and idealised view of language divorces it from the conditions in which it is actually used. In this vein, Dell Hymes's work (e.g. 1977) challenges Chomskyan linguistics, which attempts to define an autonomous realm of language as an abstract cognitive system to be studied in isolation from the contexts of use of language. Context also bears the burden of multiple interpretations: while it can refer to parts of an utterance surrounding a linguistic unit that may affect both its meaning and its grammatical contribution, context can also embrace the wider situation of either a speaker or of the accompanying activities and social situation. Language in this view is a form of social action to be viewed alongside other social activities.

As an aspect of the speaker's situation or as an aspect of the surrounding social situation, context in linguistics covers a broad range of social phenomena as well as actor-oriented characteristics. Duranti and Goodwin (1992) spell out a number of positions taken by linguists over the question of context of linguistic performance. They highlight four basic parameters of context: i) *the setting* – a social and spatial framework within which encounters are situated; ii) *the behavioural environment* – the use of bodies or behaviour for framing talk; iii) *language as context* – the way talk itself invokes context and provides context for other talk; and, iv) *the extra-situational context* or background knowledge and frames of relevance (Goodwin and Duranti 1992: 6-8). These parameters mirror to some extent those that can be detected in anthropological use, although some commentators would wish to add historical context as a major consideration.

Context as 'setting' can be seen in the work of the linguist J. L. Austin, who shifted his focus away from the analysis of words and sentences to conceive of language as a mode of action. He investigated 'how people use words to accomplish action' (Goodwin and Duranti 1992: 17), looking outside language for the way meanings are conveyed. The setting is a set of recognised conventions such as what occurs at a marriage ceremony, which involves certain kinds of behaviour – the second parameter of context. This form of contextualisation provides the surroundings by means of which an utterance such as 'I do' 'gains its force as a particular type of action' (ibid). J. Searle's work on speech acts takes a 'cognitive turn', in a manner similar to that of Grice, in that he is concerned less with external features of context (social relations or setting) and more with internal features of the speaker's state of mind. He focuses again on intentionality and a speaker's inner psychological states as relevant to meaning. Searle directs the trajectory of his analysis towards a psychological context.

All four parameters of context can be seen in Hymes's work on the ethnography of communication or speaking (*see* 1977 and Gumperz and Hymes 1986), although I will highlight only the last two. By attending to the verbal practices of human groups, language is seen as an interactive phenomenon which creates its own dynamic. Indeed, the attention given to language practices through which symbols are given meaning contrasts with Geertz's form of interpretation of cultural symbols as abstracted terms from local discourse that are then treated as static concepts or categories. (*See* Hobart's critique of

Geertz's treatment of Balinese terms and concepts.) Hymes's sensitivity to extra-linguistic and extra-situational context draws him into a consideration of a broad range of ethnographic features of the culture in question. Fabian's analysis of an ethnography of communication in Zaire/Congo draws on Hymes's earlier work, as do Fabian's earlier 1990 and 1991 publications. In his contribution here, Fabian reveals the intricacies of dealing with language as context and with the importance for social exchange of background knowledge, and sometimes what happens in the absence of such knowledge.

Finally Goodwin and Duranti themselves argue for an interactionist view of context which places the social person on centre stage. This reflects not only the view of language as context, but more generally of interaction itself as context. Their theme is 'the capacity of human beings to dynamically reshape the context that provides organisation for their actions within the interaction itself' (1992: 5). Context is both constitutive of social action and itself the outcome of social action; it is both a generative principle and a resulting outcome (cf. Harvey's argument). The definition and deployment of context is also part of actors' strategies wherein 'individual participants can actively attempt to shape context in ways that further their own interests' (1992: 6). (*See* Prince and Riches on New Agers furthering their own interests through context definition.) Context is thus 'analysed as an interactively constituted mode of praxis', and their focus on interaction links their approach to ethnomethodology's concern with face-to-face exchange as a primary exemplar of [a type of] context that is dynamic, and time-bound (1992: 22). Their argument that context and speech stand in a mutually reflexive relationship to each other (1992: 31) is developed below, particularly by Hervey and by Tabakowska, who goes on to collapse the distinction between context and meaning.

Fabian in chapter 4 deals specifically with language as an interactive phenomenon and performance, and he too argues that context and speech are mutually constitutive. Moreover, his chapter draws on the conception of an ideal speech situation from Habermas in his discussion of ethnographic misunderstandings in an exchange between him, 'the ethnographer', and a female informant-turned-interrogator/ethnographer.[22] Habermas discusses how communicative action 'relies on a cooperative process of interpretation in which participants relate spontaneously to something in the objective, the social and the subjective worlds' (quoted in Lechte 1994: 188). Fabian shows how each party in his interaction co-operated in the process of interpretation and misinterpretation until, through the processes of talk, mutual contexts emerged for the understanding of each person's particular position. Thus, something akin to an ideal speech situation developed in a public sphere where uncoerced participants debate and exchange.

It is through this process too, for Habermas, that the values of truth and rational consensus might achieve their fullest expression.

Hobart discusses the possibility of ever achieving such an ideal speech situation. Another intriguing question arises too. Is an ideal speech situation the context for the achievement of a particular type of social relationship, or is it itself the outcome of social relations, the grounds of which are constituted through the play of power? Harvey and Hobart argue for the comprehension of questions of power in the definition of context.

To dwell on Habermas further, his concept of 'lifeworld' might be considered to be close to some renditions of context. Lifeworld is the immediate environment of an individual person, a world of everyday life and a total sphere of an individual's experience. It is a taken-for-granted world, the 'horizon of consciousness'. The lifeworld is ideally that sphere in which individuals can find recognition for the validity of their communication. Communication is, moreover, an important aspect of the lifeworld as it is also the means through which the lifeworld can be modified (*see* Lechte 1994). The lifeworld is then the context for communication, and communication can in turn create new contexts or redefinitions of the lifeworld. Rapport discusses a similar kind of process – although not in the same vocabulary – for the individuals who populate Wanet, for their lifeworlds and for the communicative acts that bring them into mutual adjustments of their own personal as well as public contexts.

Two broad areas of concern for social anthropology have not been touched upon in this consideration of context within linguistics. The first, as Duranti and Goodwin note, is their silence on anthropological interpretative approaches, and the second is the question of literacy and written texts. The salience of the idea of interactive context, as they deal with it, is diminished with respect to literacy and writing in particular. These are two of the main procedures, they argue, 'through which the ground within which language emerges is systematically erased' (1992: 32 fn 8). I will now turn to consider some of these areas of interest.

The View from Structuralism, Post-structuralism and Literary Theory

In contrast to the interactionist, language-as-social-action schools of thought which invoke specific senses of context in their interpretative search for meaning, structuralist and post-structuralist approaches have often been criticised for their neglect of social context. They have been accused of taking things 'out of context'. Lévi-Strauss's work on myth, for example, can be seen as removing the processes of retelling of such oral accounts from their performative contexts, from the way in which recitation is embedded within a broader set of interactive processes (1979, and 1986 and Sturrock 1979). Lévi-Strauss's structuralism is a universalist approach that tries to establish the salience of pan-cultural features of the human mind by viewing its expression across a range of cultural variability (1972). The specificity of local cultural contexts becomes the object of his generalising project that seeks certain kinds of symbolic phenomena in particular localities, seen simply as the moulds which give shape to fundamental principles. However, if Lévi-Strauss's structuralism is not a form of contextualism, it does entail specific 'contextualising moves' as a means of seeking to structure material in a particular way (Hobart 1985: 49). Thus the analytical procedures of structuralism can be regarded as processes of contextualisation. That is, the way in which 'meaning' is given to evidence under study implies a conception of context in one form or another.

I introduced above the distinction between types of contextualising move, the way analytical attention may be directed towards 'internal' or 'external' contexts. Attention may be directed outwards and given to external features, or attention may be directed inwards and given to internal elements within a closed system (see Hervey for an argument on the greater defensibility of the circularity of internal contextualisation than the infinite regression of external contextualisation). Put simply, the meaning of a word can be considered in its relation to things in the external world or to other words within the system of a language. A third direction was also suggested for the definition of 'psychological' or mental contexts, in which attention is given to 'inner' private cognitive, intentional or even existential states (see Rapport).

Structuralism and Saussurean linguistics throw up exemplars of internal, closed-system contexts. Saussure saw meaning linked not only to the relation between a signifier and a signified, but also to the value of a sign or its connection to other signs that might be substituted for it, or against which it stands in contrast (see Hervey 1982). Structuralist developments based on Saussure's insight tended to discard the relation between signifier and signified, and sought meaning instead in terms of a closed system of signs.[23] Hobart states a similar view for semiotics in general: 'meaning is no longer to be defined by either an external "reality" or an external context' (1982: 48), but shifts the problem to one of an internal context.

Like structuralism and semiotics, branches of literary theory and criticism posit internal contexts of a particular sort. Kristeva's idea of 'intertextuality' (see above) is a concept that refers to how the meaning of a text is dependent upon a prior knowledge of other texts, and not necessarily upon the text's reference to or representation of an external reality. Culler points out (1988) that literary criticism as a discipline has been a net exporter of theoretical discourse in the 1980s, leading to developments in the concept of context. This has been achieved through the investigation of the processes of signification and the production and play of meaning.

Jacques Derrida's challenge to J. L. Austin's speech act theory is an early example of a critique centred on the problem of context (Derrida 1977). He attacks Austin on the latter's re-introduction of speaker's intention as a means of controlling or arresting the infinite regress in the process of contextualisation, the contextualising of context and so on. Austin re-introduces precisely those assumptions he is trying to question at the outset of his project. Derrida focuses on how this re-introduction of 'the presence of a signifying intention in the consciousness of the speaker' occurs. He declares: 'This is my starting point: no meaning can be determined out of context, but no context permits saturation' (quoted in Culler 1983: 123, who also discusses this debate in pp. 110-34). Culler concludes that 'total context is unmasterable, both in principle and practice. Meaning is context-bound but context is boundless' (1983: 123). Context is boundless, he argues, in two senses: first, there is no limit to its contents, it is unsaturable and is always open to further description; second, any definition of context can itself be contextualised by means of a new context, and the process is open to infinite regression.

What does Derrida offer as an alternative? Culler comments that Derrida's method does not offer a theory that defines meaning, nor does it show you how to find it. Instead, it demonstrates the difficulties attached to the definition of meaning in a univocal manner (1983: 131). Hobart's examination of Geertz's and Boon's interpretive writings on Bali suggest something of this method, although he does not leave us without the clink of light that is his proposition to consider more closely native exegetic practices and rhetorical definitions of context as social action.

If 'univocal meaning grounded in presence' is not a viable option for Derrida, then the affirmation of the free-play of meaning is. The deconstructive method, which Culler identifies with 'the twin principles of the contextual determination of meaning and the infinite extendibility of context' (1983: 215), does nonetheless suggest a hidden internal context for signifying relevance. Deconstruction is the 'turning of the text against itself' in order to investigate how a particular perspective is produced through the connections within texts. Moreover, Derrida's concept of *différance*, combining the sense of Saussurean difference with the idea of deferral, points to the endless deferral of any fixed point or privileged relationship with the external world (outside the text or language) from which meaning might be apprehended. Hobart captures this sense in his arresting description of Derrida's 'glum world where we shunt around forever in the prison of our own metaphysic' (1985: 44). For Derrida *'il n'y rien de hors texte'*, 'there is no outside-the-text'. Culler adds another dimension to the contextualising moves Derrida employs, by pointing out his paradoxical use of privileging first history to challenge philosophy, and then using philosophy against history (1983: 129).

If Derrida's method moves us into the text and into a world of other texts, then Foucault moves us in and out, that is according to Said (quoted in Culler 1988: 62). Culler suggests an imaginary dialogue between Derrida and Foucault, which can be represented thus:

Derrida: There is no outside-the-text.
Foucault: There is so! There's history, there's power.
Foucault again: We must not go from discourse towards its interior, hidden nucleus...; but, on the basis of discourse itself, its appearance and its regularity, go towards its external conditions of possibility. (Adapted from Culler 1988: 62)

Foucault can be seen to provide a background against which knowledge, language and texts can be interpreted. This background of discursive formations is particular to specific historical periods, he argues (1989). For Foucault, frameworks of knowledge and modes of understanding are themselves changing, and with them the sense of what is relevant. Indeed, Foucault's conception of the conditions of possibility and his focus on the exercise of power and knowledge reveal the way in which objects become framed as objects, and how distinctions between figure and ground, species and its environment and so on emerge as historical and cultural processes (*see* Foucault 1977 and 1989, and Rabinow 1984).

Foucault's analytical method is reminiscent of the work of the historian R. G. Collingwood, a comparison also pointed out by Hobart with regard to a common concern for the changes in ideas within history (1985: 47). What has become known as the idea of 'historical context' was developed in the work of Collingwood in *The Idea of History* (1946). He was influenced by Dilthey's idea of *verstehen* or hermeneutic understanding, such that the historian's task was to rethink or inwardly re-live the actions of historical agents in the spirit of imaginative sympathy, and with a view to rendering intelligible their behaviour and the products of human endeavour.[24] Collingwood's view of history aimed at the delineation of uniqueness and particularity of actions, events and things, was developed in contrast to a natural science epistemology for history. This latter was developed, for example, in the work of historians such as A. Toynbee or O. Spengler, in which a scientific stance towards human affairs was developed by means of speculative histories and the discovery of laws and theories (*see* Honderich 1995: 360-64). Collingwood's explicit contextualism stood as a counter to scientific historicism. His conception of context became influential in social anthropology via the work of Evans-Pritchard (1962) and of Gregory Bateson, who developed the

concept of frame and of ecological context. Bateson referred to Collingwood as 'the first man to recognise the nature of context' (1973: 20). I
will turn to consider specific versions of context in social anthropology
shortly. Before that I will briefly, and lastly, turn in this review of context
from elsewhere to Baudrillard.

J. Baudrillard's concept of the hyperreal, 'the generation ... of a real
without origin or reality: a hyperreal' (quoted in Poster 1988: 166),[25]
collapses the distinction between the real and the imaginary. Objects
become signs in a self-referential world, where the realm of necessity
is left behind and natural objects are no longer credible. Hobart uses
the idea of hyperreality to suggest the kind of world created by the
over-interpretation by anthropologists and others of images of Balinese life. As a counter, he suggests instead that the under-determina-
tion and inscrutability of the world are central, and these are best
summed up in the idea of 'hyporeality', an unsaturated reality.

Baudrillard points to a world where nothing lays outside of a system,
now not a system of texts as with Derrida, but rather one of signs,
coded signals and formulae. He goes on to argue in *Simulations* (1983)
that the code, which entails the reproduction of an object without
reference to an original natural object, enables reality to be by-passed.
Poster states of Baudrillard's vision that a new world is constructed 'out
of models or simulacra which have no referent or ground in any "reality" except their own' (1988: 6). Contextualisation, for Baudrillard, certainly does not involve the placing of phenomena in relation to external
natural objects, for 'objects are best understood ... as a network of float-
ing signifiers that are inexhaustible in their ability to incite desire'
(Poster 1988: 3) The distinction between the real and its representation
is erased, and along with this other oppositions such as text and context
collapse as well. This results in everything becoming undecidable. Baudrillard's work in one sense, therefore, heralds the collapse of context,
whereas Derrida's approach retains context as a playful thing that gives
rise to the possibility of the free-play of meanings. The situation Harvey
describes for Expo 92 represents in one sense a collapse of context, especially in terms of a conventional anthropology searching for a stable
cultural milieu. In another sense, Expo involves playing with context,
particularly on the part of the organisers who through the use of irony
expose the very contexts which are supposed to provide the foundations of the exhibition.

Views of Context in Social Anthropology

I have tried to achieve in the preceding sections a movement between
perspectives as part of a 'transdisciplinary exercise' to address the prob-

lem of context (Strathern 1987: 268). It is with this sense of movement between disciplines that diverse perspectives might be gained on the problem of context. I have aimed to elucidate the way in which other disciplines and specific analysts have come to a view on context and on the processes of contextualisation. The sets of connections that have been revealed point towards common ground shared by philosophy, linguistics and literary criticism. Indeed, there has been a good deal of cross-fertilisation across disciplinary boundaries, a point I wish to elaborate in this section with particular reference to social anthropology. Having plotted something of the 'life of context', I wish now to trace some of the disguises under which it passes in social anthropology.

Malinowski pioneered work on the problem of context in social anthropology in two publications in particular: 'The Problem of Meaning in Primitive Languages' in 1923 [1938], and *Coral Gardens and Their Magic* in 1935. He laid the foundations not only for the way the problem was conceived for generations of social anthropologists, but also influenced developments in other disciplines, particularly linguistics. These elaborations subsequently fed back into anthropology.

The first of Malinowski's publications on this topic appeared in a volume written by two philosophers, Ogden and Richards, on the meaning of meaning. The authors confronted the claims of causal theories of reference which posited meaning as the result of direct knowledge between minds and things. Meaning, they argued instead, is to be linked to context. Malinowski coined the phrase 'context of situation' (a parallel to Ogden and Richard's concept of 'sign-situation', or the context of original, immediate and direct experience [1938: 53]) in order to address the pragmatic circumstances in which language – as a mode of action and not a 'countersign to thought' – was used and articulated. He argued against the idea that a word contains a meaning as one of its essential features: '... the meaning of a word must always be gathered, not from passive contemplation of this word, but from an analysis of its functions, with reference to the given culture' (1938: 309). Only by referring a word to its given culture, therefore, could its meaning be properly assigned.

The conception of culture had to be broadened, he argued, to include the immediate and direct situation in which the word under investigation was used. In his later publication he developed much more fully the stages through which contextualisation proceeds in the course of the translation of native terms and meanings. The process starts with the 'context of words', a linguistic context referring to the properties of language, its vocabulary as well as the structure of the utterance and so on. The 'context of situation' is now rephrased as the 'context of culture' such that translation takes place with reference to it and against a 'cultural background of a society (1935: 17-18). He goes on to argue that ' ... it is very profitable ... to widen the concept of context so that it embraces not only spoken words but facial expression, gesture, bodily activities, the whole group of people present during an exchange of utterances and the part of the environment on which these people are engaged'. He refers to these features later as 'the context of cultural reality', by which he means 'the natural equipment, the activities and interests and aesthetic values with which the words are correlated' (1935: 22). It is well to bear in mind that this commentary was stimulated by his reflections on how to translate specific Kiriwinian words set within networks of associations that might be simplistically glossed as, for example, 'garden' or 'famine' etc. The twists and turns through which the 'concept of context' has been taken by all manner of hermeneuts who have reified the concept and frozen it as 'text' contrasts starkly with Malinowski's original context of use of the term.

Hervey discusses the way in which the linguist Firth develops Malinowski's ideas about context. Another inheritor of this fine-grained examination of language in use is Hymes' work on the ethnography of speaking in which he develops Malinowski's concept of 'context of situation'. While Malinowski was one of the first social anthropologists to take seriously the problem of native language, its use and its translation, Hymes was one of the first linguists to elaborate non- and extra-linguistic frames of reference for the interpretation of speech events. An ethnographic project is now seen to be part of linguistic analysis, such that a wide range of social and cultural features are considered relevant to analysis (see Duranti and Goodwin 1992).

The concept of culture became the defining feature of social anthropology after Malinowski, and it came to represent that which is local, particular and distinctive, compared to the global, general and common. The word context became part of a stock anthropological vocabulary used to denote a bewildering variety of characteristics, domains and environments. Contexts could be cultural, social, political, ritual and religious, economic or ecological; they could be interactional, systemic or historical.[26] The term, it seems, is sufficiently elastic to be stretched in numerous directions for diverse purposes. Morris attempts to impose some limitation on the explosion of context in anthropological study by referring back to four classical analytical strategies, and reviews in his chapter a range of contextualisations (historical, mythological, sociological and essentialist) concerning Malawian ritual.

One of the first to express disquiet over context was Roger Keesing, particularly in his 1972 publication on kinship. Here he pondered the need for a 'formal theory of context definition', and for 'a grammar for creating contexts' (1972: 28). He recognised the 'positivity of context' (Fabian) by stating that they are 'in our heads, not out there' (ibid). Holy later repeated these calls for anthropological attention to be given to the subject (*see* especially 1989) and he develops these themes below.[27]

The Geertzian developments within interpretive anthropology exposed the frailty of the anthropological grasp on the concept as conceived by the textual hermeneuts, whose increasing focus on text paradoxically left context unexamined. Hobart over many years has sustained a series of searching critiques against the excesses of interpretivism and continues that critique here (*see* especially 1982, 1985, 1986b and 1990). The identification of social life with text is now well documented and discussed, but there remains an ambiguity in the interpretive approach about what exactly a context is. Texts appear everywhere without accompanying contexts in reference to which the analyst's interpreted meanings take shape or gain prominence. Geertz describes various processes in textual terms: a) what the ethnographer does is produce text, turning passing events into accounts, thus inscribing social discourse (1973: 19); b) 'the culture of a people is an ensemble of texts' which the anthropologist strains to read over the shoulders of others (1973: 452), and this ensemble presumably comprises the individual 'texts' of social activities and the actions of individual agents; c) culture is not just an ensemble of texts but an integral document, a kind of script in itself ('culture, this acted document' [1973: 10]); d) culture also stands as a context that frames the meanings actors themselves attach to their lives and experiences ('culture ... [is] the structure of meaning through which men give shape to their experience' [1973: 312]). Not only might Geertz be seen to 'lose sight of the contextual wood for the textual trees' to borrow Hobart's phrase (1985: 46), but he neglects to examine the relationship between types of text, how they may articulate one with another, and how they relate to context.

If the concept of culture came to stand for many as the modernist anthropological conception of context par excellence, then the certainty of both master concepts has been shaken. Harvey introduces her chapter with a discussion of the way in which the undermining of the conventional views of culture has posed problems for the definition of an appropriate and relevant sense of anthropological context. Clifford highlights the idea that the culture concept has served its time, and he argues recently for a shift in perspective from a fixed, static and holistic notion of culture to one focusing on travel as the locus of human experience (1997).[28] He still finds it necessary to retain 'some sets of relations which preserves the concept's [culture's] differential and relativistic functions' (quoted in Fardon 1990: 11), that is precisely those functions earmarked as the task of context in challenging universalism, formalism and so on. The crisis about the certainty of modernist social anthropological context has led to a 'post-modern mood', the attitude of which is 'to make deliberate play with context' (Strath-

ern 1987: 265). One consequence of this play is that the conventional
distinction between 'us and them', the distance between the object of
interpretation and the interpreter is discredited.[29] Moreover, in this
view, ethnography should become a dialogue such that no one position
or context of any particular agent is privileged, and the reader is
allowed a degree of free play, in a Derridean sense, in reading meanings
into the text. As Strathern suggests, a new relationship between reader,
writer and subject matter is contemplated (1987: 265), such that the
reader is invited to interact with the text and 'exotica' itself. This play
with context is a feature described by Harvey in her analysis of Expo 92
in which the exhibitors played with the idea of context in their national
presentations, and where visitors framed their experiences not simply
by reference to the features of the exhibition in Spain, but sought contrasts and comparisons within their own experience from similar types
of exhibition or leisure-world setting in other places. Their interpretations referred to previous interpretations of parallel experiences elsewhere. This suggests the idea of a series of self-referential signifiers and
the idea of a type of 'inter-textuality'; or the idea expressed by Derrida
that 'everything begins by referring back ... to other traces and the
traces of others' (quoted in Ormiston and Schrift 1990: 25). The shift
from modernist context to a post-modern play with context appears to
be part of a movement from 'external' context to an 'internal' one in
which there is a deferral of immediate signification.

Fardon (1990) points to a shift in context in the analysis of anthropological monographs. This shift is from a conventional modernist
view in which the subject of ethnography is the object of our attention
to one in which it is the ethnographic account itself as literature that
is the focus. The construction of the account now becomes the object
of investigation in terms of written literary composition, style, genre
and so on, seen against the backdrop of the field encounter between
anthropologist and native. Fardon's image for this is: 'Text and context
have been reversed to focus upon the illocutionary devices which
frame and validate what is presented to be content', suggesting that
what was background or frame now becomes the foregrounded figure
for inspection and scrutiny (1990: 7).[30] The teasing out of the literary
fictions, narrative devices and textual genres inherent in an account
imply a contextualising move that remains situated within the domain
of other texts and modes of expression, and is not directed in an external trajectory towards the lives of those so described.

Critics of the conventional usage of context in social anthropology
appear equally reliant upon contextualisation, in the sense of giving
order to material, as do those they criticise. The nature of the context
invoked, however, is radically different. The new critics of ethnography
have brought about a paradigm shift in anthropology associated with a

redefinition of relevant context. But the fear is that the new knowledge generated by this shift is reduced to self-knowledge (Strathern 1987: 268). Hobart voices a similar concern when he accuses these critics of smuggling in a number of essentialisms in their re-contextualisation of anthropological enquiry, not least in viewing 'the nature of the evoking self [of the ethnographer] as curiously unproblematic' (1990: 311).

Taussig heralds the collapse, even the irrelevance, of context in the following passage:

> One could, I suppose, do the usual thing and 'analyze them' [Cuna figurines] as anthropologists do, as things to be layered with context, then stripped, but that would seem to be an evasion and miss the point – that something crucial about what made oneself was implicated and imperilled in the object of study, in its power to change reality, no less. (1993: 252-3)

It is the relationship between the self and the object of study that provides the frame for analysis, particularly the way in which it gives on to self-knowledge.

Taussig states again, more specifically:

> I know next to nothing of the 'context' of ritual, belief, or of social practice in which an older anthropology, eager for the 'native's point of view', would enmesh this African [Igbo representation of a] white man, 'explain' him (away), 'Africanize' him (as opposed to 'whitenize' him). All I have is the image and its brief caption [from a 1967 publication by Cole], and I am my own gaping subject of analysis... (1993: 238)

He does not explain why self-knowledge – that he is his own gaping subject of analysis – is any less problematic than the native's point of view, which might, one could well imagine, be a good deal more interesting and engaging. A view similar to Taussig's is echoed in Marcus and Cushman's assertion that 'through the writer's [ethnographer's] self-reflection as a narrative vehicle', a reader will be able to identify more readily with anthropological fieldwork, an identification also claimed to be facilitated by a shift from the 'classic us-them didactic form' to the 'me-them form of contrast' (1982). Again, Marcus and Fischer argue that: 'Anthropology is not the mindless collection of the exotic, but the use of cultural richness for self-reflection and self-growth' 1986: ix-x).

The literary turn in anthropology, stimulated in large part by the Derridean notions of the free-play of meaning and the boundlessness of context, ends up proposing a kind of project that Derrida would not himself want to identify with. That is, the project revolves around a set of contextualising moves that invoke an essential self that becomes the centre piece of anthropological investigation. It is one thing to argue that our 'selves' should become research objects alongside other selves rendered as objects in our enquiry (Crick 1992); it is another to define anthropology in terms of self-growth.

The self becomes, furthermore, explicitly identified as the new interpretative context in social anthropology. Cohen argues, for example, that: 'There is no option for us ... as social anthropologists but to proceed from the premise of self', for the self is 'our most potent interpretative resource' (1992: 237). This self is, indeed, a 'self-driven self' not a 'socially driven self', as Cohen explains. This latest version of anthropological interpretivism that posits as the relevant context for interpretation the anthropologist's own sense of self, as an essential self-driven self, is a development on the Geertzian textualism which rarely offered a firm grasp of context. This could at least be seen as an improvement. However, where Geertz's texts (and sometimes contexts) were located 'externally' in a world of cultural activity, the contextualising move of the 'self-essentialists' is in the direction of an inner 'psychological' context of private stirrings and processes.[31]

A similar problem is confronted in what might be broadly glossed as the constructionist view of social reality. Constructionism holds that human beings actively engage in the social construction of reality. Holy articulates such a line of argument here by arguing that 'phenomena do not in any sense exist without being meaningful' (*infra* p. 69), and it is through ascribing meaning to them that we in fact constitute them as such.[32] But if meaning is context-dependent, what is the context for this attribution of meaning? Presumably it is not any aspect of 'reality' – social or otherwise – since these only come into being through our processes of meaning-making. One might respond by saying that meanings are inherent in phenomena, but this neo-Platonic argument would sink the constructivist's ship before even the firing of the first salvo. Another line of defence might be to argue, something akin to Rapport, that it is part of the existential condition of being human that provides the framework for such attributions of meaning. Such an argument is developed by Nietzsche, for whom 'interpretation is being' and 'being is interpretation' (*see* Ormiston and Schrift 1990: 20). In this view, the interpretation of the world, 'a process in infinitum', is an active affirmation of life itself. The death of interpretation for Nietzsche involves the practice of a hermeneutic in which signs refer to that 'arcane object, the signified', when the 'real world' creeps back after its abolition in the 'Twilight of the Idols' (see ibid. for this discussion). These two types of interpretation, or contextualising move, could be seen to be reflected in Rapport's distinction between tautological and evolutionary knowledge.

The interpretative context within an extreme constructionist perspective holds that nothing can be conceived as existing without being an object of human consciousness. As a form of idealism, constructivism holds that external contexts as 'reality' only have meaning as the intentional meaning processes of a transcendental subjectivity, a universal and essential subjectivity that is the foundation for this position. We have witnessed again what Ardener alerted to us as 'parameter collapse' or 'twist', namely the involution or implosion of extreme contextualisation, which results yet again in positing a form of essential individualism.

M. Jackson's writings suggests a re-definition of context and a new direction in social anthropology (1989 and 1996). This new context is construed in terms of a phenomenology that emphasises the primacy of human experience in the lived world, without necessary recourse to an essential self.[33] 'If there is a context in which we can usefully compare', he argues, '... it is an existential one, the context of lived experience' (1989: 50). Jackson's version of phenomenology resists the idea of transcendence, for it is only another 'Western myth of context-free phenomena' (1996: 5). Instead, the contexts he is concerned with are those constituted by the world of things as it is presented to human experience. He quotes Goethe approvingly: 'Do not look behind phenomena; they themselves are the truth' (1996: 11). The connection between things and human experience constitutes relevant context for Jackson.

Knowledge and Context

The semantic turn in British social anthropology in the 1980s was a crucially reflexive moment for the consideration of the parallels between the interpretative, meaning-making processes of anthropologists and those of whom anthropologists study (*see*, for example, Parkin 1982, Overing 1985). A greater transparency was given to how our interpretative frameworks were constructed and how we had the power to describe and control contexts (Parkin 1982: xlvi-xlvii). This emphasis opened up for examination questions about forms of knowledge, and alerted us to the distinction between our own contextualising moves as analysts and the types of moves native interpreters might make. Holy and Stuchlik (1981 and 1983) suggested that there was a problem of context in the relative treatment of bodies of native knowledge and of anthropological analytical knowledge respectively.

The problem of context is therefore duplicated: how has anthropology as an interpretative discipline composed its own analytical contexts that give shape to its explanations and interpretations? How and in what ways do those people whom we study invoke context as part of their own local practices of attaching meaning to the processes and events in social life? These questions give on to the problem of commensurability between the two domains of interpretation and contextualisation. Hobart talks of the 'double account of knowledge' involved in anthropological interpretation, and this involves depicting native knowledge as distinct from anthropological knowledge, and then giving an account of the former in terms of the latter (*see infra* p. 151). The question, however, and its various conceptions underlies the problem of context. If paradigm shifts in anthropology are shifts in contexts which generate new knowledge; then different bodies of knowledge imply differing views on context. Fardon's *Counterworks* (1995) exemplifies the way in which a shift in context or frame suggests new perspectives for the generation of knowledge. The 'local' is usually seen against the backdrop of the 'global', but by shifting these interrelated elements framed as figure and ground, new bodies of knowledge might be thus generated.

Strathern points out that one of the epistemological foundations of twentieth-century anthropology has been the contextualisation of knowledge (1995a: 3); and the way in which, through this process of contextualisation, context itself was made one of its objects of knowledge (1995b: 160; 1987: 276). Native knowledge was conventionally contextualised in terms of integrated local cultures, and anthropological knowledge was set against the background of western ethnocentrism and the Malinowskian-inspired vision of the 'detection of civilisation under savagery' (Strathern 1987: 256). Culture as an item of knowledge has become part of local native discourse as much as of anthropological discourse. The local appropriations of the idea of culture have 'out-contextualised the anthropologist' (Strathern 1995a: 11). Strathern makes the point (1995a and b) that when people shift contexts they thus make knowledge for themselves, and indeed her 1991 publication *Partial Connections* is in one sense a play with context in the absence of a totalising context of 'culture'. An analysis of ethnography of the New Guinea Highlands, the work summons only 'partial' contexts in the form of partial connections wherein different frames or 'scales', as she calls them, are adopted to generate competing orders of knowledge that each make some sense of social life.[34]

The investigation of context in terms of orders of knowledge is developed in a number of the chapters which follow. A number of them address the implications for the concept of context that result from differing views of knowledge. At an ethnographic level, Prince and Riches argue that New Agers' knowledge of 'mainstream individualism' has consequences for the way in which they themselves construe their own explanatory and interpretative contexts. Morris describes the different orders of knowledge implicated by construing a body of Malawian rituals in terms of different contexts, and Hobart is concerned with the varieties of Balinese knowledge and how this gives on to certain types of local interpretative process and practice. He also describes how too much knowledge is brought to bear on a situation or state of affairs, particularly though not exclusively by outside analysts at the expense of local exegeses. The double account of knowledge that he recognises becomes therefore skewed in one direction.

Fabian and Harvey both argue for a distinction to be made between conceptions of knowledge. They contrast knowledge as representation with knowledge as practice, process or performance. Many of the problems of context discussed above are connected with the issue of knowledge as representation of the world. Indeed, writers such as Baudrillard or Derrida have disposed of the conventional sense of context, since their aim is to disengage with a view of knowledge as representation and have substituted concepts such as the 'hyperreal' or *différance*. Knowledge as practice removes us from the immediate problems of interpreting or explaining what or how things represent. Hobart argues that certain Balinese dance movements have no 'meaning' for the dancers, but are performed to have an effect and not to communicate a meaning. Rapport discusses 'external' contextualisation as being achieved either via tropes in language or via the body as a kind of 'technology'. Harvey talks of 'embodied knowledge' which has an immediate effect as practice, that things are known in terms of consequences and results, not necessarily through the hermeneutic interpretation of meaning. Context, in this respect, becomes not an aspect of a 'logico-methodological perspective' wherein knowledge is a form of representation and an accumulation, as Fabian argues; but instead when knowledge is viewed processually as praxis then context becomes performative, dialectic and interactive.

Tabakowska too distinguishes between knowledge as an accumulation of structures referring to an objective reality and knowledge as a network of relations which itself constitutes the world as reality. She argues, along with Fabian, that context is an emergent property arising through interaction and practice, although for her what is produced are new 'cognitive domains' 'conditioned by culture'. She thus proposes that context and meaning rest within a cognitive domain. A comparable 'cognitivist' argument is developed by Rapport who proposes not only a distinction between what he calls tautological and evolutionary knowledge, but indeed suggests a theory of knowledge itself in terms of the connections between the mind and the world. These links are effected through a series of 'externalisations', one central aspect of which is the definition of individually unique contexts of 'personal provenance'. These 'existential contexts' are not primarily the result of social interaction; broader, more public, less personally proximate contexts are the result of such interaction. These have a greater potential for being shared and for mutually influencing each other. Rapport could be seen in this respect to be trying to draw together the views of the deconstructionists of context, who leave only the self and self-knowledge as the grounds for analysis, with the views of those for whom social relationships and exchange constitute the grounds for contextualisation, such that contexts are both the results of interactions and the grounds for future possible actions.

Native Definitions of Context

How local social agents themselves define relevant contexts in connection with their own interpretative practices is presented in a number of case studies here. Holy gives insight into ways Berti marriage practices might be interpreted locally. Prince and Riches investigate New Agers' constructions of their sense of identity through the frame of a holistic individualism relative to 'mainstream society'. Morris suggests, among other contextualisations of Malawian ritual practice, a view which attempts to retain the promise that each interpretation offers, while he develops the idea of the ritual's relations to gender and the cultural creation of male affines. Hobart sheds light on the disjunction between a variety of interpretative practices, and focuses on how Balinese agents discuss and make sense of a medium's seance, a concern over the ownership of a temple, and a theatre performance. Harvey reveals the local definitions of context in an Andean courtroom as well as the ironic use of context in Expo 92. Fabian presents a sensitive account of the fluidity and fragility of contextualisation and interpretation in the process of dialogue and misunderstanding between himself and others in Zaire/Congo. Rapport takes us into the worlds of people in the English village of Wanet whose personal frames of reference take them through the life of the dales.

The invoking of essential objects, persons and relations is evident in a number of contributions. New Agers construct an essentialist discourse regarding themselves as spiritual beings located in a world represented as Gaia (Prince and Riches).[35] Harvey's Andean judge essentialises the categories of indian and *misti* or mestizo, and Morris deals critically with an essentialist view of ritual. Hobart also describes here and elsewhere the ability to essentialise in Bali is not simply an epistemological claim but a political manoeuvre (1986b).[36]

Power and Context Definition

Culler in a discussion of literary criticism prefers to use the expression 'framing the sign' rather than contextualising to describe the process of signification. He states that his phrase 'reminds us that framing is something we do; it hints of the "frame-up" ... and it eludes the incipient positivism of "context"' (1988: ix).[37] It reminds us in short that the agents who frame or contextualise perform a social practice. It recognises context as a process, and its definition as a species of social action entails relations of power. The very act of interpretation, evoking a specific frame in preference to another, is an act of power.

The ability to define contexts in essential or any other terms involves the issue of power. The ability of one agent to impose his or her definition of relevant context upon others as a kind of hermeneutic hegemony is a political act. Hobart notes that as a kind of social action, contextualisation requires a social agent, and hence implies the operation of power (*see* his discussion in Hobart 1986a and b). The agents in the definition of context are in most of the cases here individual social persons: a judge, an actor, a New Ager, or even Fabian himself and his interlocutor who negotiate the mutual definition of context as equal partners during the act of communication. Rapport too notes how contexts become shared through communication and interaction between Fred and Doris. While Rapport argues that it is not possible to force contextual definitions upon other individuals, he does nonetheless describe the agency of the actions of others upon individual definitions.

If the agents of context definition are sometimes taken to be individual human beings, there are a number of cases here that point to other forms of social agency. While Rapport, for example, argues for the view that context is wholly an individual affair, Hobart both here and elsewhere presents the case for the idea that individual human agents alone cannot account for all – indeed for very few – forms of context definition. A number of contributors below point to institutional contexts in their chapters: such as the Andean courtroom, the webs and politics of language that ensnare speakers (Harvey), or the form of New Age identity shaped in the face of 'mainstream society' (Prince and Riches). Moreover, many of the chapters argue that systems of knowledge are implicated in our sense of what a context might look like, and furthermore what contextualising moves may or may not be possible (*see* Holy, Hervey, Tabakowska, Fabian, Hobart, Morris and Harvey). Indeed, it is a particular version of metaphysics and a specific form of knowledge that provide us with the spatial metaphors of 'external' and 'internal' trajectories relevant to the analytical moves of contextualisation. While contextualising moves as a form of interpretative practice may be exercised by individual agents, by contrast, the form, the content and the direction of these moves, as well as the condition of possibility of contextualisation itself, rarely if ever are the product of individual agents.

A second aspect of power beyond the agency of individuals, therefore, relates to its more diffuse operation in a Foucauldian sense, and it takes us back to the issue of knowledge that I just raised above. If power and knowledge are mutually implicated, then specific orders of knowledge entail specific kinds of contexts as relevant. Indeed, Foucault has illustrated the way in which objects have been constituted as subjects of analysis during different epistemes and through different knowledge practices (1977 and 1989). The question of the conditions of possibility of interpretation and the issue of relevance are thus connected to this broader view of context as historical and systemic or epistemic. But here we start to slip into an infinite regression in tracing the relevant contexts as possibilities of power and (over)determination.

If 'context is boundless', as Culler suggests, how if at all is context to be bounded? In his analogy with lawyers he states that contextualisation is limited only by the lawyer's own resourcefulness, their client's resources and the patience of the judge (1988: 148). The limits placed upon contextualisation are the social relations that link those engaged in interaction. We are all involved in the making of connections that is context and the drawing of boundaries that put certain things out of context. We engage in and then halt investigations and re-descriptions of context for practical reasons and purposes. 'The meanings we determine are generally sufficient for our purposes', Culler states (1983: 130). One of the purposes of anthropological contextualism – the invoking of local cultural contexts – has been to produce a counter to universalist, context-free knowledge. Both approaches to knowledge – via contextualism or 'context-freeism' – are mutually implicated and necessary, for one makes little sense without the other. Moreover, as interpretative anthropologists, it is our professional specialism to produce meanings through the infinite array of contexts we might care to muster.

Evans-Pritchard warned many years ago, and Hobart reminds us again here, that 'there is only one method in social anthropology, the interpretative method – and that is impossible'. The indeterminacy of meaning that follows from these reflections, is founded upon the twin features of contextualism: meaning is context-dependent, but context is boundless. As Culler points out, such an indeterminacy does not stop mathematicians or scientists in their endeavours, nor should the ultimate indeterminacy of meaning make all efforts pointless, leading only to 'impetuous nihilism' (1983: 133). We are confronted by the McGarrigle conundrum. Persee McGarrigle, a central character in David Lodge's novel *Small World*, asks of a distinguished panel of literary critics at an international conference: 'What happens if everybody agrees with you?' What follows, in other words, if everyone agrees with the particular meanings fixed by any one of the distinguished analysts? What if analytical meanings of a given body of material were fixed, determinate and no longer subject to indeterminacy? The result was that academic debate stopped and chaos ensued in the conference room. Culler urges an optimistic view that the task continues of elucidating the conditions of signification, under whatever guise. Perhaps Nietzsche had a point when he declared that interpretation is itself life-affirming, which might be particularly true of an academic discipline such as ours and true too of people's reputations which ride on it.

Articulation of Contexts and Connections

Interpretation and contextualisation involve the making of connections. What context does is define where and which connections are made, and where disconnections, ruptures and discontinuities begin. As Keesing said, contexts are in our heads not out there; and Culler alludes to something more when he says that 'the frame [or context] itself may be nothing tangible', but 'pure articulation' (1988: ix). What is articulated is a particular mode of knowledge and a set of relevant connections. I proposed elsewhere the concept of 'mode of accountability' as a type of discursive formation or form of articulation which connects particular attributes of things, in that case, objects, exchange relations and exchange partners in an example of free market theorising (Dilley 1992). The notion of articulation has been developed by writers such as Stuart Hall, Ernesto Laclau and Jennifer Daryl Slack (see for example Morley and Chen 1996) to confront the problem of context, to attempt to map context – 'not in the sense of situating a phenomenon *in a context*, but in mapping a context, mapping the very identity that brings the context into focus' (Daryl Slack 1996: 125).[38] As a response, a theory and method of articulation replaces context as the focus of analysis. Articulation is 'the form of connection that can be made a unity of two different elements, under certain conditions. It is a linkage which is not necessary, determined, absolute and essential for all time' (Hall quoted in Daryl Slack 1996: 115). Articulation is the process of creating connections. The double meaning of articulation (Hall 1996) lends further significance to the term as used here. It has the sense of 'to utter', 'to speak forth', 'to articulate', as well as the sense of connecting two parts, namely articulation as linkage.

The kinds of hermeneutic context we have in the main been dealing with above involve the sense of interpretation as the expression or the articulation of particular kinds of meaning, especially in academic discourse. Hermeneutic interpretation is not just social action, it is a very specific form of social action. The modes of articulation I have sought to shed light on plot what might be called the 'life of contextualisation', the contextualisation of contexts, the interpretation of interpretations (Ormiston and Schrift 1990). There can be no definitive conclusion to the problem of context, only a heightened sense of awareness about the articulations and connections that we ourselves make in the process of anthropological contextualisation. However, since the concept of articulation has now come to stand for contextualisation itself, it is important to note that articulation as utterance or mode of expression must take its form within a particular language. This language form that any articulation necessitates thus brings in its train a set of conditions that situate it as a social and cultural process.

Each of the contributors here has been urged to reflect upon how they have conjured the object of analysis, how this implies a frame against which the chosen object is set, how their figure stands against a ground of surrounding detail. These frames or backgrounds not only connect and give form to the chosen analytical figure, but they also disconnect and demarcate domains of relevance. A frame implies a disjunction; it excludes as much as it includes. This process of inclusion and exclusion is a process of power. It is our sense of relevance, driven by our theoretical outlooks and practical dispositions towards the world, that defines where these frames are to be placed. Moreover, to sharpen our own sense of the way we fabricate contexts in the processes of our own analyses might help us to become aware, in turn, of the interpretative practices and contextualising moves used by others situated elsewhere and outside the academy.

The task of anthropology is to investigate the conditions of possibility of context within not only our own bodies of knowledge but also the bodies of knowledge of native interpreters and commentators. The best that anthropological accounts can hope to do is to bring these two sets of conditions together into a relationship that is dialogic. Context has been shown to be an emergent as well as a generative property of knowledge. Indeed, contexts are sets of relations and not self-evident things in themselves. We must therefore be alive to the possibility that there are two parallel processes of construing context: for us from within our own bodies of knowledge; and for them within theirs. The conjunction of these parallel processes in the course of fieldwork or in our writing about the field and its subsequent dissemination to other readers may generate further contexts of knowledge through a dialogical relationship.

Anthropologists cannot kid themselves into believing that there is a position they can readily adopt that does not rely on context or a frame of reference. Rapport quotes Bateson who states that context depends on the questions that are asked. But a question cannot be posed without a context, without a language in which to articulate it, without a location from which to bring forth the question, or without an audience – real or imagined – who might hear and respond to it. Transparency is needed in analysis such that its frames of reference are revealed. I have attempted to contextualise the problem of context with reference to the body and the history of knowledge that is the discipline of anthropology, its connections to other neighbouring traditions, and with respect to the chapters that constitute this volume. Even those who claim to offer context-free explanations and interpretations cannot adopt a position outside time and space in which their claims or articulations are made. One cannot escape the Ishmael effect, the character who in Melville's *Moby Dick* is the only one to return to recount the tale. In other words, one cannot escape the claims that some theories make to release them from the fate to which they condemn others. Contextualising social anthropologists cannot escape from the confines of context. But context is expandable, infinitely so; and we must never lose sight of the fact that a claim about context is precisely that – an articulation concerning a set of connections and disconnections thought to be relevant to a specific agent that is socially and historically situated, and to a particular purpose.

Notes

1. I would like to thank Mark Hobart, Joanna Overing, David Riches and Nigel Rapport for taking the time to read and comment constructively upon an early draft of this Introduction. Any errors or excesses in argument, and any remaining infelicities in style are, however, my own responsibility.
2. *See* in particular M. Hobart 1982, 1985, 1986a and 1986b and M. Strathern 1987 and 1995a.
3. I use the convention of quoting only a name with no date when referring to chapters in this collection.
4. Hobart's series of writings on the related questions of meaning, text, context and interpretation have been a source of much inspiration in my thinking about and writing this Introduction (*see* for example 1982, 1985, 1986a, 1986b, 1990 and 1995). Readers familiar with his body of work will recognise its influence at many points in this Introduction. I would like to acknowledge this debt to him, and to express my appreciation for the many discussions we have had on this topic.
5. All these definitions are taken from the Shorter Oxford English Dictionary; see also Hobart 1985a for a parallel treatment.
6. I use the term 'contextualism' to designate the conventional anthropological practice, for example, which places phenomena in a social or cultural context. I contrast it with the broader term 'contextualising' or 'contextualisation', which I use to refer more generally to the processes of ordering material in analysis whether via contextualism or any other theoretical stance towards the world, such as universalism, formalism and so on.
7. Not only has Gellner failed to politicise either of these two 'concepts' or philosophical perspectives, he also fails to problematise the concept of context – although he does put great stress on its importance for social anthropology.
8. Universalism, a version of which is a doctrine or belief of universal salvation for all mankind, holds more generally to principles or propositions that comprehend or extend to the whole of mankind. Language or thought, in this view, is taken to be underwritten by a universal grammar or rationality. Formalism, in the area of ethics for example, is a doctrine that morality should be structured by a set of

abstract principles, in the manner of Kant. Scharfstein uses the term 'Absolutism', to denote one of a cluster of stances along with universalism that oppose relativism. One form of absolutism is moral absolutism, the view that certain kinds of action are always wrong or always obligatory.

9. *See* Duranti and Goodwin (1992) for a similar discussion. I am not concerned nor am I equipped to discuss in any depth the philosophical intricacies of Wittgenstein's work. I am instead interested in how anthropologists and others have read him and used him for their purposes. This account draws heavily on Gregory 1987 and Honderich 1995.

10. Philosophers conventionally characterise these two approaches to meaning as follows: meaning as a function of the relation between language and the world or between language and the mind. A third approach suggests that meaning must be studied with respect to the relation between three terms: the mind, the world and language (*see* 'Meaning' in Gregory 1987: 450-54). The concept of 'mind' is, it should be pointed out, equally as problematic as that of meaning.

11. Essentialism is a doctrine that attempts to establish a basic or primary element in the being of a thing, as the thing's nature.

12. Morris points out in relation to Durkheim's work that the conception of the abstract human being or agent is unacceptable, for Durkheim's 'real man' is 'of time and place, he has family, a city, a religious and political faith' (1991: 242). Morris adds that Durkheim argued against the idea of an 'individual or subject divorced from any specific social context' (1991: 253). In this view all philosophies are developed by philosophers who, as social agents, can be situated like Durkheim's 'real man'.

13. Geertz states: '...I want not to defend relativism, which is a drained term anyway [?], ... but to attack anti-relativism' (1984: 263).

14. For discussions of the connections between social anthropology and relativism, *see* for example Parkin (1982: xiii), Holy and Stuchlik (1983 and 1981: 30), and Overing (1985). Gellner (1985) is a sustained treatment of the subject within the social sciences. Pascal Engel raised the question of the principle of charity in his paper at the St Andrews workshop to illustrate how certain assumptions about intelligibility must be made as a prior step to interpretation.

15. This discussion draws heavily on Honderich (1995: 757-58). *See* also Hollis and Lukes (1982) for a discussion of different forms of relativism: ethical, conceptual and perceptual. The latter two might be loosely connected with 'epistemological relativism'.

16. In aesthetics, for example, contextualism as opposed to 'isolationism' involves two possible analytical directions: a work of art can be understood in the context of its historical or cultural circumstances or in the context of other works of art by the same artist or author or by those in comparable artistic traditions. Again a distinction between external and internal context emerges.

17. The work of the philosophers Quine, Davidson and Grice is relevant here, and is discussed in Gregory 1987: 450-54.

18. Ogden and Richards (1938) coin the term 'psychological context' to refer to a range of inner cognitive processes and states.

19. *See* Honderich 1995 for a discussion of Russell's philosophy.

20. *See* Hobart 1982 and Parkin 1982 for alternative renderings of the hermeneutic circle.

21. Again, I claim no specialist insight into the philosophy of Heidegger, but base this discussion on the writings of those with a broad appreciation of his work.

22. *See* Fabian 1991 in which he draws explicitly from Habermas.

23. Bakhtin remains close to a structuralist position in refusing to take the author's intentions as a way of explaining a text or a work of art, but rejects the structuralist tendency to analyse texts as though they were completely self-contained units whose meaning could be established independently of external contexts (see Lechte's discussion [1994]). Goodwin and Duranti also point out his stipulation

that in order to understand verbal communication a concrete situation needs to be specified (1992: 19). Lechte argues that for Bakhtin, context refers in his study of Dostoyevsky to the relationships between words that create meanings – which in turn become contexts for other words and meanings – and also to the contextual relations conceived in terms of a dialogue of languages, 'an intersection of meanings rather than a fixed point or single meaning' (1994: 10).

24. Some commentators view Collingwood as an interpretivist in the hermeneutic tradition (see Honderich 1995). The debate about whether he is a hermeneut, a pragmatist or whatever is too large to enter into here. I would note simply that in his *Essay of philosophical method* he advocates a method of analysis as a practical activity, an act of engagement with human experience. This human experience is embodied in the writings of philosophers whose ideas must be tested against our own, the reader's, experience (1933).

25. The more complete quotation from which this passage is taken is as follows: 'Abstraction is no longer that of the map, the double, the mirror or the concept. Simulation is no longer that of a territory, a referential being or a substance. It is the generation by models of a real without origin or reality: the hyperreal.'

26. Chaiklin and Lave (1992) contrast two major views of the concept of context: the first involves historical or systemic relations and refers to the idea of historical epochs or Marxian conceptions of historical periods characterised by modes of production; the second refers to an interactive view of activity as its own context. Jean Lave has throughout her work been sensitive to the theoretical and methodological issues surrounding the problem of context (see also Lave and Wenger [1991]). One of her themes is to contextualise learning processes in terms not of cognitive operations but of social relations and practice.

27. Holy and Stuchlik raised versions of the problem of context in various writings, especially their 1981 and 1983 publications, in questions relating to the differences between the analyst's and native knowledge. They attempted to pose a particular solution to the problem of native cultural context by defining the concept of 'folk model', a broad, common-sense background knowledge, intersubjectively shared and often beyond the means of conscious articulation and reflection by local actors.

28. Clifford states: 'The old conception of context as a fixed framework within which social activities take place becomes stretched and even shattered by means of movements of people between "intersecting contexts"' (1997: 81).What constitutes the contexts that now intersect with each other requires further explanation; he leaves scattered hints, however, that they might, for example, be construed in terms of 'world systems' (p. 276) or via Bourdieu's concept of habitus (p. 44).

29. Ormiston and Schrift (1990) make a similar point in their discussion of two conceptions of interpretation – the Stoic and the Platonic. The former eliminates the gap between interpretation and object, the latter generates and maintains it as part of its method.

30. Marcus and Cushman argue, for example, that new experimental ethnographies involve an explicit methodological concern for how they have constructed such interpretations and how they are representing them as objective discourse (1982).

31. There are exceptions to this trend generalised here, such as Kondo's monograph *Crafting selves* (1990) in which she remarks on different linguistic conventions in English and in Japanese: 'The 'I' involved [in Japanese] is not clearly divisible from the world...' whereas '... the irreducible 'I' of the English language is relatively detached from its social context'. Is the idea of a context-free essential self in strands of Anglo-American anthropology facilitated by this linguistic characteristic?

32. *See* Holy and Stuchlik (1983) for a similar view: 'Since social reality exists only as a meaningful reality, it is through creating meaning that social reality itself is created' (120).

33. He states: 'It is the character of lived experience I want to explore, not the nature of man' (1989: 2); and goes on to argue that his stance implies no constant substantive self which can address substantive others as objects of knowledge, for ' the "self" cannot be treated as a thing among things; since the self is a function of our involvement with others in a world of diverse and ever-altering interests and situations' (1989: 3).

34. Strathern returns repeatedly in her work to the question of the appropriate context for social anthropology, and asserts on numerous occasions that attention to social relations (the implicature among parts of social life) is paramount (1995b: 170), and that relationships are specifiable only with reference to contexts (1987: 269). Context here appears to suggest a locus for the enactment of social relations, and is reminiscent of the idea that activities are seen 'as constituting their own context' (see Chaiklin and Lave 1996). The view that context might be regarded as systemic or historical is not developed.

35. Cf. Herzfeld's discussion (1987) of how contextualism and context-free absolute universalism have become two types of political strategy in Greece. Context-dependence is seen by the Greek state and in academic discourse as subordinate and inferior to universalism, and as a mark of the foreign and alien in those who purvey it or which are subject to it. By contrast, local writers and regionalist often emphasise contextualism as a means of distinguishing themselves from the centralist state with its ideology of absolute knowledge and fixed meanings. The contrast with Prince and Riches is interesting: in Greece a non-dominant group make claims for contextualism; in U.K. non-dominant New Agers make claims for absolutism.

36. Epistemological domination has often been effected through essentialisation, for as Laclau and Moffle suggest essentialism has frequently led to fundamentalist and totalitarian regimes (*see* Lechte 1995). Jackson too argues that transcendence is an ideology of state power and bureaucratic control.

37. Culler discusses the activities of lawyers in terms of their mastery over context manipulation. Lawyers know that context is produced, that it is infinitely expandable, and that contextualisation is never complete. 'Rather one reaches a point where further contextualisation seems unproductive' (1988: 148).

38. I thank Mark Hobart for bringing this reference to my attention.

BIBLIOGRAPHY

Ardener, E. 1989. *The voice of prophecy and other essays* (ed. by M. Chapman). Oxford: Blackwell.

Asad, T. 1986. 'The concept of translation in British social anthropology'. In J. Clifford and G. Marcus (eds),*Writing cultures: the poetics and politics of ethnography*. 141-64. Berkeley: University of California Press.

Bateson, G. 1973. *Steps to an ecology of mind: collected essays in anthropology, psychiatry, evolution and epistemology*. St Albans: Paladin.

Baudrillard, J. 1983. *Simulacra and simulations*. trans. P. Foss, P. Patton and P. Beitchman. New York: Sémiotext(e).

Chaiklin, S. and J. Lave (eds). 1996. *Understanding practice: perspectives on activity and context*. Cambridge: Cambridge University Press.

Clifford, J. 1997. *Routes: travel and translation in the late twentieth century*. Cambridge: Harvard University Press.

Clifford, J. and G. Marcus. 1986. (eds).*Writing cultures: the poetics and politics of ethnography*. Berkeley: University of California Press.

Cohen, A.P. 1992. 'Self-conscious anthropology'. In J. Okely and H. Callaway (eds). *Anthropology and autobiography*. 221-41. London and New York: Routledge.

Collingwood, R.G. 1933. *An essay on philosophical method*. Oxford: Clarendon Press.

———. 1946. *The idea of history*. Oxford: Clarendon Press.

Crick, M. 1992. 'Ali and me: an essay in street corner anthropology'. In J. Okely and H. Callaway (eds). *Anthropology and autobiography*. 175-192. London and New York: Routledge.

Culler, J. 1981. *The pursuit of signs: semiotics, literature, deconstruction*. London: Routledge and Kegan Paul.

———. 1983. *On deconstruction: theory and criticism after structuralism*. London: Routledge and Kegan Paul.

———. 1988. *Framing the sign: criticism and its institutions*. Oxford: Blackwell.

Daryl Slack, J. 1996. 'The theory and method of articulation in cultural studies'. In D. Morley and K.-H. Chen (eds), *Stuart Hall: critical dialogues in cultural studies*. 112-27. London: Routledge.

Derrida, J. 1977. 'Signature event context', *Glyph: John Hopkins textual studies*, 1:172-97.

Dilley, R. 1992. (ed.) 'Contesting markets: a general introduction to market ideology, imagery and discourse', in *Contesting markets: analyses of ideology, discourse and practice*. 1-34. Edinburgh: Edinburgh University Press.

Duranti, A. and C. Goodwin (eds). 1992. *Rethinking context: language as an interactive phenomenon*. Cambridge and New York: Cambridge University Press.

Evans-Pritchard, E.E. 1962. *Social anthropology and other essays*. (Combining *Social anthropology* and *Essays in social anthropology*). New York: The Free Press of Glencoe.

Fabian, J. 1990. *Power and performance: ethnographic explorations through proverbial wisdom and theater in Shaba, Zaire*. Madison: University of Wisconsin Press.

———. 1991. *Time and the work of anthropology: critical essays, 1971-91*. Chur etc: Harwood Academic.

Fardon, R. 1985. (ed.). 'Introduction: a sense of relevance', in *Power and knowledge: anthropological and sociological approaches*. Edinburgh: Scottish Academic Press.

Fardon, R. 1990. (ed.). 'General introduction', in *Localising strategies: regional traditions of ethnographic writing*. 1-35. Edinburgh: Scottish Academic Press; Washington: Smithsonian Institution Press.

Fardon, R. 1995. (ed.) 'Introduction: counterworks', in *Counterworks: managing the diversity of knowledge*. 1-22. London and New York: Routledge.

Foucault, M. 1977. *Discipline and punish: the birth of the prison*. Harmondsworth: Penguin.

———. 1989. *The order of things: an archaeology of the human sciences*. London and New York: Tavistock/Routledge.

Geertz, C. 1973. *The interpretation of cultures. Selected essays*. New York: Basic Books.

————. 1984. 'Distinguished lecture: anti anti-relativism', *American Anthropologist*, 86: 263-78.

Gellner, E. 1970. 'Concepts and society'. In B. R. Wilson (ed.), *Rationality*: 18-49. Oxford: Blackwell.

————. 1985. *Relativism and the social sciences*. Cambridge: Cambridge University Press.

Goffman, I. 1974. *Frame analysis: an essay on the organisation of experience*. New York: Harper and Row.

Goodwin C. and A. Duranti, A. 1992. 'Rethinking context: an introduction', in A. Duranti and C. Goodwin (eds). *Rethinking context: language as an interactive phenomenon*.

Gregory, R.L. 1987. (ed.). *The Oxford companion to the mind*. Oxford and New York: Oxford University Press.

Gumperz, J.J. and D. Hymes. 1986. (eds). *Directions in sociolinguistics: the ethnography of communication*. Oxford: Blackwell.

Hall, S. 1996. 'On postmodernism and articulation: an interview with Stuart Hall'. In D. Morley and K.-H. Chen (eds), *Stuart Hall: critical dialogues in cultural studies*. 133-50. London: Routledge.

Heidegger, M. 1962. *Being and time*. Transl. J. Macquarrie and E. Robinson. London: SCM Press.

Hervey, S. 1982. *Semiotic perspectives*. London: Allen and Unwin.

Herzfeld, M. 1987. *Anthropology through the looking-glass: critical ethnography in the margins of Europe*. Cambridge, Mass: Cambridge University Press.

Hobart, M. 1982. 'Meaning or moaning? An ethnographic note on a little understood tribe'. In D. Parkin, (ed.), *Semantic anthropology*. 39-64. London etc.: Academic Press.

————. 1985. 'Texte est un con'. In R.H. Barnes, Daniel de Coppet, and R.J. Parkin (eds), *Contexts and levels: Anthropological essays on hierarchy*. 33-50. Oxford: JASO.

————. 1986a. 'Introduction: context, meaning and power'. In M. Hobart and R.H. Taylor (eds). *Context, meaning and power in Southeast Asia*. 7-19. Ithaca, New York: Cornell Southeast Asia Program.

————. 1986b. 'Thinker, thespian, soldier, slave? Assumptions about human nature in the study of Balinese society'. In Hobart, M. and R.H. Taylor (eds), *Context, meaning and power in Southeast Asia*. 131-56

————. 1990. 'Who do they think they are? The authorized Balinese'. In R. Fardon (ed.), *Localising strategies: regional traditions of ethnographic writing*. 303-38. Edinburgh: Scottish Academic Press; Washington: Smithsonian Institution Press.

————. 1995. 'As I lay laughing: encountering global knowledge in Bali'. In R. Fardon (ed.), *Counterworks: managing the diversity of knowledge*. 49-72.

Hollis, M and S. Lukes. 1982. (eds). *Rationality and relativism*. Oxford: Basil Blackwell.

Holy, L. 1987. 'Description, generalization and comparison: two paradigms', in L. Holy (ed.), *Comparative anthropology*. Oxford: Basil Blackwell.

————. 1989. *Kinship, honour and solidarity: cousin marriage in the Middle East*. Manchester: Manchester University Press.

———. 1990. 'Culture, cognition and practical interaction', *Cultural dynamics*, 2: 265-85.

———. 1991. *Religion and custom in a Muslim society: the Berti of Sudan*. Cambridge etc.: Cambridge University Press.

———. 1996. *The little Czech and the great Czech nation: national identity and the post-communist transformation of society*. Cambridge etc.: Cambridge University Press.

———. and M. Stuchlik. 1981. (eds). *The structure of folk models*. ASA Monographs 20. London: Academic Press.

———. and M. Stuchlik. 1983. *Actions, norms and representations: foundations of anthropological inquiry*. Cambridge: Cambridge University Press.

Honderich, T. (ed.). 1995. *The Oxford companion to philosophy*. Oxford and New York: Oxford University Press.

Hymes, D. 1977. *Foundations in sociolinguistics: an ethnographic approach*. London: Tavistock.

Ingold, T. 1996. (ed.). 'Social anthropology is a generalizing science or it is nothing' in *Key debates in anthropology*. London and New York: Routledge.

Jackson, M. 1989. *Paths towards a clearing: radical empiricism and ethnographic inquiry*. Bloomington: Indiana University Press.

———. 1996. (ed.). 'Introduction: phenomenology, radical empiricism, and anthropological critique', in *Things as they are: new directions in phenomenological anthropology*. Bloomington and Indianapolis: Indiana University Press.

Keesing, R. 1972. 'Simple models of complexity: the lure of kinship'. In P. Reining (ed.), *Kinship studies in the Morgan centennial year*. 17-31. Washington D.C.: The Anthropological Society of Washington.

Kondo, D.K. 1990. *Crafting selves: power, gender, and discourses of identity in a Japanese workplace*. Chicago and London: University of Chicago Press.

Lave, J. and E. Wenger. 1991. *Situated learning: legitimate peripheral participation*. Cambridge: Cambridge University Press.

Lechte, J. 1994. *Fifty contemporary thinkers: from structuralism to postmodernity*. London and New York: Routledge.

Lévi-Strauss, C. 1972. *The savage mind*. London: Weidenfeld and Nicholson.

———. 1979. 'The Structural study of myth', in *Structural anthropology*, Harmondsworth: Penguin.

———. 1986. *The raw and the cooked. Introduction to the science of mythology: I*. Harmondsworth: Penguin.

Lodge, D. 1993. *A David Lodge trilogy: changing places, small world, nice work*. Harmondsworth: Penguin.

Malinowski, B. 1935. *Coral gardens and their magic: a study of the methods of tilling the soil and of agricultural rites in the Trobriand islands*. London: Allen and Unwin.

Malinowski, B. 1938 [1923]. 'The problem of meaning in primitive languages', a supplementary essay in Ogden, C.K. and I.A. Richards, *The meaning of meaning*.

Marcus, George E. and Dick Cushman. 1982. 'Ethnographies as texts', *Annual review of anthropology*, 11: 25-69.

Marcus, G. and M.M.J. Fischer. 1986. *Anthropology as cultural critique: an experimental moment in the human sciences*. Chicago: Chicago University Press.

Morley, D. and K-H. Chen. (eds). 1996. *Stuart Hall: critical dialogues in cultural studies*. London: Routledge.

Morris, B. 1991. *Western conceptions of the individual*. Oxford, New York: Berg.

Ogden, C.K. and I.A. Richards. 1938 [1923]. *The meaning of meaning: a study of the influence of language upon thought and of the science of symbolism*. London: Kegan Paul, Trench, Trubner.

Ormiston, G.L. and Alan D. Schrift. (eds). 1990. *Transforming the hermeneutic context: from Nietzsche to Nancy*. Buffalo, NY.: State University of New York Press.

Overing, J. 1985. (ed.). *Reason and morality*. London and New York: Tavistock.

Palmer, R.E. 1969. *Hermeneutics: interpretation theory in Schleiermacher, Dilthey, Heidegger, and Gadamer*. Evanston: Northwestern University Press.

Parkin, D. (ed.). 1982. 'Introduction' to *Semantic anthropology*. London etc.: Academic Press.

Parkin, D. 1995. 'Latticed knowledge: eradication and dispersal of the unpalatable in Islam, medicine, and anthropological theory'. In R. Fardon (ed.), *Counterworks: managing the diversity of knowledge*. 143-63.

Poster, M. 1988. *Jean Baudrillard: selected writings*. Oxford: Polity Press.

Rabinow, R. 1984. *The Foucault reader*. Harmondsworth: Penguin.

Scharfstein, B.-A. 1989. *The dilemma of context*. New York and London: New York University Press.

Smith, N.V. 1982. (ed.) *Mutual knowledge*. London etc.: Academic Press.

Sperber, D. and D. Wilson. 1982. 'Mutual knowledge and relevance in theories of comprehension'. In N.V. Smith (ed.), *Mutual knowledge*. 61-85. London etc.: Academic Press.

Strathern, M. 1987. 'Out of context: the persuasive fictions of anthropology', *Current anthropology*, 28: 1: 251-81.

———. 1991. *Partial connections*. Savage, Maryland: Rowman and Littlefield.

———. 1995a. (ed.). 'Foreword' to *Shifting contexts: transformations in anthropological knowledge*. London and New York: Routledge.

———. 1995b. 'The nice thing about culture is that everyone has it'. In M. Strathern, (ed.), *Shifting contexts: transformations in anthropological knowledge*. 153-77. London and New York: Routledge.

Sturrock, J. 1979. *Structuralism and since: from Lévi-Strauss to Derrida*. Oxford etc.: Oxford University Press.

Taussig, M. 1993. *Mimesis and alterity: a particular history of the senses*. New York and London: Routledge.

Wittgenstein, L. 1971 [1922]. *Tractatus logico-philosophicus*. Transl. D.F. Pears and B.F. McGuinness. London: Routledge and Kegan Paul.

———. 1972 [1958]. *Philosophical investigations*. Transl. G.E.M. Anscombe. Oxford : Blackwell.

Chapter 1

CONTEXTUALISATION AND PARADIGM SHIFTS

Ladislav Holy

A recent volume of essays by anthropological linguists edited by
Duranti and Goodwin (1992) stresses that linguists are no longer content with 'analyzing language as an encapsulated formal system that
could be isolated from the rest of a society's culture and social organization' (Goodwin and Duranti 1992: 1). There is of course a long linguistic and philosophic tradition in pragmatics which resorts to
context to account for aspects of meaning in language that could not
have been accounted for by traditional semantics. But those who work
in this tradition still use as their data mostly isolated sentences and
descriptions of contextual features which they have themselves constructed to illustrate their theoretical arguments. The present move in
linguistics is from this style of analysis to the analysis of actual utterances, conversations or talk embedded within a context.

To anthropologists, the present-day linguists' interest in actual
events (naturally occurring conversations or talk) and their attempt to
understand them within the context of their occurrence, does not
sound particularly novel. Anthropologists have always been concerned with actual events (observing actual situations and unlike linguists and philosophers not constructing them for the sake of
illustrating their theoretical arguments) and as far as their attention to
context is concerned, Gellner, among many others, repeatedly made
the point that the distinguishing feature of most social anthropology
was its stress on context in analysis (1970, 1973a and b). It would not
be controversial to say that, in spite of all the changing fashions or

epistemological shifts in the discipline, context is and always has been the key anthropological concept.

I am not sure whether most anthropologists would equally be prepared explicitly to grant the same status to interpretation, given that a specific style of anthropological enquiry, which emerged in the 1960s, styled itself as 'interpretative' anthropology. Its basic assumption has been that the interpretation of a people's culture, in the sense of properly identifying the meaning of specific cultural phenomena, is a precondition of the explanation of these phenomena in the sense of elucidating the reasons for their existence. In this connection, Ortner and Whitehead suggested that 'one of the persistent problems of social anthropology ... has been that, in the rush to connect "culture" to "society", analysts have often taken culture in bits ..., nailing each bit to some specific feature of social organization ... without going through the crucial intervening phase of analyzing what that bit means' (1981: 4). I fully subscribe to this view that it is the lack of importance ascribed to the interpretation of cultural phenomena within the overall strategy of their explanation which is responsible for the failure of many attempts at relating 'culture' to 'society'. I am, however, inclined to see the main problem of social anthropology somewhat differently.

In my view, this problem is not the neglect of interpretation or the neglect of the meaning of the studied phenomena as such. Either as human beings or as anthropologists, we cannot avoid interpretation any more than we can avoid speaking or writing in symbols. Interpretation is unavoidable in principle as no phenomenon can be contemplated independently of, or prior to, its interpretation, and anthropologists have been constantly interpreting the phenomena they study. Likewise, neglect of the meaning of the studied phenomena is not a persistent problem. For again, meaning cannot be neglected in principle since it is ontologically inseparable from the existence of the phenomenon as such. The persistent problem lies in treating the interpretation – i.e. the ascription of meaning to the phenomenon and, consequently the proper identification of the phenomenon – as non-problematic. Instead of asking what the phenomenon means, it is assumed that we know what it means in the first place (Ortner and Whitehead 1981: 1). We know what it means, of course, because we have endowed it with our own meaning in the process of preinterpretation, as Hobart calls it (see chapter 5).

The basic tenet of the anthropological study of meaning carried out by symbolic, semantic or interpretative anthropologists is that meaning of social and cultural phenomena is contextual, in the sense that it derives from the relationship to other phenomena within a particular systemic context. It is precisely this emphasis on context which keeps the semantically informed study of meaning methodologically in company with orthodox positivist approaches whose basic methodological tenet is also that social and cultural phenomena must be analysed in the context of the total system of which they are part. Different conceptualisations of what precisely constitutes the systemic context of the studied phenomena reflect the ontological differences between the anthropologists explicitly interested in the study of meaning and their more positivistically inclined colleagues; but a methodological and epistemological agreement underlies this ontological difference (Parkin 1982: xvi). As meaning is the product of interpretation, one can argue that the accounts of social and cultural phenomena formulated by orthodox positivist approaches in anthropology were as much concerned with the elucidation of their meaning as are the analyses of many symbolic, semantic or interpretative anthropologists.

In spite of all the changing epistemological traditions in anthropology, the concepts of meaning and context constitute the perennial linchpins of our interpretations. Meaning has been the subject of a considerable amount of scrutiny. Context, on the other hand, has always remained 'a wastebasket label, to explain away an array of fuzzy phenomena, too complicated to understand' (Keesing 1972: 28, n. 5). It seems to me, however, that we need to pay more attention to the process of contextualisation to understand why we interpret the studied phenomena the way we do. To my mind, neither the positivistic nor the semantic style of investigation in social anthropology has paid sufficient attention to the problem of contextualisation.

Context is a frame that surrounds the phenomenon which we try to understand and that provides resources for its appropriate interpretation. The notion of context thus implies a fundamental juxtaposition of two entities: a focal phenomenon and an environment within which it is embedded (Goodwin and Duranti 1992: 3). As the formulations which I have used in the preceding two sentences suggest, the best we have so far been able to do is to picture context metaphorically: context as a frame (Goffman 1974) surrounding the phenomenon to be understood and made meaningful, context as an environment (Scharfstein 1989: 1), as a background, as a perspective (Hobart 1985, 1986: 8) or as a stage on which the phenomenon to be understood occupies the central position. The variant of the latter imagery is the linguists' metaphor of the figure and ground (Goodwin and Duranti 1992: 9-11).

The reasons why we have such difficulties in defining context and why, when talking about it, we resort to metaphorical imagery, are not difficult to grasp. Both the purpose and the meaning of a phenomenon, like the purpose and meaning of a statement, are constructed through its interpretation. When trying to comprehend the meaning of a statement, act or object, we place it in various possible contexts in our effort to interpret it. The difficulties of specifying precisely what constitutes the relevant context and of marking the context's boundary, arise from the fact that the specification of the context is itself the result of interpretation. In this sense, meaning is as much context-dependent as context is meaning-dependent. (See chapter 3 in which Tabakowska characterises context understood in this sense as a cognitive domain.)

It seems to me that, in our effort to come to grips with the meaning of social and cultural phenomena, we have too hastily disregarded the dialectical relationship between meaning and context and tried to solve the problem of meaning by concentrating on only one aspect of this dialectical relationship: the effect of context on meaning. While meaning became problematic, context was, as it were, taken for granted. Phenomena were treated as if they were inherently part of a specific context and the problem was reduced to identifying it; we have too easily overlooked the fact that the context of the phenomenon does not exist out there for us to grasp but is itself, like the meaning, the result of our interpretation. As Hobart points out, it 'is just an analytical convenience designed for a particular purpose' (1985: 34).

In my view, the whole intellectual history of anthropology bears witness to this. However else the conceptual shifts in anthropology might be envisaged, they can be seen as shifts in the conceptualisation of what constitutes the relevant context of the phenomena which anthropologists try to explain.

For Frazer, a global culture, differentiated only through the stages of savagery and civilisation (Strathern 1987: 263), was the relevant context for the beliefs, customs and ritual practices whose rationality and motivation he tried to elucidate. When his approach was later rejected by the functionalists, the main charge levelled against him was that he removed the studied phenomena from their context. In the way in which it was formulated, the charge implied that phenomena belong intrinsically to a specific context, from which they must not be removed if they are to be properly understood, and that Frazer simply chose to ignore this inherent contextual fit.

When, in their turn, the functionalists' assumptions ceased to be universally shared, it became apparent that context is in no sense 'given', and that what Frazer actually did was to remove the studied phenomena from the context in which they made sense to the functionalists: the context of the social life in which the phenomena function. This consists, on the one hand, of all actions and practices observable in a given society and the beliefs which inform them; and on the other hand, of the multiplicity of ties which bind together their performers within the system of social relations constituting a functioning whole which can be conveniently set against other such systems for comparative purposes. As Strathern points out, 'the organising analytical ideas of anthropologists were themselves contextualised by putting into *their* social context the indigenous ideas through which people organised their experiences' (1987: 259). However, she seems to me to be guilty of reifying context or seeing it as something substantive when she characterises the modernist phase of social anthropology as a phase in which the practice of comparing beliefs, customs and practices within the context of a world culture was replaced by the practice of comparing contexts. What is context in one particular type of study may well be text in another. The whole field of social relations constituting a particular society may be the relevant context for understanding a particular belief, custom or practice of that society. The same field of social relations becomes a text when compared with another such field in the context of the global field of social relations.

It would probably be futile to speculate as to whether it was the rejection of Frazer's methodology which led to the recognition of a different context as relevant for the phenomena he tried to explain, or the recognition of a different context which led to the rejection of his methodology and his style of explanation. The role ascribed to fieldwork in functionalist anthropology would favour the latter view. But whatever the cause and whatever the effect, the novel context and the novel mode of explanation went hand in hand. The very shift from the Frazerian emphasis on notions (belief) to the emphasis on action (ritual) was indicative of the recognition of new contextual relevance.

The subsequent demise of structural-functionalism, and its replacement by various kinds of interpretative approaches, can again be envisaged as a shift in the conceptualisation of the relevant context. Irrespective again of how else the shift may be conceptualised, it was to a great extent accomplished through privileging the system of signs and symbols (culture) over the system of interaction and social relations (society). For example, myth is no longer understood as a charter for social action but as an attempt at highlighting and deflecting basic conceptual contradictions; witchcraft is no longer seen as a device for coping with tensions arising from living together in society but as one of many possible ways in which human conduct can be morally evaluated (Crick 1976: 109-29), and so on.

The change from the concern with what institutions do to the concern with how they are culturally constructed is underpinned by the change in the conceptualisation of the context in which they should be properly placed. The postmodern phase in social anthropology, which manifests itself in the rise of reflexive anthropology, critical anthropology, semantic anthropology, semiotic anthropology and poststructuralism (Crick 1985: 71), is characterised by conscious 'playing with context' (Strathern 1987: 263-70).

Invocations of different contexts during the intellectual history of
anthropology (as well as in everyday practice) can be seen as having
certain common features.

1. What leads to the different contextualisation of studied phenomena
   is neither their nature nor the internal structure of context but 'the
   prior question of what is to count as context' (Goodwin and Duranti
   1992: 13). The answer to this question is determined by the analytic interest of the researchers – what they want to know about the
   contextualised phenomena. It may seem that the phenomena we
   try to explain determine how we perceive the context in which they
   are situated. But in fact what we describe as the relevant context
   depends not only on the phenomenon as such but also on what we
   want to know about it.
2. 'Omission of what is claimed to be appropriate context is treated as
   having distorted the sense of what has been "taken out of context".
   Putting something "in context", accordingly, is treated as transforming, and correcting, our understanding' (Schegloff 1992:
   193). To rethink something thus means to recontextualise it, to
   take it out of its earlier context and to place it in a new one (Goodwin and Duranti 1992: 31-32). The contextualisation of the studied phenomenon, more than anything else, determines the
   analyst's success or failure in explaining it. At the same time, the
   way in which we conceptualise the relevant context determines
   both the formulation of what we see as problems to be explained
   and what we accept as reasonable explanations (Gellner 1970: 41).
3. When placing something in proper context, we treat that context as
   reasonably well understood. The analysis focuses on what is being
   put in context; our understanding of the context is treated as reli-
   able. Context is not so much subject to analysis as it is 'invoked'
   (Schegloff 1992: 193).

Considering the importance of context in any kind of anthropological enquiry, it is remarkable to what extent the definition and delineation of context has always been regarded as unproblematic. While
other key concepts have received close scrutiny from time to time (for
meaning, see Hobart 1982), the notion of context has remained virtually unanalysed. Although different anthropological approaches differ widely in their views about what constitutes the proper context in
which the phenomena should be placed to be understood and
explained, they have always treated context as a 'given' or self-evident
construct. Maybe anthropologists were able to get on with their job
precisely because the key concept of the discipline was treated as
unproblematic. Yet, in a sense, it is the most problematic of all the con-

cepts anthropologists employ. Ultimately, of course, the limits of context 'overlap with those of the universe', as Tabakowska points out in chapter 3. But such wide conceptualisation of context is obviously neither manageable nor very practical. The world somehow has to be divided up to arrive at a manageable context into which to place a phenomenon to make sense of it. There are, of course, many different ways in which the world can be divided, and some are more useful than others. This has been well recognised in the discussion about 'relevant context', a phrase which implies that there are many contexts into which a phenomenon may be placed but that not all of them matter. It also suggests that there is no inherent relationship between a phenomenon and its context. Phenomena may be put into different contexts, or seen in different contexts, of which only some are relevant. 'On one side the subject under discussion constrains the likely range of what is pertinent. Against this, differences in roles, interest, power and perspective make the potential contexts different for those involved' (Hobart 1985: 48).

If there is no intrinsic relationship between a phenomenon and its context, there is an intrinsic relationship between the meaning of a phenomenon and its context. All theories of meaning acknowledge this relationship in one way or another (see Hobart 1982). This has, of course, always been commonsensically recognised. The charge that the intended meaning of an utterance has been altered or deliberately distorted by quoting it 'out of context' rests on the recognition that context is essential for the correct understanding of the meaning. The same utterance carries different meanings in different contexts (Tyler 1978: 31), and different utterances carry the same meaning in the same context. Nothing has meaning in isolation, and meaning and context are inseparable. Gellner's observation along the lines that 'the range of context, and the manner in which context is seen, necessarily affect interpretation' (1970: 41) has prompted Asad to point out that 'the problem is always what kind of context?' (1986: 151). Indeed.

It has also been recognised that meaning is not simply the result of consensus and a non-problematical agreement about the context into which the phenomenon 'properly' belongs. Meanings are negotiated, challenged, argued about, imposed, altered or reinterpreted to reflect changed circumstances or changed goals and aspirations of individuals and groups. In brief, meanings are subject to manipulation. And so are contexts, because if meanings are intrinsically context-dependent, any manipulation of meaning involves, perforce, manipulation of its contextualisation. And it is precisely this manipulation, or the fact that contexts are constructed for specific purposes and thus always negotiable, which makes futile any attempts at defining contexts substantively (Hobart 1985: 48). A manipulation of context may be triggered off either by the desire to impose new meaning or to reinterpret the existing meaning of a phenomenon, or by the recognition of a new conceptual domain or a new situation as a context from which the phenomenon derives its significance. In the former case, the relevant context in which to understand the phenomenon is redefined; in the latter case, the perceived meaning of the phenomenon is reinterpreted or, at least, challenged. The former process of the manipulation of meaning is widely resorted to in political practice. The latter process is exemplified by the very history of anthropology, to which I have alluded.

The intrinsic relationship between meaning and context has yet further implications for the conceptualisation of the relevant context. If the meaning of a phenomenon is understood to derive from its relationship to other phenomena within some encompassing system, then most anthropology can be said to be preoccupied with the 'meaning' of social and cultural phenomena (Parkin 1982: xvi), even if, until recently, this preoccupation has not expressly been acknowledged. The very essence of anthropological enquiry can be said to consist of the conscious attempt to render 'meaningful' the beliefs, customs and institutions of other cultures by showing their place within an integrated encompassing system. However, two types of meaning have to be clearly distinguished. So long as the cognitive endeavour of the actors is either explicitly or implicitly disregarded, the meaning ascribed to the studied phenomena is no more than a product of the reflexive consciousness of the analyst. This type of meaning can be called 'sociological' (Meeker 1976: 257) or analytical as it is formulated by the analyst on the basis of his or her understanding of the contextual relevance. In contradistinction to this, 'cultural meaning' is produced by the reflexive consciousness of the actors. Obviously, analytical and cultural meanings will diverge when the analyst situates a studied phenomenon in a context different from that in which the actors habitually situate it. Such discrepancies have consequences for anthropological analyses which have been only partially recognised.

If anthropologists endow a studied phenomenon with their own analytical meaning – that is, if they interpret the events and beliefs, and the customs and institutions of an alien culture in terms of their own criteria of discrimination, ones different from those of the culture under study – they do more than simply ignore the cultural meaning of the studied phenomenon. It has been realised that when we ascribe meaning to phenomena, we do much more than make sense of them. These phenomena do not in any sense exist without being meaningful; through ascribing any particular meaning to them, we in fact constitute them as such. When anthropologists endow a studied phenomenon with their own analytical meaning, they invariably change the object of their interest by conceptualising it in the way they do; or put another way, they themselves create an object of study which has not had any existence prior to their analysis.

The ascription of meaning to a phenomenon is the result of the way in which the phenomenon is contextualised. If phenomena may be differently interpreted or ascribed different meanings by the analysts and the actors, it logically follows that relevant contexts may also be differently defined by them. As Hobart pointed out, 'in adopting academically fashionable criteria for selecting relevant contexts in preference to those used by the participants themselves, we may be guilty simultaneously of an act of distortion and a subtle kind of epistemological domination' (1986: 8). On top of that we may do yet something else. By 'adopting academically fashionable criteria for selecting relevant contexts in preference to those used by the participants themselves', we may effectively preclude any explanation of the object of our interest because the contextualisation of the studied phenomenon, more than anything else, determines the analyst's success or failure in explaining it. The preference for marriage with a patrilateral parallel cousin in Middle Eastern societies is a case in point. Some anthropologists have openly declared it to be a phenomenon which cannot be explained sociologically, or one which occurs in settings so widely different economically, politically and culturally that, although it is possible to explain it within the specific context of one society or community, it is impossible to formulate generalisations about it which would be cross-culturally valid (Cohen 1965: 120, n.1; Davis 1977: 218; Bourdieu 1977: 47; Goody 1983: 43). I have argued elsewhere (Holy 1989) that this pessimistic conclusion is the result of considering the preference for the patrilateral cousin marriage as an action which can be understood in its 'situational context' (Keesing 1972: 18) (i.e. of considering it as an instrumental device for achieving particular goals) and of neglecting the context of all the other notions which constitute the culture of which the preference is a part (i.e. of neglecting its expressive aspects). I argued that the preference can be explained when it is considered in the multiplicity of contexts in which the actors themselves consider it and I tried to delineate how the Berti contextualise it. When considering the pragmatic reasons for which certain marriages are better than others, they formulate these reasons by considering specific marriage choices in the multiplicity of contexts: the context of the relations between spouses, the context of economic and political relations and the context of the culturally defined pattern of marriage negotiations. At the same time, the specific marriage choices are evaluated both in the contexts of asserted norms of kinship relations and in the context of the practice of these relations. Different reasons are put forward for the same marriage preferences because different people consider each marriage in specific contexts selected from the multiplicity of contexts in which the desirability of any marriage can be evaluated. The different scales of preference expressed by men and women, for example, are the product of their different roles and social positions, whereby they see different contexts as relevant and consider different pragmatic reasons as important for their particular preferences.

However, marriage not only fulfils various pragmatic functions; it is also a culturally meaningful act and the actors habitually consider the preference for FBD within the context of the cultural notions of which it is a part. The most important among them is the emphasis on kinship and the devaluation of affinity, the recognition of the agnatic ties as the closest and most binding ones, the high value placed on agnatic solidarity and the conceptualisation of gender relations whereby men are charged with control of and responsibility for the conduct of women.

The meaning of the asserted preference derives from its place in the context of all these interrelated notions. When the analysis concentrates on locating the reasons for the expressed preference in only one of the contexts from which the preference derives its meaning for the actors themselves, it robs it inevitably of the multiplicity of its cultural meanings and ultimately renders it inexplicable. When, on the other hand, we pay full attention to the way in which the actors themselves contextualise the asserted preference for marriage with a patrilateral parallel cousin, we are able to explain it as relating to the system of gender relations in which men are charged with controlling the unharnessed female power, combined with undervaluation of affinal relationships at the expense of kinship ones, and with the conceptualisation of agnatic links as those of the closest – and in extreme cases the only – kinship. On the one hand, the preference for close agnatic marriages is a logical outcome of this system of notions; on the other hand, it itself contributes to the reproduction of this system. As it is not only the place of particular marriages within the context of social action which the actors manipulate through their marriage strategies, but also their place within the context of their cultural notions, the asserted preferences are an important factor in the decisions which underlie the actors' marriage strategies. These strategies, in their turn, constitute the key element in the continuous production of the context which gives cultural meaning to gender relations, agnatic solidarity and marriage.

My purpose in introducing this brief ethnographic example was to show that disregarding the way in which the actors contextualise phenomena which we try to understand and explain and replacing their contextualisation with our own, may result not only in distortion and epistemological domination but in outright analytical failure. There are at least two ways in which anthropologists can part company with the actors in conceptualising context. The first derives from the fact that the anthropologist's interest in elucidating any phenomenon is always a theoretical one, whereas the actors' interest, if not necessarily or strictly a practical one, is always at least partly circumscribed by their practice. The anthropologist's interest is thus qualitatively different from any possible interest of the actors: he/she studies the culture; the actors live it or live by it, they create and recreate it. They may both be interpreting it, but they are interpreting it from different positions and for different purposes. Most importantly, they are interpreting it for different audiences: the actors interpret it for themselves and other members of their culture; the anthropologists interpret it for the members of their own culture or for their fellow anthropologists. The respective interpretations are carried out from vastly different vantage points. Moreover, adopting a specific vantage point always involves a precarious balancing act for the analyst. As an ethnographer, s/he is in the business of elucidating a culture with which s/he became familiar during fieldwork; as an anthropologist, s/he is in the business of contributing to the development of anthropological knowledge and theory. As a result of this dual role, what s/he wants to say about something derives also to a considerable extent from what is perceived as being worth saying about it in terms of the current anthropological theory. Consequently, in numerous subtle ways, the anthropological theory of the day affects the anthropologists' contextualisation of the studied phenomena.

The second way in which the actors' and anthropologists' contextualisations may differ is closely connected to the first. It derives from the fact that anthropologists not only have much more freedom than the actors to put the studied phenomena in a wider range of contexts, but are also in an unique position to create their own context for them. This is the context of their comparative generalisations, to which nobody except anthropologists has access, for it is a context which they define in their position as specialists in crossing cultural boundaries and as translators of cultures.

Keesing pointed out some time ago the need for a formal theory of context definition (1970: 447). But it seems to me doubtful that any formal definition of context is possible. There are two reasons for this view. The first one stems from the fact that the range of relevant contexts in which any phenomenon can be placed is potentially infinite. The second one stems from the fact that the relevant context is not given but always constructed and that its construction differs because of the differences in roles, interests, purposes and power of those who do the contextualising, whether they be actors or analysts. Gellner pointed out a long time ago that 'there is nothing in the nature of things or societies to dictate visibly just how much context is relevant to any given utterance, or how the context should be described' (1970: 33). If context is as much the result of interpretation as meaning is, as

I have tried to suggest, the presupposition for having a formal theory of context would be to have a satisfactory or formal definition of interpretation in the first place. This would require having a formal theory of making good guesses or a theory of imagination and creativity. Even if that were possible, the problem of exploring context in an attempt to arrive at its formal theory or definition would only be beginning. Resorting to yet another metaphorical imagery of context, Schlegoff points out that '"context" can appear to be a "horizontal" phenomenon. That is, like the horizon or like peripheral vision, it by definition eludes direct examination; when examined directly, it is no longer peripheral' (1992: 223, n. 4), and it is hence no longer 'context'.

Keesing argued a long time ago that 'contexts are in our heads, not "out there", and that "grammar" for creating contexts out of perceived flux must be coded in the brain' (1972: 29). People obviously learn the skills to discriminate relevant contexts and 'which context is relevant in different discursive events is something one learns in the course of living' (Asad 1986: 149). To describe how people acquire the necessary knowledge for discriminating relevant contexts appears to me to be the urgent task of the various disciplines engaged in the study of human cognition. Linguists have already embarked on this type of research. I mentioned at the beginning of this chapter that their present-day attempt to understand naturally occurring talk within the context of its occurrence would appear to anthropologists to be closely paralleling what they themselves have always been doing. Like anthropologists, the linguists interested in context treat it as providing resources for the appropriate interpretation of actual events. What is, nevertheless, novel in the linguists' approach is that rather than restricting their analyses to the resources used by an ideal, passive observer, their research 'focuses on how participants attend to, construct and manipulate aspects of context as a constitutive feature of the activities they are engaged in' (Goodwin and Duranti 1992: 9). Their analytical endeavour is thus concentrated not on formulating the formal theory of context definition but on the processes of contextualisation as an interactively constituted mode of praxis. This is the kind of research project upon which anthropologists, with their long tradition of paying attention to context, are eminently qualified to embark. To do so, our interest has to shift from context understood as the conventional anchoring of phenomena within specific systems of relations towards the active process of contextualisation as a socially and culturally situated practice (Grillo 1989: 19-20). Our close attention to how the actors contextualise phenomena in the course of their everyday living, and in the process of learning their own culture, should be an important part of the effort of shedding light upon the cognitive processes underlying the human ability to contextualise.

Bibliography

Asad, T. 1986. 'The concept of cultural translation in British social anthropology'. In J. Clifford and G.E. Marcus (eds), *Writing culture: the politics and poetics of ethnography*: 141-64. Berkeley: University of California Press.

Bourdieu, P. 1977. *Outline of a theory of practice*. Cambridge: Cambridge University Press.

Cohen, A. 1965. *Arab border-villages in Israel: a study of continuity and change in social organization*. Manchester: Manchester University Press.

Crick, M. 1976. *Explorations in language and meaning: towards a semantic anthropology*. London: Malaby Press.

———. 1985. '"Tracing" the anthropological self: quizzical reflections on fieldwork, tourism and the ludic'. *Social Analysis*, 17: 71-92.

Davis, J. 1977. *People of the Mediterranean: an essay in comparative social anthropology*. London: Routledge and Kegan Paul.

Gellner, E. 1970. 'Concepts and society'. In B.R. Wilson (ed.), *Rationality*: 18-49. Oxford: Basil Blackwell.

———. 1973a. 'The new idealism: cause and meaning in the social sciences'. In I.C. Jarvie and J. Agassi (eds), *Cause and meaning in the social sciences*: 50-76. London: Routledge and Kegan Paul.

———. 1973b. 'Time and theory in social anthropology'. In I.C. Jarvie and J. Agassi (eds), *Cause and meaning in the social sciences*: 88-106. London: Routledge and Kegan Paul.

Goody, J. 1983. *The development of the family and marriage in Europe*. Cambridge: Cambridge University Press.

Goffman, E. 1974. *Frame analysis: an essay on the organization of experience*. New York: Harper and Row.

Goodwin, C. and A. Duranti. 1992. 'Rethinking context: an introduction'. In A. Duranti and C. Goodwin (eds), *Rethinking context: language as an interactive phenomenon*: 1-42. Cambridge: Cambridge University Press.

Grillo, R. 1989. 'Anthropology, language, politics'. In R. Grillo (ed.), *Social anthropology and the politics of language*. London: Routledge.

Hobart, M. 1982. 'Meaning or moaning?: an ethnographic note on a little understood tribe'. In D. Parkin (ed.), *Semantic anthropology* (ASA Monographs 22): 39-63. London: Academic Press.

———. 1985. 'Texte est un con'. In R. H. Barnes, D. de Coppet and R.J. Parkin (eds), *Contexts and levels: anthropological essays on hierarchy*: 33-53. Oxford: JASO.

———. 1986. 'Introduction: context, meaning and power'. In M. Hobart and R. H. Taylor (eds), *Context, meaning and power in Southeast Asia*: 7-19. Ithaca, NY: Cornell University Press.

Holy, L. 1989. *Kinship, honour and solidarity: cousin marriage in the Middle East*. Manchester: Manchester University Press.

Keesing, R.M. 1970. 'Toward a model of role analysis'. In R. Naroll and R. Cohen (eds), *A handbook of method in cultural anthropology*: 423-53. New York: Columbia University Press.

————. 1972. 'Simple models of complexity: the lure of kinship'. In P. Reining (ed.), *Kinship studies in the Morgan centennial year:* 17-31. Washington, DC: The Anthropological Society of Washington.

Meeker, M.E. 1976. 'Meaning and society in the Near East: examples from the Black Sea Turks and the Levantine Arabs'. *International Journal of Middle East Studies* 7: 243-70, 388-422.

Ortner, S.B. and H. Whitehead. 1981. 'Accounting for sexual meanings'. Introduction to S. B. Ortner and H. Whitehead (eds), *Sexual meanings: the cultural construction of gender and sexuality:* 1-27. Cambridge: Cambridge University Press.

Parkin, D. 1982. 'Introduction' to D. Parkin (ed.), *Semantic anthropology* (ASA Monographs 22): xi-li. London: Academic Press.

Scharfstein, B. 1989. *The dilemma of context.* New York: Columbia University Press.

Schegloff, E. A. 1992. 'In another context'. In A. Duranti and C. Goodwin (eds), *Rethinking context: language as an interactive phenomenon:* 191-227. Cambridge: Cambridge University Press.

Strathern, M. 1987. 'Out of context: the persuasive fictions of anthropology.' *Current anthropology* 28: 251-81.

Tyler, S. 1978. *The said and the unsaid.* London: Academic Press.

Chapter 2

CONTEXT, THE GHOST
IN THE MACHINE

Sándor G.J. Hervey

Writing in the climate of the 1990s I am likely to be damned in advance by my very choice of such a title for such a chapter in such a context as the present collection. At the very least, indeed, that title inevitably condemns me to the role of devil's advocate in the on-going debate about 'context': a paradoxical role which I, nonetheless, undertake willingly.

My role as devil's advocate dictates that my remit will not be to point forward towards an optimistic future in which various social sciences (from theoretical linguistics, through textual criticism and semiotics, to anthropology) finally manage to integrate context into their explanatory accounts, and into its predestined central place in explanation. Rather, I shall begin by pointing back to a number of quite 'old-fashioned' approaches in which, EVEN several decades ago, context was intended to hold a central place. In short, the first article of my brief is to serve a reminder of how little is new in the idea of invoking context as a device in social scientific explanation.

Long before I first became acquainted with theoretical linguistics (back in the mid-1960s) the association of the London School of Linguistics with the concept of 'context-of-situation' was already a commonplace in comparative accounts of linguistic paradigms (Robins, 1967). Thus, as a student I was taught that one of the hallmarks of the London School (tracing its intellectual ancestry from Malinowski and Firth) was the unique attention this approach paid to 'context-of-situation' as a theoretical and methodological key to the identity and the meaning of linguistic elements. Where, as my mentors were careful to point out, other approaches such as those inspired by Saussure, by Boas, Sapir and Bloomfield, or for that matter by Chomsky, treated language as a *closed* system of formal units, autonomous and hermetically sealed off from external influence, the London School had the 'advantage' of never losing sight of the fact that language operates in extra-linguistic contexts of situation and derives its meaning from these contexts. Indeed, the equation 'meaning is function in context' is a cornerstone of the linguistic approach inherited from Malinowski (1935) via Firth (1957).

Through the work of Noam Chomsky's supervisor and precursor, the American linguist Z.S. Harris (1951), I became familiar with another form of 'contextualism' dating from the first half of the twentieth century: the approach known as 'distributionalism'. The salient feature of this approach rests in the idea that linguistic units *are* what they *do*, and what they do is to occur in contexts. That is to say, the very identity of linguistic units (phonemes, words, phrases, sentences) is defined by their *distribution*, which, in turn, is defined as the total array of the environments in which each unit can occur. According to Harris' position, operations with this *formal* concept of 'distribution' can, and should, be substituted for the impossible search for 'meanings'. In short, distributionalism counts as an early exponent of 'contextualist' approaches to 'meaning'; a version of a group of approaches classed together under the unifying slogan borrowed from Wittgenstein: 'don't look for the meaning, look for the use'. In Harris's distributionalism the proviso is, of course, that 'use' (here synonymous with 'occurrence in an array of environments') can be quasi-mathematically measured by scanning the entire set of environments in which each given unit occurs. A major criticism (which I mention here only in passing, though it is a serious point to which I intend to return later in a wider connection) incurred by this operationalist method of quasi-quantitative measurement is that, ultimately, the environments in which linguistic units occur are *utterances*; and the array of utterances in which any unit can occur is in principle infinite. Consequently, in quantitative terms, the measure of the occurrences (= distribution = identity) of linguistic units (in particular, words) is a function of infinity. Needless to say, such a function of infinity is quantitatively vacuous – for the simple reason that one cannot scan, or measure, a set which is infinite. In practical terms, this vacuity is sidestepped by operationally substituting a corpus (a finite collection of utterances) for the open-ended set of real events to which utterances actually belong. In short, the ultimate 'context' of distributionalism is not the infinitely creative use of utterances in actual communication, but an artificially created and artificially closed corpus. So-called 'corpus-based' approaches prevalent in 'Bloomfieldian' structuralist linguistics (Bloomfield, 1935; *see also* Hockett, 1958; Longacre, 1964) find their shortcomings in this implicit stipulation of a restricted and ad hoc collection of data as the context that frames the methodology of linguistic description.

The formulation of 'environment' in Harris-type distributionalism is a particularly formalistic and narrowly focused one: the environment of any element X is constituted wholly by the surrounding elements, each of which must be of the same ontological type as the element X itself. An environment for a given *linguistic* unit, then, is literally a narrow frame of surrounding linguistic units of the same type: /p --- t/ is a phonemic environment, or frame, in which the phoneme /i/ can occur to create an utterance of the word 'pit'; 'The --- went home.' is a grammatical environment, or frame, in which the word 'students' can occur to create an utterance of the sentence 'The students went home.', and so on. In short, the very concept of environment is, in this version of 'contextualism', hermetically sealed into the language-system under investigation. As we shall see later, a system-bound notion of context, as typically exemplified in distributionalism, has both important advantages and serious disadvantages.

John Lyons's 1961 Ph.D. dissertation, published as *Structural Semantics* in 1967, went one inevitable step beyond distributionalism by proposing the double framing of linguistic units, first in a linguistic *environment* in which they co-occur, and contrast, with other linguistic units of the same kind; and second, in a *context* in which linguistic utterances, as self-contained wholes, are embedded. The formula for this two-layered contextualist model sets off the hierarchically lower *environment* (symbolised by E and defined as an array of linguistic co-occurrents) against *context*, symbolised by K and given as an array of extra-linguistic situational factors.

In Lyons' theory, the hierarchically successive frames are formalised as follows:

$E = (X \text{---} Y)$ (where X and Y are linguistic units constituting a frame into which linguistic unit Z, of the same ontological type, can be slotted),

$K (X \text{---} Y)$ (where K stands for an array of information about features of a given context of situation).

However, in significant contrast to distributionalism and in the spirit of an approach influenced by Firthian linguistics, relevant occurrences of linguistic units are not measured here in terms of linguistic environments alone. Rather, they are assessed in a wider extra-linguistic frame in which the narrowly linguistic environment is embedded in its own turn.

For instance, and I am freely adapting Lyons's example here, a particular environmental frame such as 'Twenty ---- please.' might, on a given occasion, be embedded in a situational frame (K_j) containing the following contextual information: 'speaker A enters a tobacconist's shop and addresses the tobacconist'. Given such a circumscription of K_j, the most probable items likely to fill the blank slot in the environment 'Twenty ---- please.' are such linguistic units as 'Kensitas', 'Embassy', 'Lambert and Butler', and the like. Items such as 'boxes of matches', 'balloons', 'packets of drawing pins' are, somehow, less immediately probable – but they remain clear possibilities. Other items such as 'pints of milk', 'loaves of bread' are not totally improbable, given the range of things stocked by tobacconists, though they may raise a few eyebrows, along with the question: why should speaker A want so much milk or so many loaves? Had we been given K_j to which is added the information that 'speaker A is intending to feed a large number of visitors', this would, of course, have removed the improbability in question. However, items such as 'pounds of steak', 'ounces of garlic sausage', would still remain entirely improbable; while items such as 'bananas' or 'first class stamps' would constitute marginal cases.

From the last observation it transpires that K_j contains far more than what is explicitly stipulated in it: namely, it contains culture-specific items of background information such as the knowledge that tobacconists do not sell steak or garlic sausage, though they may, perhaps, sell bananas or stamps. The presence, in any given context of situation, of unspoken, culturally presupposed, items of cultural information has far-reaching implications: the issue of this vitally important pointer to the open-endedness of context is yet again a consideration to be stored up for later, more general, discussion.

For the moment we remain with the particulars of Lyons's early attempt at using context as a means of semantic description. Evidently, the method envisaged was aimed at establishing the situations *in which* the use of a linguistic item (an utterance, or part of an utterance) is *applicable*. In such an approach situational applicability must, of course, be seen as a matter of probabilities: the more predictable a linguistic item is in its situational context, the more probable and semantically unexceptional its occurrence in that context. But, from this it follows that the more we know about the details of a situational context, the more probable will seem the occurrence of certain linguistic items in it, and the less probable the occurrence of certain other items. The methodological problem this poses is a further point to be stored up for more general discussion at a later stage.

One cannot help noticing in Lyons's exposition a feature that is characteristic of the type of approach to context he exemplifies: namely, the manipulation of tailor-made contexts of situation. While

Lyons's examples, and, hopefully, my elaborations of them, may seem plausibly commonplace, the fact of the matter is that these are examples entirely under the control of the analyst, since analysts invent them as they go along. Real contexts are of course not like this, but – and here lies yet another point to store up for subsequent discussion – it is doubtful whether analysts are capable of coming to terms with real contexts of situation as opposed to (at best plausible) artificially made-up ones.

Not only Lyons, but a much earlier exponent of context, the American philosopher and semiotician Charles Morris (particularly in his 1964 volume *Signification and Significance*) espouses an approach entirely given to the manipulation of self-invented examples in which, somewhat in the manner of the omniscient fiction-writer, he is in full authorial control of the details of situational context. While *semiosis*, in Morris's later work, is theoretically defined as a five-term constellation of a SIGN, an INTERPRETER, an INTERPRETANT, an OBJECT and a CONTEXT, in practice he invariably operates with context as a given, rather than as a genuine empirical analysand. The actual analysis of context of situation, as opposed to its manipulation in invented examples, must be seen as one of the weak points of contextualist approaches in general.

I have now assembled a sufficient number of significant bits and pieces – problems illustrated from a variety of fairly old sources, but problems which, I contend, persist to date – to put together a case for a devil's advocate. It is a case that, at the very least, might indicate why in the 1990s we are still discussing unsolved issues relating to the notion of context. It would not surprise me at all, though this is not a point I can substantiate, if some of these issues proved to be not merely unsolved but insoluble.

My case consists of the following general points:

1. Certain problems of meaning in linguistics, and of interpretation in anthropology, can only be dealt with by reference to situational context.
2. Even the narrowest conception of context, defined in terms of immediate linguistic environment, runs into a 'Hobson's choice' between an infinity of variables and arbitrary reductionism.
3. Even the narrowest, arbitrary formulation of a given situational context is open-ended.
4. The selection of the details relevant to a particular context of situation is, in the final analysis, a matter of arbitrary choice for the analyst.
5. Context cannot be invoked as a means of explanation unless it is brought within the scope of the analyst's theory.

6. Bringing context within the scope of the analyst's theory entails a
choice between infinite regression and inherent circularity.

The first of the above points can be dealt with by providing just one
typical example from linguistics, and just one typical example from
anthropology, to illustrate how certain types of problem cannot even
be formulated without recourse to context. A relatively simple linguistic example involves the meaning of the word 'dog'. Along with other
words like 'cat', 'sheep', 'goat' etc., this word, taken in the abstract,
seems simply to designate a particular animal species. However, unlike
the words 'cat', 'sheep' and 'goat', the word 'dog' can assume the
strictly gender-specific meaning of 'male dog': compare the perfectly
sensible sentence 'Do you want a dog or a bitch?' with the anomalous
sentences 'Do you want a cat or a she-cat?', 'Do you want a sheep or a
ewe?' and 'Do you want a goat or a nanny-goat?'. The semantic problem that lurks here cannot even be sensibly formulated unless we
assume that (unlike 'cat', 'sheep', 'goat') the word 'dog' has a semantic potential to double as a gender-neutral species term and as a male-
gender-specific term (Hervey, 1980), and that some feature or features
external to the word – features of linguistic environment and/or features of situational context – have the power to trigger one or other of
these two semantic potentials.

In general, all connotative meanings in language (without which
no text can be more than superficially understood) require such contextual triggering from outside the words and sentences endowed with
connotative potential. Thus, a full account of linguistic meaning must
at some point invoke context as an explanatory device.

As for interpretation in anthropology, the single example of 'violence' (Riches, 1986) will be sufficient to serve my present purpose
here. It is, I take it, entirely uncontentious that an act answering a
particular physical description can, in different circumstances be
counted as an act of 'violence', of 'justice', or even of 'mercy'. The formulation of problems related to 'violence' is, therefore, clearly impossible without framing them in culturally constructed contexts of
situation. What holds for 'violence' as an analytic term in anthropology holds by extension for terms used in anthropological explanation
in general: all cultural constructs in anthropology need to be interpreted and construed with the aid of context.

For my second point we need to look back briefly at Harris's distributionalism as a maximally narrow conception of context equated with
linguistic environment. It may be imagined that, by remaining firmly
locked within the narrow confines of a single language system, distributionalism has succeeded in making the occurrence of linguistic
items in linguistic contexts truly measurable. But to suppose this

would be to forget that language itself has its own inherent potential for infinity. Since, in fact, the linguistic items 'Kensitas', 'Embassy', 'Lambert and Butler' can each figure in an infinite number of utterances, what use is it to say that each of them has a measurable distribution? The measure of that distribution will always be infinity. Equally, the probability of occurrence of a linguistic item in an environment can only be a meaningful measure if it is expressed as a fraction of some real number; it is quantitatively vacuous if it has to be expressed as a fraction of infinity. The logical implications of distributionalism, if we follow this alternative, are that every meaningful linguistic unit has a meaning determined by an infinity of variables: an infinite set of variable environments. There is, of course, another alternative, which is to systematise variable environments and aim at general statements that stipulate how 'Kensitas', 'Embassy', 'Lambert and Butler' etc. *typically* appear in certain *kinds* of environment, of which 'Twenty --- please' is one. However, in the first place, this alternative is no longer *quantitative* in the way required of a distributionalist approach, but has shifted gear into a *qualitative* mode; and, in the second place, it raises the entire question of justification for the process by which the infinite array of environments is artificially reduced to a finite set of *kinds* of environment. The resulting reductionism is bound, as far as I can see, to suffer the usual fate of all reductionism: to be open to the charge of using an arbitrary, unjustified descriptive procedure driven by a ghost in the machine. In the long term, the effects of this ghost in the machine boil down to explaining the unexplained by the inexplicable. Looking at these two alternatives – that of sinking in the mire of an infinite variability and that of resorting to an arbitrary reductionism – we are indeed faced with a choice between two evils. Unless there is a third option, of whose existence I am not aware, even the most formally restricted conception of context is either a term for an imponderable infinity, or a label for a *deus ex machina* .

My third point makes a concession to the arbitrary formulation of given contexts and amplifies a remark I made earlier in connection with the invented example of a customer entering a tobacconist's shop. In this instance the analyst has been given complete freedom to elaborate a definition of the required context; yet we found that probabilities and improbabilities of events in even that narrowly framed context were not entirely governed by features explicitly stipulated in the formulation of the context. Not to put too fine a point on it, features in the formulation – such as 'tobacconist's shop' – are cross-referenced with items of cultural knowledge concerning what we can or cannot reasonably expect of such an essentially culture-specific institution. We can put no limit to this cultural cross-referencing, which may pull into the context any of an open-ended set of items of information available to cultural agents and analysts alike as part of their cultural competence. This being so, the notion of a context that is *closed*, so that its finite features can be systematically manipulated in description or interpretation, is chimeric. On the other hand, an open-ended context, whose properties and contents are inherently only known in part, is as much of a ghost in the machine when used in explanation as a context conjured into existence by the magic of artificial reductionism.

My fourth point is a critical elaboration on the reductionist alternative discussed above. Given that contexts are to be manipulated as devices for explaining linguistic or cultural events (in linguistics and anthropology, respectively), it is inevitable that the analyst will select just those features in a given context which will answer the need for what has to be explained. If, as linguists, we were seeking an extra-linguistic contextual frame for a particular utterance 'Good --- ', situational features such as 'speaker A enters a tobacconist's shop and addresses the tobacconist' would *a priori* be insufficient for our purposes, as these say nothing about the relative probability of the occurrence of 'morning', 'afternoon' or 'evening' as part of the greeting applicable in a given situation. From common sense alone, the analyst knows in advance what relevant contextual cues are missing from this description. Naturally, in such an instance, the analyst would 'top up' the stipulated context so as to read as, say, 'speaker A enters a tobacconist's shop at 10.34 a.m. and addresses the tobacconist' – a formulation that makes the occurrence of 'Good morning' highly contextually probable. That may seem fair enough, and no more than common sense. However, as a method of description and explanation, this common-sensical procedure invites serious critical comment: the analyst's formulation and reformulation of contexts of situation in such a way that they meet explanatory needs constitutes a form of begging the question. It is because the analyst knows in advance how appropriate greetings differ according to the time of day when they are uttered that cues about the time of day are selected as a relevant part of the context. The explanation is, therefore, based ultimately on the analyst's prior intuitions, which the formalisation of a pseudo-objective context of situation merely serves to disguise. The process is circular at best, and constitutes the most utterly trivial, as well as deceptive, use of what is intended to serve as a central descriptive device. Because of the element of ad hoc selection inherent in circumscribing a relevant context, it is difficult for me to imagine how context could be used in ways other than simply to confirm what analysts already know, while pretending that they are just finding this out. In this sense, yet again, context seems to figure as a ghost in the machine.

My fifth point relates back to my earlier complaint that context often seems to be a means of explaining the unexplained by the inexplicable. The substance of this objection is simply that context cannot be invoked as an explanatory concept unless the analyst invoking it can claim technical expertise in 'contextology' (i.e., in studying and understanding contexts as objects of disciplined analysis in their own right). In short, whatever falls outside the analyst's competence, because it is beyond the theoretical scope of investigation, is bound to constitute a weak point in overall approach: and all the more so when the object falling beyond this scope is a crucial ingredient to explanatory interpretation. It is in a similar vein that Thompson criticises studies of discourse analysis for failing, in their praiseworthy effort to deal with the relations between linguistic and non-linguistic activity, 'to provide a satisfactory account of the non-linguistic' (1984: 100). It is, of course, hardly surprising that the non-linguistic side of the relationship, which is largely outside the competence of discourse analysts, should constitute the weak point in their approach: a point where explanatory key concepts remain undefined. Context itself remains inevitably an ill-defined key concept in explanatory accounts that invoke it as a solution from beyond their own theoretical scope.

My final point can best be approached by comparing linguistics with anthropology. I would have no hesitation in contending that, unlike textual context, situational context (alias extra-linguistic context) can never be brought into the scope of linguistics, and that, therefore, invoking situational context in explaining linguistic behaviour will always be a case of explaining the not fully known in terms of the fully unknown. Unless a branch of linguistics is brought within the scope of anthropology – as is more-or-less the case in Dell Hymes's 'ethnography of communication' (1964) – the very fact that context (as opposed to strictly linguistic environment) is 'extra-linguistic' militates against the possibility that it might be systematically and meaningfully employed as a device in linguistic description. If context of situation were to be used as such a device, the linguist would have to be able to claim a firm analytic grasp of this analytic tool, and of the theory and methodology behind its refinement. There are two alternatives for making this claim: either the explication of context is borrowed from some other discipline credited with a higher competence (a case of 'passing the buck'), or the notion of context is restricted to a narrow domain that is within the competence of the analyst's discipline. A linguist would fare relatively poorly with either of these alternatives. Passing the buck to another discipline would merely raise the question of whether that discipline can justifiably claim a firm analytic grasp of context; staying within a restricted domain would simply instigate a circular, hermetically sealed description doomed to fail as 'a satisfactory account' of the non-linguistic factors that influence much of linguistic behaviour.

However, the situation is more problematic, and more generally problematic than even the foregoing would suggest. There is a simple argument that runs as follows: if every object of description needs to be externally contextualised in order to be interpreted, then every context used in explaining some other object is, itself, also an object that needs to be contextualised... and so on *ad infinitum*. The upshot of this argument is that the requirement for external contextualisation leads to infinite regression.

On the other hand, if every object of description needs only to be internally contextualised, relative to other objects in the same closed system, then objects of description and interpretation merely explain one another mutually and reciprocally. The conclusion from this argument is that a requirement for internal contextualisation leads to inherent descriptive circularity.

I have suggested that linguistics would fare equally badly with either of the two alternatives of external and internal contextualisation. This is due to my conviction that, although in principle internal contextualisation is the more defensible option, the domain to which this option confines linguistics (essentially the domain of linguistic, or at best textual, environment) is too narrow and impoverished to offer a satisfactory account of linguistic behaviour. Far too many factors influencing linguistic behaviour (both competence and performance) fall, as we know, outside the narrow margins of linguistic theory and into the broader domain of the social and cultural.

Following this line of thought, anthropologists should fare better on this score. Since context must surely be textured out of the very social fabric whose weaving they study, internal contextualisation does not necessarily imprison them in a domain from which vast numbers of factors necessary for explanation are known to be excluded. In other words, in principle at least, one could make out a case that the process of internal contextualisation is not *viciously* circular in anthropology. In order to argue this case, one would have to imagine that anthropology has access to the entire gamut of social and cultural factors: that is, to every feature of social context that might be required for making sense of any other social feature. While, ultimately, social factors would be used to make sense of each other in this scheme of things, the circularity would not be rendered vicious by the fact that vital (external) factors were seen to be missing. Such a conception of an anthropology capable of dealing with contexts by virtue of the fact that all contexts are, themselves, culturally constructed objects fully open to anthropological investigation, is an unashamedly idealistic, not to say utopian, one. I make no apology for this: for I consider it significant that at least in principle it is feasible to conceive of an anthropological approach in which context is, at the same time, both a valid explanatory device and an object of description. Whether such an ideal can be realised in practice is, of course, another matter: the ideal can define a direction for anthropology to follow.

However, I feel that some of my earlier stated misgivings must hold even for anthropology. To make, in a large, integrated, and intertwined scheme of culture, *one* set of cultural factors the context for *another* set seems to be one thing – and, in principle, unobjectionable. In this way, context can, indeed, be brought within the scope of anthropological theory: as simply neither more nor less than part of culture. Yet it seems more common for anthropology to look to some other discipline or theory to supply it with the means of analysing and administering context. This alternative is fraught with danger. The assumption that the external theory invoked is capable of giving an account of context is likely to be the result of a naive overestimation of the achievements of other disciplines (for instance, in the past, anthropologists have been guilty of naively overestimating the potency of linguistic theory and of social psychology). Since contexts are, in general, socially and culturally construed, it is highly unlikely that a theory outside of anthropology should hold the key to their understanding. There is also the consideration that the external theory invoked may in its own turn need to invoke context as part of its own explanatory mechanisms; in which case a chain of infinite regressions might be set up, merely shifting the responsibility for explanation from one discipline to another.

In conclusion, if anthropology insists on viewing context as something external that can be invoked for purposes of explanation, yet is itself beyond anthropological explanation, then it will fare no better than has contextualism in linguistics. That is, if anthropology looks to context as some kind of externally administered magic potion, it will find context operating as a 'ghost in the machine' – more of a hindrance than a help to rational discussion.

Bibliography

Bloomfield, L. 1935. *Language*. London: Allen and Unwin.

Firth, J.R. 1957. *Papers in linguistics*. Oxford: Oxford University Press.

Harris, Z.S. 1951. *Structural linguistics*. Chicago: University of Chicago Press.

Hervey, S. 1980. 'Rétrécissement connotatif et antonymie connotative', in M. Mahmoudian (ed.), *Linguistique fonctionnelle*: 119-44. Paris: Presses Universitaires de France.

Hockett, C. 1958. *A course in modern linguistics*. New York: Macmillan.

Hymes, D. (ed.). 1964. *Language in culture and society*. New York: Harper and Row.

Longacre, R. E. 1964. *Grammar discovery procedures*. The Hague: Mouton.

Lyons, J. 1967. *Structural semantics*. Oxford: Blackwell.

Malinowski, B. 1935. 'An ethnographic theory of language', in *Coral gardens and their magic.* vol. 2: London: Allen and Unwin.

Morris, C. 1964. *Signification and significance* . Cambridge(Mass.): M.I.T. Press.

Riches, D. 1986. 'The Phenomenon of violence', in D. Riches (ed.) *The anthropology of violence.* Oxford: Blackwell.

Robins, R.H. 1967. (1990, 3rd edn.). *A short history of linguistics.* Harlow: Longman.

Thompson, J.B. 1984. *Studies in the theory of ideology.* Cambridge: Polity Press.

NEW PARADIGM THINKING IN LINGUISTICS

MEANING IS THE CONTEXT

Elżbieta Tabakowska

Paradigm Shift: Science and Linguistics

In the late 1970s the cognitive approach to the study of language (most clearly reflected in theoretical works by Ronald Langacker and in George Lakoff's research on the nature of metaphor) emerged as the strongest opponent against contemporary mainstream linguistics inspired by Chomsky's theory of generative grammar. The fundamental opposition between Generative-Transformational Grammars on the one hand and the emerging paradigm which became known as Cognitive Linguistics on the other figures quite prominently in what happens today in American and European linguistics.

It could hardly be said that the cognitivists offer an entirely new paradigm for linguistics; rather than claiming new discoveries, they aim at providing a coherent and comprehensive theoretical framework for many old intuitions, such as can be found in the works of 'traditional' linguists and philosophers of language. Thus the paradigm is 'new' only in the relative sense: in the context of the present situation in theoretical linguistics. However, interestingly enough, its development reflects parallel developments in science, thus marking what seems to be the advance of a more general paradigm shift, in the sense of Kuhn, 1962.

In Kuhn's terms, the phase of 'normal science' (or steady accumulation of facts and statements within the existing structuralist paradigm: 'growth without change') could be seen as coming to an end,
giving way to a 'pre-paradigmatic period', in which opposing views
begin to compete.

Obvious limitations of the 'old paradigm' make the proponents of
transformational and generative frameworks face certain insurmountable problems. Their fundamental dogma (i.e. autonomy of language, of
its individual components and, finally, of linguistics itself as a branch of
science) means strict separation from all other domains of cognition, as
well as total abstraction from all extra-linguistic context. The final objective of the formalisation of grammars as systems of rules (with particular emphasis on autonomous syntax), has been proving increasingly
unrealistic. The model has been repeatedly (and justifiably) accused of
being too abstract to be useful in dealing with natural languages, and
too Anglocentric to cope with the diversity of empirical evidence coming
from the many 'exotic' languages of the world. More importantly, the
'old paradigm' has so far failed to propose an integrated theory such as
could re-unite the constituents of language which it had been striving to
single out, namely, phonology, syntax, lexicon and semantics.

In what follows I would like to justify the claim that the cognitive
approach in linguistics should indeed be considered as an emerging
'new paradigm', and that it stands a good chance of gaining the upper
hand in an approaching 'scientific revolution'.

In their most interesting and inspiring discussion on modern
physics and new theology, Capra *et al.* (1991) claim that a general paradigm shift in science may be seen to take five basic directions:

1. from *structure* to *process*;
2. from *part* to *whole*;
3. from *objective science* to *epistemic science*;
4. from 'building' to 'network' model of knowledge;
5. from the *search for truth* to *approximate description* as the final objective of research.

The first two criteria are ontological; the third one pertains to the
epistemology of science; the last two involve methodology.

The first change implies a shift from the assumption that structures
are objects on which certain forces act in order to bring about certain
processes to the assumption that every structure must be seen as a
'manifestation of an undergoing process' (Capra *et al.* 1991: xii).
Applied to the study of language it means, for instance, bridging the
methodological gap between diachrony and synchrony, which was
carefully maintained (and sustained) by de Saussurian structuralism

(cf. Winters 1992: 504). Cognitive Linguistics postulates full integration of these two aspects of language: it claims that the investigation of the diachronic development of language reveals certain cognitive mechanisms which motivate seemingly arbitrary synchronic structures. Such mechanisms prove much more intricate than those governing the well-known semantic changes of lexical meaning. To quote just one example, an attempt at tracing down the history of conditional constructions in languages as unrelated as English and Polish not only reveals the common motivating principle behind the structuring and arrangement of protasis and apodosis, but consistently explains a more general process of grammaticalisation, by showing the analogous development of English and Polish conditional conjunctions from expressions of spatial deixis to abstract means of textual organisation (for discussion, see Tabakowska 1997; Traugott 1997). Ultimately, the 'new paradigm' challenges the postulate of strict arbitrariness of language, which is the cornerstone of classical linguistic structuralism. On the other hand, by claiming experiential and/or cognitive motivation for large areas of language, it brings linguistics closer to a reconciliation with cognitive and social anthropology.

The second ontological aspect of what Capra *et al.* consider as the oncoming paradigm shift, i.e. the shift from part to whole, means rejecting the old assumption that the workings of a whole can only be understood following the scrutiny of constituent elements. Similar to movements in such disparate disciplines as medicine or the science of remote control systems, in cognitive linguistics the shift is in favour of the network model. A *part* is defined as a recurring and recognisable pattern that can be identified within a network of interrelationships. Every act of separating a part from the whole necessarily means cutting off at least some of the interconnections, and thus must lead to a false, or at best only partial, description. Things have no absolutely intrinsic properties, and nothing exists as an *isolated part* of some other thing. These assumptions, formulated by scientists (but also adopted by, for instance, the proponents of an analogous changed paradigm in theology, *see* Capra *et al.* 1991), are readily recognised by linguists of the cognitive persuasion. Such phenomena as verbal deixis or referentiality (now defined as linguistic means which serve the purpose of locating entities in physical or mental space), are generally recognised as definable only in terms of interrelational properties, while the application of the network model to the description of both grammatical and semantic categories is a fundamental theoretical principle of linguistic investigation: it is only too natural to assume that the organisation of human language should be the reflection of the overall psychological organisation of human cognition.

What applies to the structure of language applies in the same measure to the structure of linguistics; within the cognitive framework, language makes sense only in so far as it fits into a larger network, and so does linguistics as a scholarly discipline. Language must be placed in a physical, psychological, social and cultural context, and therefore the context for linguistics must be heterogeneous. This approach entails obvious methodological problems: if one adheres to the network model and accepts that '[m]eaning is context. It is the way things fit into the larger whole' (Capra *et al.* 1991: 97), then one also has to admit that the limits of *context* ultimately overlap those of the universe. It is therefore necessary to postulate certain methodological restrictions: to define the scope of human cognition that underlies human creation and use of language, to isolate speech events as 'chunks' of social interaction, and to delimit the area of linguistic investigation. The interpretations and the definitions follow from epistemological principles that underlie the 'new paradigm' (*see* sections 2-4 below).

In epistemology, the shift from objective to epistemic science means emphasis on the role of the human observer and the process of knowledge, i.e. acceptance of a basically 'constructivist approach': gaining knowledge means building the world. The assumption that the world does not 'exist' in an objective sense, but is created, or brought to existence, in the process of knowing, finds direct reflection in language. Thus, for instance, people who speak English talk about the sun 'setting in the west' and 'rising in the east' almost half a millennium after Copernicus, and whether the time 'flows' like a river (as it does in English), 'grows' like a tree or 'falls' like a waterfall (as it does in Mandarin Chinese; cf. Lee Chen 1993) depends on how the 'individual human observer' responsible for first creating an expression that with time became the linguistic convention happened to see the things around him. Human knowledge (the way humans make their world) is mirrored by human language (the way humans speak about their world) (Goodman 1979).

The same principle applies to how human language deals with de Saussurian 'semantic coverage': it reflects the way people see things. 'There is a reality, but there are not things, no trees, no birds. The patterns are what we create. As we focus on a particular pattern and then cut it out from the rest, it becomes an object. ... What we see depends on how we look' (Capra *et al.* 1991: 124). Fritjof Capra said this in relation to modern theoretical physics, but the quotation could well be used as the opening sentence in an introduction to cognitive linguistics.

Applied to methodology, the constructivist approach implies a radical shift from the traditional assumption that knowledge is based on certain unchanging 'fundaments', sanctioned by the objectivity of 'things': 'fundamental' laws, 'fundamental' principles (Capra *et al.* 1991: xiii). In the 'new paradigm' the old metaphor 'knowledge is a building' is being replaced with the metaphor of 'network': like the reality itself, which is the object of our perception, our description of reality constitutes a network of interrelationships. In the new paradigm, what is 'fundamental' ultimately becomes 'a matter of scientific strategy. It depends on the scientist, and it's not permanent' (Capra *et al.* 1991: 137). Moreover, things chosen as 'fundamental' for one theory may well find explanation within another. For instance, in cognitive linguistics the psychological theory of categorisation by prototype underlies the theory of grammatical categorisation: nouns and verbs prove to be just as 'prototypical' or 'peripheral' as Rosch's birds or Labov's cups, and the two systems of categorisation are found to be governed by the same cognitive principle. In lexical studies, traditional principles of the organisation of lexicon (hierarchies based on logic, semantic fields) are abolished in favour of those founded on the psychological concept of basic level terms. Basic levels cut across lexical hierarchies, because the emergence of prototypes is conditioned by pragmatic rather than formal semantic factors.

Finally, the recognition of epistemology as an integral part of a scientific theory results in a shift from certainty and search for the absolute truth as the scholar's final objective to an a priori limited and approximate description of his or her reality. Such is the necessary consequence of cutting parts out of wholes, and severing at least some of the interconnections in the process. The more of those interconnections can be subsequently restored and included in the description, the closer the approximation. Thus gradual improvement of the approximation ultimately becomes the measure of scientific progress.

As in science, in theoretical linguistics the shift from the search for the (absolute) truth to an approximation means replacing controlled experiments (i.e. linguist-made samples of pre-sanitised language 'tested' in linguist-made contexts) with systematic observation (i.e. real language in actual use), with the resulting reversal of the traditional ordering of research strategies: from objects to relationships, or from the 'meaning in context' to the 'basic meaning' (see Senft 1991).

To sum up, the oncoming paradigm shift in theoretical linguistics as marked by the development of the cognitive approach means the emergence of a model for which biology is a better metaphor than mathematics (cf. Langacker 1991b). In consequence, the issue of the habitat, or context, becomes crucial in formulating definitions of networks relevant for linguistic units of differing sizes, in describing the uses to which these units are put, and, finally, in setting the scope of linguistic investigation.

Context: Linguistic Units

'It is a premise of cognitive grammar that all linguistic units are defined, and all linguistic expressions assessed, relative to some context' (Langacker 1987: 38). The language user's recognition of context – physical, social, and linguistic – is a crucial aspect of conceptualisation, which in Cognitive Grammar becomes equated with meaning (Langacker 1991b: 2)

Langacker's discussion of linguistic context resides in de Saussurian opposition between syntagmatic and paradigmatic relations. Thus the process of linear combination of linguistic units to form complex linguistic expressions is defined in terms of *syntagmatic context* (Langacker 1987: 405-8). Grammatical constructions are described by means of abstract schemas that grasp individual patterns of semantic composition, but the 'model neither claims nor requires that composite structures be exhaustively definable or algorithmically computable from their components' (Langacker 1987: 158, fn.8). Conversely, the components are not mere elements out of which a structure has been assembled in a purely mechanical way: the semantic structure is only partially compositional. The 'doctrine of partial compositionality' (Langacker 1994) claims that components of a composite structure are not comparable to building blocks, of which the structure is built through mere addition. Composite structures regularly incorporate elements of meaning that are not actually brought in by their individual components. This is clearly seen in derivation and morphology; to quote just one example, while the lexeme *going is* easily analysable as an instance of an action (*go + ing*), the notion of action is much less prominent in *wedding*, and even less so in *building*, although all the three lexemes are instantiations of the same structural schema, or conventional grammatical pattern.

The same fundamental principle of partial compositionality underlies structures of higher syntactic complexity. To quote one of Langacker's examples, the English expression '*pencil sharpener* has a conventional meaning which is considerably more specific than anything derivable compositionally from the meaning of its parts – a pencil sharpener is not simply "something that sharpens pencils"' (Langacker 1991b: 17). Syntagmatic context is responsible only for a fairly schematic categorisation of the resulting expression (compare the function of selectional features in transformational-generative models).

In contrast to the syntagmatic context, *systemic context* (Langacker 1987: 401-3) establishes the position of a linguistic unit within the network of interrelations which taken together constitute the grammar of a language. Used in its particular setting, a linguistic unit derives its value from its relation to relevant aspects of this network. Thus, for instance, the creation of a novel composite structure *chalk sharpener* (example from Langacker 1991b: 18) is preconditioned by the existence in the system of the constructional schema itself, the components that make up the structure, and their grammatical categorisation. The structure *chalk sharpener* is structured analogously to the structure *pencil sharpener*, but as is immediately obvious to a speaker of English, the latter 'means more' than the former. Therefore other types of context must be recognised to supplement the general conception of linguistic structure. The full meaning of an expression can only arise by including relevant situational elements of the particular situation which is being described, i.e. pragmatic circumstances (physical and social context, in Langacker's terms) that condition a particular usage event. It is this *situational context* that finally establishes the overall *contextual meaning* of an expression: the meaning which 'includes all relevant aspects of the conceived situation' (Langacker 1987:157), and thus guarantees proper understanding. Such meaning is obviously encyclopaedic in scope, and as such it can be neither algorithmised nor computed through componential analysis.

In the process of conventionalisation of linguistic expressions, contextual meaning becomes the conventional meaning of the new linguistic unit. Thus, to come back to Langacker's example, through repeated use over a long time, the expression *pencil sharpener* finally becomes associated with a particular (prototypical) shape and size of the contraption to which the name refers, the material it is made of, the way and the circumstances in which it is used, etc. In short, it becomes associated with the relevant features of its situational context. When these features become permanently 'built into' the expression, its status changes to that of a *conventional linguistic unit*, endowed with an expected default reading.

Conversely, the expression *chalk sharpener* does not regularly associate with any particular situation such as would include analogous details, and therefore it can only be understood in a very schematic way (i.e. as 'somebody who sharpens chalk' or 'something that is/may be used to sharpen chalk with'). In short, the English expression *chalk sharpener* is not (yet?) a conventional linguistic unit. In terms of linguistic diachrony, the process of 'conventionalisation through decontextualisation' may be seen as an explanation of most fundamental mechanisms of semantic change.

In consequence, linguistic expressions do not *convey* the contextual meaning, but, to use Langacker's term, *sanction* it as one of many possible conceptualisations motivated by their schematicity (Langacker 1987: 158). For instance, the English expression *go for a walk* sanctions the contextual meaning of *walking on foot*, as one preferred over all other potential interpretations, just because that is what English speaking people do when they go for a walk.

Within Langacker's theory of language, systemic and syntagmatic contexts are directly reflected in the structure of linguistic expressions. Langacker describes linguistic expressions in terms of the relation between a *trajector* (which he defines as the most salient substructure

within the *profile*, i.e. the particular aspect of the cognitive domain chosen as subject of an utterance), a *landmark* (i.e. some other salient substructure within the profile) and the *setting* (i.e. all other non-salient
substructures). For instance, the sentence *Yesterday I sharpened all my pencils with my new pencil sharpener,* profiles a particular relationship between
me and *all my pencils,* with the instrument (*my new pencil sharpener*) and
the time anchoring (*-ed, yesterday*) providing elements of the setting.

The relationship between trajectors, landmarks and settings reveals
each linguistic expression as a particular arrangement of elements, in
which some substructures (trajectors and landmarks) function as *figures*, and other (setting) as the *ground* (as the terms are defined in
Gestalt psychology; for the relevance of the distinction in linguistic
analysis, see e.g., Langacker 1987, passim).

The same general principle of figure/ground organisation underlies
the concept of situational context, defined in terms of Langacker's distinction between *profile* (i.e. the entity designated by a given semantic
structure) and *base* (i.e. the cognitive domain which serves as a 'ground'
for the designatum; cf. above). To use another standard example, the
expression *door knob* profiles the concept *door* as its immediate scope, that
is, brings in the amount of semantic content directly relevant at a particular level (for instance, to enable the right processing of the sentence *Just
turn the knob,* please). At the same time, the same expression profiles such
concepts as *wall, room, house,* etc. as its overall scope, that is the domain
required for full characterisation of the profile (for instance, in the sentence: *Even the door knobs were changed to fit the taste of the new owners*).

The notions of *figure* in opposition to *ground* and *profile* in opposition
to *base* could be considered as mere additions to a fairly large collection
of convenient pictorial metaphors for non-linguistic context ('frame',
'stage', 'environment', etc.; *see also* chapter 3). What is helpful, however, is not so much the creation of yet another metaphor, but the
incorporation into linguistics of the dialectic relationship between the
unit of language and the circumstances of its use. The elusive relation
between the two can be now seen as a diachronically changing pro-
portion: the more conventionalised an expression of a profile, the less
need for the elaboration of the base.

Context: Usage Events

The problem of defining situational context recurs on the level of
larger composite structures built of linguistic units: these are expressions constructed by speakers in 'a particular set of circumstances for
a particular purpose', which embody 'detailed, context-dependent con-
ceptualizations' (Langacker 1987: 66). In Langacker's terminology,

they are referred to as *usage events*. The 'context-dependence' brings back the notorious problem of scope.

Attempts to formulate theoretical principles such as might help to reduce the scope of 'context' to a manageable size have been repeatedly undertaken by linguists working within the framework of the young discipline of linguistic pragmatics. The most comprehensive proposal is perhaps that put forward by Sperber and Wilson and known as the theory of relevance (1986). Rejecting the traditional view that envisages context as something that is uniquely determined and given a priori, i.e. prior to comprehension, Sperber and Wilson offer a characterisation of factors that contribute to the interpretation of utterances by the hearer and propose that the principle of communicative relevance be decisive for the choice and subsequent delimitation of 'context'. In consequence, 'it is relevance that is treated as given, and context which is treated as a variable' (Sperber and Wilson 1986: 142).

Sperber and Wilson construe their theory from the perspective of the hearer; they focus on the comprehension of verbal messages, which means viewing language mainly as being grounded in social interaction. They give an analysis of psychological factors that are operative in the process of comprehension, and their definition of 'chunks' of context relevant for the interpretation of a given usage event is based upon psychological and functional rather than purely cognitive criteria. Conversely, Langacker's main interest is in the process of conceptualisation, which results in his focusing on the perspective of the speaker; in his theoretical work language is seen mainly as being grounded in human cognition. The two viewpoints are of course two sides of the same coin, and *'cognitive* linguistics and *functional* linguistics (with its emphasis on discourse and social interaction) should be regarded as complementary and mutually dependent aspects of a single overall enterprise' (Langacker 1994: 1). Indeed, undertaking such a 'single overall enterprise' would be a welcome step towards the re-integration of the cognate disciplines which had suffered much from the scientific apartheid of the last decades.

Sperber and Wilson talk mainly about mechanisms which underlie the process of inferencing; in Langacker's theory man's 'inferencing ability' is recognised as one among the 'multiple resources' on which the hearer draws when looking for an interpretation of an expression (cf. e.g. Langacker 1994: 5). However, Langacker's main interest is in grammar of natural language, i.e. in ways in which linguistic structures symbolise concepts. As a prerequisite to his explanation of such linguistic entities as the English definite article (Langacker 1991a: 97) or pronominal anaphora (1994: 2), he introduces the notion of the *current discourse space*: a mental space (in the sense of Fauconnier 1985), shared by the speaker and the hearer at a given stage of the discourse. Entities with which the current discourse space is furnished are immediately available to the participants in the discourse, and the repertoire changes as the discourse progresses, with new elements being added, and others 'fading from awareness'. As a theoretical construct, the current discourse space could probably be seen as a possible supplement (refinement?) of Sperber and Wilson's notion of context.

Context: Language and Linguistics

Within the theoretical framework of Cognitive Linguistics the notion of *situational context* ultimately becomes tantamount to that of *cognitive domain*. Cognitive domains pertain to 'mental experiences, representational spaces, concepts or conceptual complexes' (Langacker 1987: 147). The psychological character of the definition of context must necessarily follow from the cognitivist approach to natural language: 'context' is no longer external to either the speaker or the utterance, but becomes 'located in the mind of the hearer' (Sinclair 1993: 535). Cognitive domains arise from man's mental experience in the process of concept formation, which in turn comes as the result of perception. While the sensuous dimension of perceptual processes should most probably be considered as universal ('global'), the physical, psychological and sociological dimensions which constitute the basis for concept formation emerge as a network of socio-cultural factors and personal predispositions of language users, such as intelligence, education, emotions, beliefs, values, attitudes, motivation, etc.; in short, they are idiosyncratic and/or culture-specific (or 'local'). Ultimately, cognitive domains emerge as products of cognition conditioned by culture. The two are closely connected: the twin keys to interpretation – both linguistic and anthropological.

The interrelationship between the cognitivist universalism on the one hand and the specificity on the other underlies most recent work done within the framework of Cognitive Linguistics. It may be reasonably argued that while strategies for categorisation and the resulting conceptual structures may well be products of the universal ability of the human mind, semantic (that is, grammatical) categories will be context-dependent, and therefore language-specific. Consequently, universalism may be postulated on the perceptual level, but not on the linguistic level (cf. also the discussion in Dirven and Taylor 1988). By the same token, the process of conventionalisation in language will yield specific rather than universal results: the fact that the expression *pencil sharpener* – but not *chalk sharpener* – enjoys the status of a linguistic unit in English may only be seen as being conditioned by that particular culture. Thus, on the highest level, it is also reasonable to talk about the context in which human language functions and develops: the context of language.

The opposition between the 'universal' and the 'specific' components of this context manifests itself most clearly in the cognitive approach to metaphor, which is no longer considered as a figure of speech (and therefore, as a phenomenon of only marginal interest to a linguist), but as a way of thinking that underlies a great majority of (linguistic) expressions of man's empirical experience. Using metaphor means using simpler, more basic cognitive domains as points of reference for other, more complex and abstract ones. Universal source domains, which are rooted in man's primitive bodily experience, underlie what is defined as *conceptual metaphors*. Conceptual metaphors are highly schematic, and they give rise to 'families' of more specific metaphorical expressions. For instance, the conceptual metaphor LIFE IS A JOURNEY is the source of many specific metaphors, such as *the point of no return, we've come a long way,* etc. (see Lakoff 1990).

On the other hand, *single image metaphors* (or, as Lakoff [1990] calls them, *one-shot metaphors*) arise via idiosyncratic or culture-specific perception (cf. *To be born with a silver spoon in one's mouth,* or *Something is rotten in the state of Denmark*). In the cognitivist view of metaphor, 'context' becomes tantamount to 'cognition conditioned by culture'.

Like every theory, in its search for generalisation Cognitive Linguistics looks for 'similarities in diversity', that is for universals. However, they are radically different from those postulated within the transformational-generative paradigm. They are no longer the extremely abstract 'linguistic universals', as the universalism proclaimed by linguists of the cognitivist persuasion pertains to the very processes of cognition, which are not specific to language but characterise perception and information processing in general. In terms of the context of language and language in context, universals are norms and patterns: 'the sources of universals, and the constraints on diversity, are situated not in the hypothetical depths of the mind or the genes, but in the social world of the speakers' (Keesing 1992: 601). In the same world, anthropology looks mainly for cultural differences, to which linguists of the cognitivist persuasion pay much more attention than do most representatives of today's mainstream linguistics. Since the former assume that linguistic theory can only emerge from broad and solid empirical and descriptive foundations, they look for the diversity among 'exotic' languages, which the latter traditionally relegated to anthropologists. Thus it seems only too natural that a rapprochement between the two disciplines must mean a compromise: 'diversity and universals are seen as two sides of the same coin, each side illuminating the other' (Keesing 1992: 601).

A linguist who believes that the object of his professional interest should be located in a social and cultural context will naturally assume that anthropology should constitute an obvious context for linguistics.

Bibliography

Capra, F., D. Steindl-Rast and T. Matus. 1991. *Belonging to the universe. (Explorations on the frontiers of science and spirituality)* San Francisco: Harper.

Dirven, R. and J. Taylor, 1988. 'The conceptualization of vertical space in English: the case of "tall"'. In B. Rudzka-Ostyn (ed.) *Topics in cognitive linguistics* : 379-402. Amsterdam: John Benjamins.

Fauconnier, G. 1985. *Mental spaces: aspects of meaning construction in natural language.*. Cambridge, Mass.: MIT Press.

Goodman, N. 1979. *Ways of worldmaking.* Cambridge, Mass.: Hackett Publishing Co.

Keesing, R. M. 1992. 'Linguistics and anthropology'. In M. Putz (ed.), *Thirty years of linguistic revolution. Studies in honour of René Dirven on the occasion of his sixtieth birthday*: 593-610. Amsterdam: John Benjamins.

Kuhn, T. 1962. *The structure of scientific revolutions.* Chicago: University of Chicago Press.

Lakoff, G. 1990. 'The invariance hypothesis: is abstract reason based on image-schemas? '*Cognitive linguistics*: 1 (1): 39-74.

Langacker, R.W. 1987. *Foundations of cognitive grammar. Vol.I: Theoretical prerequisites.* Stanford: Stanford University Press.

———. 1991a. *Foundations of cognitive grammar. Vol.II: Descriptive application.* Stanford: Stanford University Press.

———. 1991b. *Concept, image and symbol: the cognitive basis of grammar.* Berlin: Mouton de Gruyter.

———. 1994. 'Conceptual grouping and pronominal anaphora'. MS.

Lee Chen, L. 1993. 'Iconicity and complementary opposition: time expressions in Chinese'. MS. Paper read at Third International Cognitive Conference, Leuven, 18-23 July 1993.

Senft, G. 1991. 'Everything we always thought we knew about space – but did not bother to question'. MS. Paper read at the Workshop 'Concepts of space and spatial reference in Austronesian and Papuan languages', Nijmegen, 30 September – 1 October 1991.

Sinclair, M. 1993. 'Are academic texts really decontextualized and fully explicit? A pragmatic perspective on the role of context in written communication'. *Text* : 13 (4): 529-58.

Sperber, D. and D. Wilson. 1986. *Relevance: communication and cognition.* Oxford: Basil Blackwell.

Tabakowska, E. 1997. 'Conceptualization: conditionals as an instance of figure/ground aligment'. In A. Athanasiadou and R. Dirven (eds), *On conditionals again*: 373-87. Amsterdam: John Benjamins.

Traugott, E. 1997. 'UNLESS and BUT: a historical perspective.' In A. Athanasiadou and R. Dirven (eds), *On conditionals again*: 145-68. Amsterdam: John Benjamins.

Winters, M.E. 1992. 'Diachrony within synchrony: the challenge of cognitive grammar'. In M. Putz (ed.), *Thirty years of linguistic revolution. Studies in honour of René Dirven on the occasion of his sixtieth birthday*: 503-12. Amsterdam: John Benjamins.

Chapter 4

ETHNOGRAPHIC MISUNDERSTANDING AND THE PERILS OF CONTEXT

Johannes Fabian

Alles Verstehen ist daher immer zugleich ein Nicht-Verstehen, alle Über-
einstimmung in Gedanken und Gefühlen zugleich ein Auseinandergehen.

Wilhelm von Humboldt[1]

Ethnographers report what they understand: sounds are transcribed
into texts; utterances are presented as stories or conversations; events
and processes are interpreted or explained. If what is reported is not to
be dismissed as mere recording or description, it must be recognised as
understanding. Understanding must be relevant to what the discipline
wants to understand and it must be shown to have been arrived at by
methods and procedures that are accepted as valid. After all, our
efforts are expected to result in some kind of enlightenment, even if
analysts and hermeneuts, explainers and interpreters disagree, sometimes vehemently, about what constitutes enlightenment.

Where there is light, and where there are objects, there are shadows.
On the dark side of understanding there is not-understanding and misunderstanding.[2] The conventions of scientific discourse make provi-
sions for this, but always in such a way that light apparently prevails in
the end. Misunderstanding, by the very logic of the concept, can be
envisaged neither as the goal nor as the result of scientific work. Even
those who maintain that falsification, not verification, is all that science can accomplish, and those who state that all interpretation is partial, strive for some kind of positive gain in knowledge. In presentations

of anthropological knowledge, misunderstandings may be focused on and reported, though not very often, and discussions of misunderstandings usually serve as methodological or rhetorical strategies destined to enhance the discipline's (or the writer's) authority.

I will begin by discussing a few examples of ethnographic misunderstanding from my own work, which has been language-centred in two respects: first, almost all my empirical inquiries were conducted through speaking and listening to (and recording) speech; second, language and communication have been central to me in conceiving a theoretical approach within anthropology.[3] Needless to say, I never made an inventory, much less a systematic study, of misunderstandings in my work. Therefore, my examples will be necessarily anecdotal. Nevertheless, I have tried to strengthen my case by considering misunderstandings on not just one but several levels that are conventionally distinguished in the study of language. It did not take much searching to find instances that involved phonology, grammar, semantics, and pragmatics.

One hesitates to point out the obvious: by the time they have been made to serve as examples, misunderstandings have been understood. Or have they? We begin to suspect that what happens when we (mis)understand cannot be envisaged adequately as a flow through a chart of binary branches marked either + or –. Should the question be rephrased? Do misunderstanding and understanding relate to each other like error and truth? Perhaps a case could be made for misunderstanding as committing an error, but not for understanding as attaining truth. Scientific, discursive understanding is both less and more than truth: less than truth, because understanding is related to a 'discipline' and expressed in the language of that discipline. Always doubly limited, it is thus removed from any absolute notion of truth. There does not seem to be any other notion worth positing; 'relative truth' is a compromise, not a solution. Scientific understanding is about more than truth, since when we speak of understanding, we do not merely signal the presence of an abstract quality; we offer specific content, statements about the world as experienced, whether direct or reported.

Because a myriad of possible questions can arise on every level of (mis)understanding, I shall try to give my comments on the examples some focus by concentrating on one issue: different ways to repair ethnographic misunderstanding which have in common that they summon context as a corrective. In anthropology, context is usually invoked to point out shortcomings or misconceptions that arise when analysis falsely reifies items or entities, confuses logic with explanation, or sells generalisations as cultural universals. Examples of false reifications can be easily found, for instance, in semantic approaches to kinship studies, but a similar critique can be levelled against formalist linguistics in general. As a field, sociolinguistics, or the ethnography of communication, has resounded with appeals to context. When, in what follows, I speak of the perils of context, I draw partly on self-observation. Precisely because I sympathise with the 'contextualisers' in linguistics and language-centred anthropology, I feel that critical reflection is called for.

I will conclude this essay with a more ambitious argument: the significance of misunderstanding can be appreciated when we begin to struggle with the notion of not-understanding. Only then will it be possible to proceed from questions of method and rhetoric to epistemology.

Ethnographic Misunderstanding and Not-Understanding

Transcription: Sounds

In ethnographic work based on the documentation of speech, understanding begins, as every practitioner of that approach has painfully experienced, with work that has often been considered problematic only in a technical sense: transcribing recorded sounds.[4] This is not the place to face the multitude of problems that arise, ranging from distinguishing speech sound from noise to deciding what must go into a reasonably accurate graphic representation of recorded speech.[5] Instead, I propose to look at an instance of misunderstanding that is of particular interest regarding the role of context in misunderstanding. The task at hand was to transcribe a brief passage of dialogue, followed by a song from *Le pouvoir se mange entier*, a play created by a group of popular actors in Lubumbashi/Zaire.[6] The language in this, as in all the other examples to be discussed, is a local variety of Swahili. The general theme is power, a story of its exercise, corruption, and restoration. Here is the fragment as it appears in translation:

> *Notable* : Stop it, stop it ... but what is this noise here?
> *Villagers* : [vociferous protest; impossible to transcribe]
> *Notable* : What is all this rejoicing about? This is what ought be done, what ought to be done [. ..] everyone cultivates his fields. When the fields are worked you can take a rest and a little glass, isn't that [... ? ...] pass the ladle.
> *Woman* : Let them first give you a small one.
> *Man* : He should first sit down in the furrow over there.
> *Others* : In the furrow. That's how we see it [...]
> *Woman* : Singing! Singing! Get into the dance!

Both the scene and the speaking are thoroughly performative rather than discursive, which makes the recording quite difficult to transcribe. In our translation, gaps and incomprehensible passages are marked by dots between square brackets. The text that can be recuperated is elliptical but sufficient to get the gist of the exchange: An elder (notable) is sent by the chief to remind the villagers of their duty to work in the fields. He finds them feasting and decides to join the drinking and dancing. The scene ends with a song expressing resolve to defy the chief. The songs that were interspersed in the play posed special problems. In addition to the fact that it is always difficult to lift the lyrics from a musical performance, most songs were in languages other than Swahili. I therefore settled for transcribing just a few lines of each and then indicating the content as best I could. In the case we are considering here, I initially noted, at the end of the scene, 'A sort of fighting-song is intoned, consisting mainly of repetitions of *tutabawina*, we shall beat them (in local Swahili; derived, possibly via Bemba, from English "to win").' I later checked my transcriptions with the help of that provider of context par excellence – a native speaker of Shaba Swahili. He confirmed my reading of *tutabawina*. Not only that, he volunteered additional information to the effect that this is the type of song intoned by supporters of a soccer team.

But we had both misunderstood what we heard. Because I continued to have difficulties with other songs, I wrote to the theatre group in Lubumbashi to ask for help. They responded with a letter giving the opening lines of five of the songs, together with a French translation. As it turned out, the song in question was not in Swahili but in Kizela (a language spoken east of Lake Moero). And it was not a fighting song but a marching song. According to the letter, it goes:

> TUTA MAWILA, LUMUNDU
> KWA MWENGE I KULA
> March on, Lumundu
> It is still a long way to Mwenge's.[7]

As misunderstandings go, failure to identify the language (Kizela rather than Swahili) as well as the genre (a marching rather than fighting song), certainly constitutes one. The point of giving this case our attention is to show that failure to understand can be due precisely to the kinds of sources on which we base claims to understanding: language competence and knowledge of context. This is how it worked in our case: because Shaba Swahili was the language of the play, it was to be expected that its sounds would be heard in this song. That a string of sounds was identified as *tutabawina* was, if not demanded, at least encouraged by context. *Context* here means the semantic environment of the song in a text that expresses defiance. Context also evokes a cultural environment that has fighting songs in its repertoire, constructed around the expression *kuwina*.

It could be argued that correction was in this case provided by a double break with context. One break was the decision to suspend trust in the 'natural' workings of context (through linguistic and cultural competence), a trust that would normally seem to be required to make the task of transcription possible. The other break consisted in leaving the context of orality and of the ethnographic routines developed in working with oral 'data'. Rectification was demanded by a written document that was not a transcript; the recorded play itself was improvised, without a script to quote from.

Translation: Grammar and Semantics

On 15 April 1973, I recorded a conversation with the painter Kanyemba Yav at Kolwezi/Shaba. In the course of discussing his life history we came to a passage where he recounted his involvement with the Bapostolo, a religious movement that originated in Zimbabwe and had reached the Kolwezi area by 1953. At one point I told him that I had often seen Bapostolo walking around in their colourful biblical attire and had observed some of their open-air meetings from a distance. I said that I found it difficult to make contact with them. This led to the following exchange:

Kanyemba: It is not difficult because right now we have a white person from America who is a member of our group.

Self: Of the Bapostolo?

Kanyemba: Of the Bapostolo movement, yes.

Self: Here in Kolwezi?

Kanyemba: Not here in Kolwezi, I think [the person] made the contact first during a trip to the Kasai region. From the Kasai region they took [the person] to Lusaka in Zambia because the Bapostolo religion is a religion that came there from Southern Rhodesia. That's what I think, yes. That is where this religion came from.

Self: Was it not Yoanne ...

Kanyemba: ... Malangu, yes John Malangu [John Maranke, the founder]. And thus it arrived in Lusaka. Now, some of the local leaders [from Zaire] went there to Lusaka to fetch [the person] and then they arrived here. That is where they met this [person who was like a] white person. This is now the first white person here among us. [The person] had to get to Lusaka because that is where the leaders are.

Self: I see.

Kanyemba: They arrived there and baptised [the person]; now we are with that person in our community.

The translation, which is as literal as possible, poses several problems of understanding. The most obvious one is caused by the fact that in Swahili neither nouns nor pronouns (or pronominal infixes) are marked for gender. Grammar (in this case morphology) is no help in

deciding whether the person that is reported to have joined the movement is male or female. I signal this uncertainty by enclosing references to that person in square brackets. A few other passages require
paraphrases or explanations (some are provided), but they are marginal to the point illustrated by this example.

I transcribed this text from a recording some time in 1975 without
translating it (other than the kind of translation that is involved when
one transcribes from a language he or she understands). However, I
distinctly remember storing the information as, 'A white man joined
the Bapostolo movement'. At about the same time, Bennetta Jules-
Rosette published *African Apostles* (1975), her dissertation on the
church of John Maranke, which must have come to my attention during the same year or early in 1976, when I was asked to review it
(Fabian 1977). In this book, Jules-Rosette describes her conversion to
that church. I do not remember exactly when I made the connection,
but eventually it became clear to me that she must have been the person I had taken to be a white man. That revealed a first misunderstanding: the person was a woman, not a man. But there is another
twist to this story: Bennetta Jules-Rosette is an African American. That
signals the problems with translating the Swahili term *muzungu*. It distinguishes one class of non-Africans (there are others) on the bases of
origin, socioeconomic status, and political position, but not of colour.[8]

What brought about the misunderstanding I had stored in my
memory? When I recorded the conversation with Kanyemba I knew
that Swahili pronouns and pro-nominal infixes are not marked for
gender and that *muzungu* does not correspond exactly to 'White'. Yet,
when decisions had to be made in order to translate the phrase into
English – where pronouns have gender and European means 'White' –
I let myself be guided by context; not, of course, the specific context of
this particular utterance, but the context of 'normal' expectations,
derived both from experience and from prejudice.

The point I want to make with this case of misunderstanding is not
that we should mistrust our expectations and improve our competence
as translators. We should, of course; but we must, as I have said, make
decisions and settle for a version we can live with. Otherwise we will
end up with unreadable texts like the one quoted, full of gaps and cau-
tionary paraphrases. So the useful lesson to be learned from this case
must be elsewhere. I would argue that it demonstrates, even on the
level of interpreting grammatical and lexical meaning, that translation requires *historical* background knowledge. In this case, such
knowledge was obtained after the fact, though it could have been
obtained during the original exchange, had I been bothered by ambiguities of gender and the meaning of *muzungu*. History, despite expressions such as 'historical context' that come easily to most of us,

provides connections that are contingent, unpredictable, and unsystematic, and are therefore not really 'con-text' in either the linguistic or literary sense of the term.

Interpretation: Speech Event

As we have seen so far, misunderstanding may be due to a failure to decode sounds or to reduce grammatical and semantic ambiguity. I have tried to show how such misunderstandings far from being merely failures, can become ethnographically relevant. When they are made the object of reflection, they reveal what should have happened to make us understand what we in fact misunderstood. Misunderstandings can reveal conditions of understanding.

Misunderstandings, whether or not productive, are usually identified after the fact. Their occurrence is reconstructed from a record available to us in the present: the recorded text. This means, strictly speaking, that recourse to a corrective context is dependent on the availability of a text. In this perspective, a hermeneutic stance is not all that different from a positivist view stipulating that a theory needs to be tested against data; if theory is the text, data become the corrective context.[9] Doubts about such an approach caused us to reflect on misunderstanding. These doubts concern the notion that ethnographic understanding happens always after the fact and that it is possible to distinguish the collection of information from interpretation or analysis. Opposed to this is the idea that collecting does not (or not adequately) express what happens when anthropologists do field research. The founding acts of ethnography are communicative events. Hence, to confront misunderstanding must be a task that poses itself already in those moments in which the knowledge process gets under way – that is, in those verbal exchanges of which a selection eventually becomes documented as ethnographic texts. When we participate in speech events, our questions regarding misunderstandings are not addressed to information deposited in texts but to potential breakdowns in an ongoing process of communication. Perhaps the difference can be marked terminologically if we distinguish misunderstandings of texts from mistakes in communication. On the other hand, every textual misunderstanding was once (part of) an event. As we shall see, communicative mistakes occur when some sort of text invades the event. We should add that mistakes can in turn be communicated only when they have been turned into texts.

Elsewhere I took a mistake in communication – a wrong choice of what Dell Hymes calls the 'code' component of a speech event – as the point of departure for a critique of reified sociolinguisitcs (Fabian 1991 [1979a]: ch. 5). Here I want to confront a similar key experience which has taught me that in ethnography things sometimes go right when they go wrong. I must admit, however, that my comprehension of what happened remains incomplete and that my interpretation of the text I am about to quote is tentative.

In 1986 I undertook, as a sideline to other projects, some rather incidental research on Catholic charismatics (the neo-Pentecostal *renouveau charismatique*). The research was conducted in the same language (Swahili) and in more or less the same area (Lubumbashi/Shaba) from which I took my other examples. I had made contacts with several persons involved in the charismatic movement, and made a number of recordings, something that had become a routine in my way of doing ethnography. Matters were everything but routine when I met Mama Régine, leader of one of the 'prayer groups', as the charismatics are known locally. We hit it off, as the saying goes. There may have been other reasons, but in the end it was a case of kinship of mind that, I felt, allowed us to transcend gender, culture, politics – and religion. Whenever we talked at her place, one or several other persons were present and, as the recordings show, they occasionally intervened. Nevertheless, in my memory I carried the impression of conversations between only the two of us.

Not that the beginning of our exchanges was especially auspicious. Mama Régine, then a statuesque lady in her forties, received me because I came with a friend who was among her followers.[10] She took control, as it were, by reciting a brief prayer before we sat down around a coffee table. I began by making conversation, telling of my past work with the Jamaa, another Shaba religious movement with a Catholic background. Eventually, her husband came and joined us; drinks and cake were offered. This could have been the end of our meeting. But then our conversation came to a critical point and took a new turn. Régine must have had some information about me before we met, because she now confronted me with my past (more about that later). Whatever she knew about me, it did not stop her from asking me a question that I immediately felt was loaded with significance beyond the meaning of the words that were spoken: 'Do you pray?' This head-on challenge made me uncomfortable. I did say 'no' but basically I stalled. I suppose ethnographers of religious enthusiasm acquire the ability to hang on in moments when they sense that an important conversation might otherwise be cut off. To bridge what I feared was becoming a gap, I countered with a question, 'You want to know who sent me?' She did indeed, and that gave me an occasion to direct our attention from her work, prayer, to mine, research sponsored by my university (not, as she had obviously feared, by the church).[11] 'Empty research [*recherches ya bule*],' she muttered. Then she insisted on telling me her life history. When she had finished we took our leave, but not before agreeing that I would come back soon for more questions.

Before I continue my account of conversations with Régine, I want to stop for an ethnographic aside. It should illustrate why I find the notoriously difficult study of religious enthusiasm theoretically rewarding. As we left Régine's house, my friend, an eminent folklorist, expressed his surprise at not seeing me taking notes. This had been his first occasion to watch me at work, and I felt there was gentle professional chiding implied in his reaction. Two reasons account for my unscientific behaviour. One was habit. I have always found the posture of the scribe extremely embarrassing. Except when the subject matter was very specific and technical – eliciting, say, a terminology – I have never taken notes while I have conversed with people during field research. My notes are assembled as soon as possible after the event, sometimes assisted by tiny scribblings that I make to aid my memory, but not necessarily at the time or place to which the notes refer. I have been able to cultivate that habit because, in the end, I always tape what I consider truly important – after learning what is important. That this may leave bits of information un-noted is a small price to pay for the richness of well-prepared recordings.

But there is another reason to abstain from note-taking, which is epistemological. If what I was after in a conversation such as the one with Mama Régine was primarily knowledge in the sense of something *known* (such as a folktale, a genealogy or a historical recollection), then what I learned could and should be noted immediately. But if I was primarily after knowledge as process, if I sought to learn *how* charismatics know what they know and how I can know what they know, then I would be involved in a social undertaking, and it would be crucial not to disturb the dialogue situation (for epistemological rather than ethical reasons). In practice, this means that one must refrain from turning process into product too early. The risk of missing information is small compared to the risk of being excluded from a practice of knowing.

The preceding, by the way, is an elaboration of thoughts I noted in my diary right after the event. That entry was followed by reflections, which I now want to quote (slightly edited):

One of the questions M. Régine asked me was whether I 'pray.' Being put on the spot I had no choice but to say no. She responded with a smile and a gesture saying 'I thought so'. Why, damn it, should I be put on the spot? And am I reacting the way I do only because I fear losing contact and rapport? I only have to imagine someone in my everyday surroundings asking such a question [meaning: I would express resentment and brush off questions of that kind]. Nor is this sort of challenge – because Régine's question is *not* a question of information but a challenge – simply a matter of religion. Would it be put up by a practitioner of 'traditional' religion? He/she might ask me to *do* things. M. Régine's question was not about whether or not I *do* something but whether I do it as an expression of faith, with the implication that we will never have a common understanding except on the level of faith. Therefore, her invitation to participate in the next meeting [of her group] is aimed at *conversion* not *conversation*. But what if all that is just a projection? Yes, there might be a challenge to convert – but perhaps not to a faith but to *doing* (Lubumbashi, 15 June 1986).

Three days later I made a partial recording of a séance of Mama Régine's group: two-and-a-half hours of song, prayer, preaching, and testimony. Afterwards, we sat together for a while and talked about this and that. Before I left, another meeting was scheduled. 'We part on good terms', I noted in my diary, without being able to say why. At first, not much came of this next meeting. I arrived at the appointed time but I caught Mama Régine just as she was leaving. I gave her a lift to the market, where she had to see after her business, and we agreed to meet again in the afternoon. We did, and this time I asked permission to use my cassette recorder (taking some time to explain the purpose). Régine did not hesitate for a moment. Once again she began with her life history, dwelling especially on early experiences that made her certain that she had the gift of prayer, as well as other gifts. This took up about one-third of the 130 minutes of the recording. A second part was devoted mainly to events since 1973, when she began to gather a group together. A third part, in which her husband joined us, was spent, as Mama Régine put it, discussing the 'conclusions' from her life story. It was in this reflexive meta-perspective that she resumed the line of questioning that had provoked the angry reaction I noted above. As it turns out, the rather timid suspicion I formulated then – that I might be projecting rather than understanding – was proven correct.[12]

> *Régine:* All right, Now I have a question for you... You told me, excuse me, you see things from a distance – aren't you a Catholic?
> *Self:* Hm.
> 5 *Régine:* [taking several starts] Even though you have... I am asking you. You are...
> *Self:* We were talking about that with your son, the one who studies statistics.
> *Régine:* Yes.
> 10 *Self:* He asked me the same question.
> *Régine:* So, did you give him an answer?
> *Self:* Tsk [I click my tongue]. We looked at each other... He asked me: Are you a Catholic?
> *Régine:* Ah.
> 15 *Self:* So I said: Hm, tsk. And he, too, said: Hm. [I laugh] He understood. We are searching, mama.
> *Régine:* Are you searching for God? [chuckles] Is that what you understood there [when you questioned each other]?

Self: Yes.

20 *Régine:* Voilà, and I, when you questioned me, did I not give you answers?
Self: Ask, go ahead, ask. So, your first question was: Am I a Catholic?
Régine: [repeats] Am I Catholic. Now, earlier you used to
25 be a [Catholic].
Self: I was, I was...
Régine: You were a Catholic.
Self: I worked very hard...
Régine: Amen! [passage omitted]... In the end you
30 did everything. Now [pauses] – you see farther. The matters of God go
on outside. You used to be a Catholic; [now] you are in the world.
Self: Mm.
Régine: You see further.
35 *Self:* Mm.
Régine: [somewhat obscurely] We haven't died yet, we are still alive.
Self: Mm.
Régine: You see further. As far as that is concerned, I also
40 speak the way you spoke. As when you made your 'Mm'. That is what
I said, too. I told you about that. When they [the official supervisors of
the charismatics] call me to a meeting, then I don't tell myself first that
this is not a Catholic meeting. I go and listen, I come home and I go to
sleep.
45 *Self:* True
Régine: Mm.
Self: That's how it is.
Régine: [sighs]
Self: But these are difficult matters, mama.
50 *Régine:* [chuckles]
Self: Go on, ask. Ask.
Régine: [Laughs out loud, turns to her husband.] Nestor, what else do
you want to ask?
Nestor: No, you ask [him]: When you finished every-
55 thing...
Régine: When you finished everything, sorry, you finished everything...
Nestor: ... did you enter?
Régine: He entered. He entered...
60 *Nestor:* All right, after you had entered, did you leave, did you return to
what was before?
Self: I left.
Nestor: Why?
Self: That's the question [laughs].
65 *Régine:* That's what I am trying to ask.
Self: [Sigh] To begin with, I did not think a lot about it.
Régine: Right.
Nestor: Yes.
Self: It was like growing up. I was thinking, now I left this
70 behind me. I have my work, my work as a professor. I am going to put a
lot of effort into this work. It's going to be all right.

Régine: Right... [passage omitted] I know. This is why I asked you: Those
people whom you saw [when you were a
75 Catholic], they say they are Catholics. Right?
Self: Mm.
Régine: [Chuckles] But – I just use my eyes.
Self: Yes, indeed.
Régine: That's what I kept telling you the other day. You
80 were sitting here [when I said]: They should stop going on my nerves.
They should stop going on my nerves. Here I am, to pray to God, and
that's it.

In this episode Régine confronts me for the second time with a question I experience as embarrassing. No longer being a Catholic, I fear
that my answer may be embarrassing to her. Hence the clever dodges
(lines 7-16) that help me avoid giving a direct and clear answer. Régine
is not fooled by this and insists: the questions you asked me were of the
same kind as those I am asking you – did I not give you answers? (line
20 f.). But this is still allusion. Only in lines 39 ff. does she put into
words what had begun to dawn on me a few moments earlier. In my
reaction to her question and in my anticipation of her reaction to my
response I had been mistaken. She had no intention whatsoever of
criticising me for my past, or of bringing me back into the fold; she was
quite simply interested in how one gets away from Catholicism and
how one acquires the ability 'to see farther' (a notion expressed at the
very beginning of this exchange in line 2). Once I realised that, we had
a new basis for our conversation and we therefore started again with
another version of the first question (lines 23 ff.). Accordingly, my
answer was more detailed. Régine could identify with my recollections
(see lines 39 ff.). At the very end of the exchange quoted here, she
announced, as it were, that she intended to put her cards on the table
(lines 69 ff.). The rest of our conversation (recorded until the tape ran
out) consisted of one example after the other of ways, direct or indi-
rect, subtle or rude, in which the Catholic church, as represented by
the local hierarchy, had become an intolerable burden for this devoutly
religious woman.

Before I get further embroiled in this episode, let me stop and consider what it can contribute to our inquiry into ethnographic misunderstanding. In this instance, there were no problems with phonetic
decoding or semantic interpretation. The misunderstanding that I felt
had occurred concerned the interpretation of intentions. Conventionally speaking, something went wrong on a meta-linguistic level (the
mistake that was made was perhaps akin to a failure to recognise irony
or parody). On the other hand, the 'ethnography of speaking' holds
that the 'linguistic' includes, above the levels of phonemes, mor-
phemes, lexemes, and sentences, those of speech events and genres of

communication. And this is where we might locate the mistake: although I should have known better from previous experience,[13] I simply misunderstood the nature of the event. I approached this conversation as an 'interview', certainly not preset and hardly directed, but nevertheless as an exchange whose purpose was to elicit and record information about charismatics. Hence my concern, expressed textually in what I called dodges, about not endangering the flow of information. While I was pursuing an interview, Mama Régine was engaged, and was trying to engage me, in a different genre: testimony. Had this been clear to me, my communicative competence should have included knowledge of the fact that the 'rules of speaking' for defining testimony among charismatics require that those who give testimony and those who receive it assume positions of absolute, perhaps utopian, equality. The Jamaa movement, whose teaching is quite explicit about these matters, often expressed the required attitude as one of self-humiliation (*kujishusha*). That gave the event a moral tinge and eventually resulted in a ritualisation of testimony exchanges as 'encounter' (*mapatano*), a necessary step in the process of initiation. With charismatics, the definition of this genre is somewhat different. But here again it is ritualised in form and often also in content, and is part of the typical meeting of a prayer group. Incidentally, our text contains a discursive marker to confirm this. Just when I begin to respond to her question about my Catholic background with an account, Mama Régine responds with a typically charismatic expression of assent and encouragement: 'Amen!' (line 29).

Ritualised or not, speech we classify as testimony has intellectual functions we should briefly consider. Testimony/witness is given when there is something to prove or verify. Proof/verification is needed when there is an argument, when something is contested. The more precarious faith becomes – because it is more and more isolated in an individual, or because it goes more and more against common sense – the stronger the need for testimony. Through the years, I have become convinced that there can come a moment when testimonies can be exchanged between ethnographers and the people who are being researched. The result need not be agreement or conversion, and it seldom is; but it can be the promise of nontrivial understanding that is produced by researcher and researched together (see Fabian 1979b).

This means (returning to our reflections on the significance of ethnographic misunderstandings) that this kind of mistake can be repaired by invoking as context certain culturally defined rules of communication. But it is also clear that here, context is not 'given'.[14] What is not given cannot be called upon or applied; it must first be created. Furthermore, there is nothing inherent in context that makes it a corrective for misunderstanding. A text 'reduced to writing' may give us the illusion of an inside and an outside, of a part and a whole, or of lower and higher levels of understanding. In reality, in acts that produce ethnographic knowledge, creations of text and creations of context are of the same kind. This is an insight now accepted widely in literary and cultural studies. Jonathan Culler wrote some years ago:

> [The] notion of context frequently oversimplifies rather than enriches discussion, since the opposition between an act and its context seems to presume that the context is given and determines the meaning of the act. We know, of course, that things are not so simple: context is not given but produced ... contexts are just as much in need of elucidation as events; and the meaning of a context is determined by events. [1988: xiv][15]

The particular route by which we came to a similar conclusion – that the problem was misunderstanding rather than a matter of interpreting meanings – can, I believe, be travelled further. From examining misunderstandings and their repair with the help of context, we can, having overcome the positivity of context, go on to direct our attention to the significance of not-understanding in the production of (ethnographic) knowledge.

The Significance of Not-Understanding

At this point I should address a likely objection. In my examples, misunderstanding was identified reflexively – the same person was involved in misunderstanding and in understanding that something was misunderstood. What about situations where one person 'corrects' the misunderstandings of another? Can understanding be collective? Is reflexivity collective? In order to get a grip on these questions we should briefly stop to consider reflexivity. I would argue that at least three aspects of reflexive understanding need to be attended to: critical intent and memory, yes, but above all, a personally situated process of knowing. By 'critical intent' I mean an intellectual habit directing attention not just to the possibility of misunderstanding but to actual cases of it. 'Memory' I take to be the capacity to connect present with past understanding (every misunderstanding was once an understanding). Finally, 'process of knowing' signals a notion of understanding as a praxis of constant transformation, rather than as the accumulation of understandings and the elimination of misunderstandings. The latter view would pre-suppose a position of distance or transcendence outside the process of understanding, one that does not seem attainable if that process is, as I said, personally situated. Contrary to the endearing ethnoscientist fiction of an 'omniscient ethnographer', our work is necessarily historical and contingent because it is autobiographical.

It seems to be a different matter when another person catches or diagnoses the misunderstanding. But critical intent, although individually mobilised, is a socially shared habit connecting both analytical and reflexive practices. How is memory involved? I must remember that someone reported something as understanding in order to confront this with evidence that is available to me but not, or not yet, to the author of the reported understanding. But whose is the misunderstanding in that case? Whatever the answer may be, it will necessarily point to a communicative view of the pursuit of understanding. After all, even in cases where I am the author of both the misunderstanding and the understanding, I act with communicative intent as soon as I report my (mis)understanding.

I realise that choosing to address the problem of ethnographic misunderstanding has led me onto dangerous ground. As a matter of elementary logic, it is impossible to determine the significance of a negative proposition with any degree of exactitude. To establish that something was misunderstood tells us nothing about how it should be understood. But my examples should have shown that, in practice, the diagnosis of ethnographic misunderstanding is certainly not a matter of logic alone. The reason is, of course, that it is impossible to specify axiomatic truth conditions for anthropology. Unless we are able to deal with statements such as 'a white person is black' in ways other than rejecting them as contradictory, there is no point in doing anthropology. What I want to argue is that misunderstanding needs to be considered epistemologically and that it is but one kind of not-understanding.

Misunderstanding, with its conceptual aura of mistake, error, failure, and falsity, serves conceptions of knowledge that measure validity with a standard, if not of absolute truth, then of the degree of match between representations (ethnography in this case) and realities. If this measure is applied rigorously, validity becomes a matter of either/or (true or false). The very rigor of such a position requires that the idea of approximation be introduced if knowledge is to expand beyond first assumptions. Approximation, however, reaffirms what it qualifies: proximate to what? To the truth. Although such an approach to knowledge can subjectively be experienced as continual search, as the never-ending work of eliminating misunderstanding, it does not really conceive of knowledge as process. How one gets from one state of grace to another is not part of what is known, but belongs to the realm of rules, of method or theory, all of which are posited as being outside of the 'context' of intentions, communicative purposes, and historical conditions, at least while knowledge of (a) reality is being established.

In a processual, dialectical theory, knowing is not envisaged as a succession (and accumulation) of states of agreement between representation and reality, but rather as the production of knowledge through practices of interacting with, or confronting, reality. It is essential for such a process, and not a regrettable weakness, that negativity be involved in every conceivable step: not-knowing, as I think of it here, is not a logical but a dialectical negation. It is that which makes of knowing a process and of knowledge a product. Hegel could be invoked here, but we may as well stay with Humboldt, who provided the epigraph for this essay. He makes his intriguing statement that all understanding is not-understanding in a discussion of the dialectic relationship between language and speaking. We may speak of the individuality of a language when we distinguish one language from another, but 'true individuality' – that is, true actualisation, realisation – is achieved only by the individual speaker (1963 [1830-35]: 439). On that level:

> Nobody means by a word precisely and exactly what his neighbour does, and the difference, be it ever so small, vibrates, like a ripple in water, throughout the entire language. Thus all understanding is always at the same time a not-understanding. [1988: 63][16]

Let me now bring these reflections down to earth, and consider our problems with misunderstanding in language-based ethnography. I embarked on my argument by limiting what would otherwise have been a scope too vast to be addressed within the confines of an article. I suggested that we might get a better understanding of the epistemological significance of ethnographic misunderstanding if we were to concentrate on a claim that presumably is accepted by those who are theoretically inspired by the ethnography of speaking, namely that full understanding, and consequently overcoming failures to understand, requires recourse to context. What I have been struggling to make clear is that the potential of the ethnography of speaking to go beyond semiotic (and certainly beyond purely methodological) uses of language in ethnography – the potential, that is, to move ethnography from a position that takes knowledge as representation to one that takes knowledge as praxis – may be endangered precisely by unreflected appeals to that which distinguishes it from other 'linguistic' approaches: context.[17] Context, I have argued, works in a dialectical, not a logical-methodological, way. Context cannot, except trivially, be 'cited' (as con-text). Context does not coexist with text 'synchronically' – a qualifier that, rather than affirming temporal coexistence, really asserts the irrelevance of time. A 'synchronous' or paradigmatic notion of context may be involved, for instance, when Dell Hymes appears to use 'context' and 'setting' synonymously in his discussion of the components of a speech event (1974:13).[18] If there is a conclusion to be drawn from our reflections on examples of ethnographic misunderstanding, then it is something like the following: Context must be constituted in a practice that is individually and therefore historically situated and determined. Ethnography is biography is historiography – a position that can escape tautology if it rests on a dialectical conception of knowledge. The point of insisting on dialectics is to overcome facticity through overcoming positivity. The positivist definition of facts as *choses* (that is, 'things') needs negating, not just breaking down or refining. Dialectics opens up a view of history as uniting the general and the specific in a process. Positive social science, on the other hand, ends up with something like 'pluralism'. Historiography/ethnography is then envisaged, at best, as a matter of negotiation and, at worst, as a game of classification. Of course, if a dialectical theory of knowledge is descriptive, not just programmatic, then positivists produce knowledge dialectically like everyone else. But the problem is not one of ontology – not of what knowledge *is*, but of how it can be presented and communicated. This is what can be discussed by people holding different theoretical positions. I hope the cases I have discussed show that we stand to lose a great deal if we deal with misunderstanding by sweeping our failures under the rug of invariably positive accounts of success.

Notes

1. *Tr.* Thus all understanding is always at the same time a not-understanding, all concurrence in thought and feeling at the same time divergence (Humboldt 1988: 63).

   This essay was originally prepared as a discussion paper for a workshop on *Les rhétoriques due quotidien*, organised by Bertrand Masquelier and Jean-Louis Siran, Paris, 22-23 May 1992. I thank Vincent de Rooij for bringing several important references to my attention.

   [Editor's note] It was first published in *American anthropologist* 1995, 97 (1): 41-50 and is re-printed here with the kind permission of the American Anthropological Association: '*Reproduced by the permission of the American Anthropological Association from American anthropologist 97: 1, March 1995. Not for further reproduction.*' My thanks are also extended to Johannes Fabian for agreeing to allow his paper to be circulated at the St Andrews workshop and for it to be included in this volume.

2. At this point, so as to avoid making an already difficult reflection even more complex, I use the terms synonymously. That they may have to be distinguished is a question that can be addressed more profitably after I have provided examples of ethnographic understanding gone wrong. In the meantime I must ask for indulgence when I use 'misunderstanding' in an undifferentiated sense, covering both not- and mis-.

3. Like others I was inspired by a movement variously designated as sociolinguistics, ethnography of communication, or ethnography of speaking, and most convincingly advanced by Dell Hymes (see 1974 as a convenient collection of his essays).

Philosophically I was influenced by J. Habermas's early writing on the logic of the social sciences (1988[1967]). Although the ethnography of speaking forms a background for these reflections it is not what I am discussing here.

Contextualisation and (mis)communication in conversations are widely debated issues in current sociolinguistics (see, for instance, Auer and Di Luzio 1992 and Goodwin and Duranti 1992) but, as far as I can see, sociolinguistics are not concerned with the issue of ethnographic knowledge production as such. Just as earlier 'ethnography of communication' did not give us a method for producing ethnography (just a better understanding of what we were doing), so it is also unlikely that sociolinguistic studies of conversational strategies will provide us with rules for dealing with ethnographic misunderstandings. For an earlier paper in which I discuss a misunderstanding or mistake that made me rethink 'ethnography as communication', see Fabian 1979a (reprinted in Fabian 1990: chapter 5).

4. For the sake of the argument, let us omit the fact that understanding is already required in the preceding phase, that of deciding what to record and what not.

5. D. Tedlock's essays (1983) are still the most complete discussion of the matter. My own current comprehension of the task is formulated in Fabian 1990. A most perceptive and comprehensive treatment of 'context presentation' in transcribing may be found in Cook 1990. See also the more broadly formulated arguments against naive conceptions of transcription in Mishler 1991.

6. From a recording made on 30 June 1986 at Kawama village near Lubumbashi/Shaba.

7. I am unable to ascertain whether the transcription and translation provided by the group are correct. But that they call for a correction of what we had heard cannot be doubted.

8. This is not to say that Africans such as Kanyemba are 'colour blind' – shades and hues of skin colour are constantly distinguished and remarked upon. Incidentally, our text contains at least a hint of uncertainty that I failed to notice when I did the transcription. At one point the person is referred to as *ule kama ni muzungu*, a Shaba Swahili idiom signalling a hedge on the part of the speaker.

9. This is how I understand Bourdieu when he qualifies, or denounces, anthropological structuralism as 'hermeneutic' because it is objectivist (1977: 1 f. and elsewhere).

10. We first met on 14 June 1986 at her home.

11. In Lubumbashi, relationships between the prayer groups and the official church hierarchy have been precarious, to say the least.

12. Note that the following excerpt, although edited to prevent autobiographic detail from distracting from the argument, is translated as faithfully as possible; it is just that faithfulness is not enough when it comes to meeting the challenge of this sort of text. Matters are further complicated by two factors. Mama Régine, although fluent in Swahili, is not very articulate in this language. She resorts to intonation, gestures, and other means to compensate for shortcomings in vocabulary and idioms. Furthermore, our conversation had reached the point at which performative elements begin to prevail over referential discourse. Both of us worked with allusions, innuendoes, and ellipsis; we used phonations and gestures, changes in intonation, and pauses. The difficulties that such texts pose are dealt with in Fabian 1990: chapter 5.

13. Reported and analysed in Fabian 1974, reprinted in 1991: chapter 3 under the heading of 'testimony'. I refer to this essay also for the remarks that follow.

14. And that, incidentally, has been a reason for me not to invoke 'pragmatics' as if it were merely another level of linguistic analysis. For the problems I have with (mis)understanding utterances and texts, little seems to be gained by considering pragmatics abstractly.

15. Mieke Bal, to whom I owe attention to this statement, goes on to state: 'Context, in other words, is a text and thus presents the same difficulty of interpretation as any other text' (1991: 6).

16. Actually, Humboldt does not say 'nobody means' the same but 'nobody thinks' the same – a nuance that signals his concern with language as activity of the mind rather than system of significations.

17. I only note, but cannot adequately discuss here, a further complication: in cultural and social anthropology, context, more so than other 'technical terms', has an evocative and rhetorical rather than referential meaning. It does not really belong among the terms designating the object, or aspects of the object, we study, such as culture, religion, kinship, economy, and so forth. Nor is it usually part of a conceptual scheme constructed of opposites or contrasts such as structure (versus event) or meaning (versus function). In fact, now that anthropology has developed more or less holistic approaches to whatever it studies, a call for consideration of context often turns out to be preaching to the converted.

18. Hymes refers to other authors who speak of 'context of situation', which I take to imply a view of context *as* situation, that is, as a state of affairs (1974: 20). He points approvingly to Malinowski's use of context as something that underlies (again a static notion) acts and events (p. 61). But notice also a shift of meaning when Hymes speaks of the event itself as 'context' (p. 13).

Bibliography

Auer, P. and A. di Luzio (eds) 1992. *The contextualization of language.* Amsterdam and Philadelphia: John Benjamins.

Bal, M. 1991. *Reading 'Rembrandt': beyond the word-image opposition.* Cambridge: Cambridge University Press.

Bourdieu, P. 1977. *Outline of a theory of practice.* Cambridge: Cambridge University Press.

Cook, G. 1990. 'Transcribing infinity: problems of context presentation'. *Journal of Pragmatics* 14: 1-24.

Culler, J. 1988. *Framing the sign: criticism and its institutions.* Norman, OK: University of Oklahoma Press.

Fabian, J. 1974. 'Genres in an emerging tradition: an approach to religious communication'. In A.W. Eister (ed.), *Changing perspectives in the scientific study of religion*: 249-72. New York: Wiley Interscience.

———. 1977. 'Charisma: theory and practice'. *ASA Review of Books* 3: 122-34.

———. 1979a. 'Rule and process: thoughts on ethnography as communication'. *Philosophy of the Social Sciences* 9: 1-26.

———. 1979b. 'Introduction' to *Beyond charisma: religious movements as discourse..* Special issue of *Social Research* 46(1): 4-35. New York: Graduate Faculty of the New School for Social Research.

———. 1990. *Power and performance: ethnographic explorations through proverbial wisdom and theater in Shaba, Zaire.* Madison: University of Wisconsin Press.

———. 1991. *Time and the work of anthropology: critical essays 1971-1991.* Chur and Philadelphia: Harwood Academic Publishers.

Goodwin, C. and A. Duranti (eds). 1992. *Rethinking context: language as an interactive phenomenon*. Cambridge: Cambridge University Press.

Habermas, Jürgen 1988. *On the logic of the social sciences*. Cambridge, MA.: MIT Press.

Humboldt, W. von. 1963. *Schriften zur Sprachphilosophie*. Andreas Flitner and Klaus Giel (eds.). Stuttgart: Cotta.

————. 1988[1836]. *On language: the diversity of human language – structure and its influence on the mental development of mankind*. Peter Heath (trans.). Cambridge: Cambridge University Press.

Hymes, D. 1974. *Foundations in sociolinguistics: an ethnographic approach*. Philadelphia: University of Pennsylvania Press.

Jules-Rosette, B. 1975. *African apostles: ritual and conversion in the church of John Maranke*. Ithaca, NY: Cornell University Press.

Mishler, E. G. 1991. 'Representing discourse: the rhetoric of transcription'. *Journal of Narrative and Life History* 1: 255-80.

Tedlock, D. 1983. *The spoken word and the work of interpretation*. Philadelphia: University of Pennsylvania Press.

Chapter 5

AS THEY LIKE IT

OVERINTERPRETATION AND HYPOREALITY IN BALI

Mark Hobart

Bali overflows with meaning. As the illustration overleaf shows, meaning has even found its way into exported Indonesian representations of themselves. A glorious intellectual genealogy climaxing with Bateson and Mead, Geertz and Boon, ends limply in advertising copy for Bank Bumi Daya. In Bali even capitalism has been aestheticised. Or is it aesthetics commoditised? In the advertisement Balinese epitomise Indonesia; while dance epitomises Bali. And meaning is what motivates Balinese dance. But how did meaning get into the dance? And according to whom?

The problem these days, to paraphrase Evans-Pritchard, is that there is only one method in social anthropology, the interpretive method – and that is impossible (Needham 1975: 365). It is not however self-evident that social actions are either interpretable or, what follows, meaningful, except in a trivial sense. For instance, there is a well known and very difficult movement in Balinese dance, *magulu (w)angsul*, which involves moving the head from side to side smoothly, while keeping it vertical. I once asked some dancers what the meaning (*arti*) was to be greeted with a laugh and told it had none! It was appreciated because it was so difficult to do well.[1] To succeed was to be *tekek*, firm, precise; just as good speech should be *seken*, clear, definite. Only when a dancer has mastered the use of the body can they assume a *sebeng bingar*, an expression of deep inner contentment, radiate light

(*masinar becik*) when dancing, so that the audience feel *buka girik*, as if
it has been tickled and aroused. It is about achieving an effect. Balinese
are highly critical commentators on what is considered good or bad,
but do so largely without recourse to meaning. Such Balinese reflections on their own practices though stand in stark contrast to what
scholars insufflate into them. Interpretation is so central to the definition of the anthropologist as knowing subject, of the object of study
and the required disciplinary practices however that questioning its
universal applicability must be rather like questioning the existence of
God in the Vatican. The result is to preempt inquiry into the conditions under which it is justifiable or appropriate to rely on interpretation or to impute meaning.

On Interpretation

In anthropological practice, interpreting has come, profligately, to embrace any activity from expounding the meaning of something abstruse, to making clear, to giving a particular explanation.[2] In short, it is what anthropologists do. The word has a more specialist sense: the method, goal or subject matter of hermeneutics. This is not just an obscure German philosophical genealogy culminating in Habermas, but by routes as diverse as Weber and Freud has permeated human scientific thinking; and has even had a significant impact via Heidegger on post-structuralists such as Foucault and on Derrida. My interest however is especially in anthropological uses of hermeneutics. It so happens that the doyen of Interpretive Anthropology, Clifford Geertz, has used Bali to illustrate his method. Geertz's work expounds and exemplifies many of the kinds of interpretive methods and assumptions invoked by other anthropologists. So, rather than engage in sweeping generalisations, I confine myself to interpretation as it has actually been practised on Balinese.

Interpretation creates a dilemma for anthropologists. As Dan Sperber notes

> the project of a scientific anthropology meets with a major difficulty: it is impossible to describe a cultural phenomenon...without taking into account the ideas of the participants. However, ideas cannot be observed, but only intuitively understood: they cannot be described but only interpreted. (1985: 9)

Sperber's task therefore is to get from intuitive understandings to true descriptions which may be falsified and so are scientific. Taking examples from Evans-Pritchard's *Nuer Religion*, Sperber argues the extent to which an anthropologist reworks supposed observations in the course of even the most apparently raw factual account. What mediates is

> anthropologists' technical vocabulary...a medley of words to be used where straightforward translations are wanting: 'sacrifice', 'divination', 'priest'... 'symbol', 'marriage'... When they seem to be developing a theory of sacrifice, they are, actually, pursuing [the] work of second (or nth) degree interpretation' etc. (1985: 25, 27)

This is what makes

> interpretive generalizations differ radically from descriptive generalizations. An interpretation is adequate when it is faithful, a description is adequate when it is true. (1985: 29)

As usual I find myself agreeing heartily with the first half of what Sperber writes and disagreeing furiously with the second. Not only description and explanation involve interpretation in some sense or other, but so do translation and even transcription. The idea, however, that you can drive a wedge between fidelity to ideas and true descriptions looks gently dated and unnecessarily dualistic (Quine 1953; Davidson 1973), although the vision still seems to excite the occasional analytical philosopher. For some reason, even quite intelligent anthropologists retain a touching affection in the powers of impartial observation, when we spend so much time asking people to explain what it is we have just seen. Sperber attempts to escape by resort to a scientised epidemiology of representations, which is a subtle form of representationism and semiological regression (Fabian 1991a). His 'participants' however turn out to be the usual passive, de-fanged objects of anthropological inquiry, whose ideas conveniently reflect or instantiate collective representations, the raw materials of the thinking anthropologist.

The Prize for Good Guesses

Considering how broad the claims made for interpretation, it turns out to be quite a difficult animal to track down. When it comes to spelling out what is involved in the approach he has made his own, Geertz becomes rather coy. What does come across though is that an interpretive theory of culture is 'essentially a semiotic one' (1973a: 5). As Geertz relies very heavily for his theory on the work of Ricoeur, it is worth quoting the organ-grinder himself:

> the primary sense of the word 'hermeneutics' concerns the rules required for the interpretation of the written documents of our culture... *Auslegung* (interpretation, exegesis)...covers only a limited category of signs, those which are fixed by writing, including all the sorts of documents and monuments which entail a fixation similar to writing. (1981a: 197)

The difficulty is that this interpretation or exegesis is not confined to the analysis of signs in any obviously Saussurean manner. Hermeneutics is redolent of supplementarity: it promises more than semiotics, a 'surplus of meaning'. It is this more that worries me.

The supplement which is promised derives from the workings of that delightfully arcane notion: the hermeneutic circle. Geertz wields his semiotic trowel with some panache:

> Cultural analysis is (or should be) guessing at meanings, assessing the guesses, and drawing explanatory conclusions from the better guesses, not discovering the Continent of Meaning and mapping out its bodiless landscape. (1973a: 20)

This is odd in a way, because there are not many bodies, or people, in Geertz's analyses, except occasionally as props to get the narrative going (Crapanzano 1986: 69-71). Ricoeur is more prosaic:

We have to guess the meaning of the text because the author's intention is beyond our reach...if there are no rules for making good guesses, there are methods for validating those guesses we do make...[which] are closer to a logic of probability than to a logic of empirical verification. To show that an interpretation is more probable in the light of what we know is something other than showing that a conclusion is true. So in the relevant sense, validation is not verification. It is an argumentative discipline comparable to the juridical procedures used in legal interpretation, a logic of uncertainty and of qualitative probability...we are also enabled to give an acceptable meaning to the famous concept of the hermeneutic circle. Guess and validation are in a sense circularly related as subjective and objective approaches to the text. But this circle is not a vicious one...the role of falsification is played by the conflict between competing interpretations. An interpretation must not only be probable, but more probable than another interpretation. (1976: 75-79, my parentheses)

The whole juggernaut is driven by the will-o'-the-wisp of the almost unbelievably probable interpretation. In the last resort though, there is no yardstick for judging the quality of an interpretation which is not recursively defined by the interpretive method itself.

Ricoeur is admirably explicit and so highlights what tends to be submerged in Geertz's suasive prose. Once again there is a convenient Cartesian split of truth about the world and what pertains to the higher reaches of Mind. Mind however is oddly passive. On the crucial question of how you decide between rival interpretations, it is 'the conflict' which is supposed to do the work. An approach which purports to clarify the intricacies of forms of argumentation ends up in this instance by muddying the waters to the point that Jonathan Spencer has remarked of this strain of American anthropology that there has been 'the abandonment of *any* consideration of problems of validation' (1989: 159). One of the drawbacks of a postmodern, post-interpretive, post-global world is an abandonment of critical thinking to a spurious democracy of argument in which anything goes: *lasciate ogni discernimento voi ch'entrate.*

For Ricoeur, the meaning of the text originates in, but becomes detached from, the author's mind. It turns into public property to do with what one will; but few are qualified to do so. For interpretation 'presupposes a discrepancy between the clear meaning of the text and the demands of (later) readers' (Sontag 1961: 6). By postulating an ironic doubling with a wealth of hidden deep meaning (Foucault 1973: 303-387), gerundively hermeneuts create a potentially inexhaustible resource to be exploited and where they effectively exercise unregulated control. A semantic free market is declared, with procedures (guessing and checking guesses) supposed to ensure that all works out for the best.[3]

A difficulty of interpretation is that you cannot begin guessing without some background of prior texts (pre-text or inter-text) and without determining beforehand what kind of object you are dealing with in the light of what you already know (a further determination). In short, hermeneutic methods require preinterpretation, with little restriction on how you procure the results. As we can never approach something innocently, we inevitably introduce assumptions and presuppositions. We begin preinterpreting in the act of listening. The reason so much of this paper is devoted to a critique of interpretation is I am still trying to free myself to the degree I can from yet more unthinking preinterpretation.

The text instead is passive: it awaits the active resourceful interpreter (commonly male) to prize open and enjoy its riches. Ricoeur's juridical metaphor develops the theme. For the interpreter assumes further powers as judge to interrogate, and conduct whatever forensic procedures he (use of a male term again seems appropriate in this instance) will on the objectified products of mind by a mind set apart in judgement, knowing, superior. The findings are not subjective however, for objectivity then grafts itself onto validation in a manner which is far from clear. The connection rests upon the assumption that this mind approaches objectivity through its all-encompassing superiority, which transcends subjectivity and objectivity (unlike Geertz, Ricoeur is concerned to avoid the traps of a 'Romanticist' grounding of interpretation in the subject and intersubjectivity, 1981b). But whose subjectivity, whose objectivity and whose criteria of validation are these? The answer is the interpreters'. Finally, Ricoeur leaves the choice between probable interpretations remarkably open, uncontextualised and unsituated. Who decides which interpretation is more probable and by what criteria? On Geertz's and Ricoeur's account, for all their demotic imagery and show of humility, the power quietly abrogated by the interpreter is a dictator's dream. The familiar language of reason and reasonableness clouds an epistemological battlefield, on which, through their own choosing, the odds are stacked in favour of the big battalions.

In trying to defend the unrestrained freedom of the interpreter against all-comers, Geertz's former student and apologist, James Boon, delivers the approach and himself an accidental *coup de grâce*.

> Metaphors of text and of reading applied to anthropological fieldwork strike some critics as fancy devices to silence or disempower the interlocutor. I would reply that 'read texts' radically construed, certainly speak back; they may, moreover, change their mind's message on each re-reading. (1990: 52)

There is a serious problem of agency here. Texts have minds. But this still leaves the question: who 'radically construes' the texts, or rather 'the constructed understanding of the constructed native's constructed point of view (Crapanzano 1986: 74)? Perhaps this is why, in the end, the texts' minds look strangely like their interpreter's. The autonomy granted to 'the interlocutor', as opposed to a person as agent, resembles a pheasant bred for shooting or the icons in an interactive video game or virtual reality machine.

Textuality

What is the object of anthropological interpretation? Famously, it is culture inscribed as a text. Interpreting

> the flow of social discourse...consists in trying to rescue the 'said' of such discourse from its perishing occasions and fix it in perusable terms (Geertz 1973a: 20).
>
> The human sciences may be said to be hermeneutical (1) inasmuch as their object displays some of the features constitutive of a text as text, and (2) inasmuch as their methodology develops the same kind of procedures as those of Auslegung or text-interpretation. (Ricoeur 1981a: 197)

Social action becomes a text by the act of ethnographic inscription (Geertz 1973a: 19). There is the further extension though that this is possible only if action – or what humans make of events themselves – have some at least of the features of a text (Ricoeur 1981: 197-210). Further, texts (or text-like productions) *contain* meanings, their '*propositional* content' (Ricoeur 1981: 204; invoking the conduit metaphor, see Reddy 1979). Put this way, however, meaning as a concept and in its particular ascriptions becomes open to critical consideration. It must be reclaimed and mystified. In a neat three thimble trick, Boon therefore announces that meaning is 'fundamentally transposed, converted, substituted' (1990: 209). Displacing the problem, just as declaring 'culture' to be 'multiple constructions that are *at base* contrastive' (1990: 209), is somehow supposed to resolve the difficulties.

However, 'events only *seem* to be intelligible. Actually they have no meaning without interpretation' (Sontag 1961: 7). There are two senses of 'text' here. In the narrower one, text refers to what Barthes called 'work' which 'is a fragment of substance, occupying a part of the space of books' (1977: 156-57). In the broader one, text 'is a methodological field...*the Text is experienced only in an activity of production*' (1977: 157, original emphasis). In the latter sense, it is of a higher logical order than Ricoeur's text, which is itself a complex whole built out of sentences (1976: 1-23).

There are two obvious problems. First you cannot write an epistemological space. Second, it conflates culture and work/text. Unless you inhabit a peculiarly recondite world, culture is not a text. Before Boon declares me yet again a vulgar positivist, let me explain what I wish to say by this. It may be fruitful to treat culture heuristically (one of my least favourite words) *as if* it were a text. I doubt it. But many postmodernists have made great reputations (and brought about the felling of many trees) to celebrate the catachresis. It has become conventional in the last decade or so among those suffering PMT (postmodernist trendiness) cheerfully to talk about how texts have constituted people in ever more ambiguous ways. Quite what being constituted by a text – be it a book, a methodological field or a condition of intelligibility – would actually involve is charmingly mind-boggling.

The problem with subsuming the whole strange eventful gamut of human actions and events across history under the sobriquet of 'Text' is not only that it hypostatises and homogenises whatever has happened, but that, if everything is Text, the notion is vapid (cf. Baudrillard on Foucault's idea of power, 1987). It becomes an abstract substance, empowered with amazing, if largely imaginary, qualities. In short, it becomes a 'Transcendental Agent', beyond history, and with thrasonical hermeneuts and deconstructionists as its immanent intelligence to tell us what It is up to. Text becomes an excuse not just for pastiche but to make what you please of other peoples' lives and how they represent themselves, to mix and match at will in a consumers' utopia.[4]

There is something pleasantly amateurish, indeed Frankensteinian, about the attempts of anthropologists such as Geertz (with assistance from Boon) to jolt the cachexic corpse of culture into textual life. Since then, however, a consortium of Literary Critics has taken over the business of transmuting the whole gamut of human and social activities into texts on an industrial scale.[5]

Overinterpreting

Treating culture, or life itself, as a text avoids a recognition of textualising as a cultural practice. People write, speak, read and listen; textualise events and actions in circumstances which depend on the existence of previous practices of textualising. The Literary Tendency is itself part of such practices; but solipsistically its practitioners hypostatise practices into abstract objects (texts) and imagine particular practices to be constitutive, essential or even universal. The sort of approach I prefer however treats practices as particular, historical, situated and varying in degree and kind. I assume that, far from having a determinate, extractable essence, facts are underdetermined by explanation (Quine 1953, 1960) or, put another way, that 'reality transcends the knower' (Inden 1986: 402). On this account, any activity or practice, the agents who engage in them and the patients who are their subjects, are themselves partly a consequence of, but are not fully determined by, past practices and activities. Among practices, some rework past practices (e.g. commenting, criticising, correcting); others aim at transforming patients (e.g. graduating, curing, managing) and the agents themselves (e.g. crowning, praying, self-disciplining; cf. Foucault 1986). Yet other practices are concerned with trying to eliminate the underdetermination of actions and events, including much academic writing and 'ritual' (see Hobart forthcoming). I choose therefore to treat both explaining and interpreting as often practices of determination, or essentialising, in some form.

What I call overinterpreting is overdetermining one interpretation where alternative equally plausible interpretations are possible, or have in fact been put forward. As a practice, overinterpreting usually starts with preinterpreting prior to any engagement with what is actually to be interpreted and concludes in defending the interpretation against criticism. Evidently Balinese, for instance, may well on occasion also overinterpret for whatever reasons. Where they differ from hermeneuts is that the latter's justification for existing is that they somehow add more to what the locals are perfectly capable of saying for themselves. This something is a logical method for validating probable interpretations, presumed – in a fine example of preinterpretation – to be so superior to Balinese methods that no interpreter has bothered to inquire what they are (cf. Hobart 1985) or if they even exist.

One of the best ways of clarifying what I wish to suggest by overinterpreting is to put forward a null hypothesis. It is that no act of anthropological interpretation takes place dialogically and dialectically during fieldwork between ethnographer and local intellectuals – let alone centrally involving local intellectuals arguing among themselves – but rather before the ethnographer's arrival in, and after departure from, the field. It is then possible to distinguish anthropologists by the degree to which they breach the null hypothesis in their work. In my experience of an island crowded with expatriate experts, sadly it holds up remarkably well. If it makes a mockery of most anthropologists' and other specialists' pretensions, that is their problem. If you stop and think about how many anthropologists or others speak the vernacular language well enough to engage in the critical exchange necessary to argue through rival interpretations, far less understand Balinese arguing amongst themselves, the imaginary nature of much interpretation *as a practice* rather than as a posture stands out with grim clarity.

Two practices among others related to interpreting are textualising and contextualising,[6] which I take to be always situated acts. (On this account, context and situation are not Cartesian mental and physical domains within semantics. All actions are situated; and contextualising is one kind of action.) By contrast to recourse to Text, or even textuality, (con-)textualising is a historically situated action aimed at changing the *status quo ante*. To develop Goodman's analysis of representation (1968: 27-31), some agent represents, textualises or contextualises something as something else, commonly to some subject on an occasion for a purpose. The relevance of this argument here is that it enables us to reconsider interpretation not as a finished product, we are to admire, believe or even criticise, but as a practice which takes place on an occasion for a purpose. Anthropologists very rarely ask what is the purpose of what they do.

They are not alone in this, nor in glossing fast over what it is that they actually spend much of their professional time doing. One practice is textualising, reworking events into writing through a double process. The author articulates the events in question with previous descriptions and writing practices, in so doing making the events discursive, interpretable and understandable (Hall 1980: 129). The author also reproduces the events, commonly in writing, for the delectation of her peers and the Advancement of Knowledge. Taken to absurd lengths, you end up overtextualising people (Boon) or the world (Appadurai, Bhabha), and recursively anthropomorphising the texts. Now there are many occasions when people textualise events and actions, but they do much else besides.[7] As they seem to find texts realer, or at least cosier, than life, perhaps it is not so odd that afficionados of the Literary Turn in the human sciences should project their own practices and predilections onto the rest of the known and, in their case, knowable world. This world is there *to be read* and contextualised. Anthropologists often appeal to context. What appears as an exercise in interpretive charity and anti-essentialism depends, however, on furbishing the natives first with a rich realm of Textuality in which their strange remarks make sense ('Birds are twins' is the paradigm case). Then their utterances and actions can be reinscribed using the familiar language of textual procedures (metaphor, synecdoche etc., the stock in trade *inter alia* of both structuralism and hermeneutics). Historians and literary experts specialise more literally in reconstructing how people read texts, and so to constructing Texts.[8]

Either way, as anthropologists engage in it as a practice, contextual interpretation often becomes a way of idealising specific social actions. Contextualising the text or weird statements shows how the native Mind instantiates or insinuates itself into the world. I am not referring here to actual minds on particular occasions: what people did or said. That is purely contingent. It is not clear what contextualising that would consist of. Contextualising highlights what is essential, general, indeed generic, not to particular persons, but a Culture or People (the Nuer, the Balinese), which is the politically acceptable synonym for Mind. Anthropologists have long used context as an authenticating and emancipatory strategy. 'Understanding something in context' confirms you were really there, saw and understood. (The idealist rejoinder is to turn 'being there' effectively into a question of literary genre, Geertz 1988.) Contextualising easily becomes emancipatory from the critical evaluation of evidence; and so permits anthropologists to write themselves interpretive blank cheques. It culminates in Baron Münchhausen's Syndrome, first identified by Raspe in 1785.

Overinterpreting Bali

How does an interpretive analysis actually work as against ideal statements of method? Let us take examples from two of Clifford Geertz's most celebrated essays into interpretive anthropology and one from Boon, who has adapted Geertz's method in a distinctive way.

In *Person, time, and conduct in Bali*, Geertz elaborated upon the work of Bateson and Mead (e.g., 1942). 'The anonymization of persons and the immobilisation of time are thus but two sides of the same cultural process', the third being 'the ceremoniousness of so much of Balinese daily life' (1973b: 398-99). The crucial means in achieving this is *lek*. Geertz argued

> that *lek*, which is far and away the most important of such regulators, culturally the most intensely emphasized, ought therefore not to be translated as 'shame,' but rather, to follow out our theatrical image, as 'stage fright'. ([1966] 1973b: 402)

Nearly twenty years later nothing had happened to make Geertz question his interpretation or its assumptions.

> Nor is this sense the Balinese have of always being on stage a vague and ineffable one either. It is, in fact, exactly summed up in what is surely one of their experience-nearest concepts: *lek*. *Lek* has been variously translated or mistranslated ('shame' is the most common attempt); but what it really means is close to what we call stage fright... When this occurs, as it sometimes does, the immediacy of the moment is felt with excruciating intensity and men become suddenly and unwillingly creatural, locked in mutual embarrassment, as though they had happened upon each other's nakedness. It is the fear of faux pas, rendered only that much more probably by the extraordinary ritualization of daily life, that keeps social intercourse on its deliberately narrowed rails and protects the dramatistical sense of self against the disruptive threat implicit in the immediacy and spontaneity even the most passionate ceremoniousness cannot fully eradicate from face-to-face encounters. (1983a: 64; cf. 1973b: 401-2)

What though is the ethnographic evidence upon which Geertz validates his guesses? We do not know. How did Geertz know what Balinese felt? Did they participate in this analysis of their essential being? Or was it despite them? We are not told.

The remaining examples are from Geertz's most sustained interpretive foray, *Negara: the theatre state in nineteenth-century Bali*. Epitomising the king as the centre of the state (a much recycled Orientalist theme in South East Asia), Geertz develops a series of dichotomies around the contrast of inside *versus* outside:

> So is body to mind, countryside to settlement, circle circumference to circle center, word to meaning, sound to music, coconut shell to coconut juice. (1980: 108)

What is Geertz's evidence, for instance, that body is opposed to mind, or word to meaning? And what word does Geertz have in mind for 'meaning'? Once again the reader is not told, nor can you work it out even if you are familiar with the literature on Bali.

A central part is Geertz's analysis of kingship rests on the link between three symbols or imaged ideas: '*padmasana*, the lotus seat (or throne) of god; *lingga*, his phallus, or potency; and *sekti* [misspelt by any convention], the energy he infuses into his particular expressions, most especially into the person of the ruler' (1980: 104; the second parentheses are mine). Of the *lingga*, he announces:

> On earth, the ruler acts on behalf of Śiva, and the essence of his royal power is embodied in the *lingga* [which] the brahman...obtains...from Śiva and hands...over to them founder of the dynasty as the palladium of his royalty. The image summarizes the deep spiritual connection (Hooykaas calls it an 'indivisible trinity') between the supreme god, the reigning king, and the state high priest. (1980: 106)

This seems exemplary stuff. What is Geertz's evidence for his analysis though? It is in fact a quotation from the Dutch philologist, Hooykaas (1964: 143) citing another Dutch scholar, Krom (1931: 124). A review of what Hooykaas wrote however suggests matters are not quite so straightforward.

Textual Extremities

My last example is from Boon's *Affinities and Extremes*, which offers an Aladdin's cave of choice. Given his interest in Balinese textuality, the following passage is apposite:

> Outside reformist circles, Balinese textual practices minimize neutralized commentary. Reading groups (*sekaha mebasan*) may discuss distinct episodes from favored narratives; but their busywork is ideally another

ingredient of ritual celebrations. To enact, cite, or even refer to a text may unleash its power. Exegesis in any strict sense does not number among the functions of traditional textual and ritual experts... Just as Bali has little ascetic remove from life-in-society, so it demonstrates little interpretive remove from texts that would make them partly alienated objects of exegetical reflection. In Bali's 'interpretive scene' the restricted role of exegesis proper facilitates a play of affinities, analogies, and contradictions across social forms, performance genres, and ritual registers. (1990: 84)

I love the smack of the 'strict' disciplinary proprieties, the natives evidently need so badly. But, what are Boon's grounds, first, for this sweeping summation of Balinese textual practices as anti-interpretive and ritualistic? He cites my old teacher, Hooykaas: 'temple priests, exorcists, and puppet masters alike "have some share in the brahman's panoply of magic weapons"' (1990: 84, citing Hooykaas 1980: 20). This hardly underwrites Boon's assertion. Further, on what evidence does Boon justify his statement that Balinese textual practices are not exegetical but about the melding of genres? It is shadow theatre (*wayang*).

Wayang's epistemology resembles Western examples of so-called Menippean satire, a form of parodic rhetoric that multiplies voices and viewpoints, tongues, citations, pastiches, and etymologies. (1990: 86)

Oddly the sources cited are for Java, not Bali at all. Presumably shadow theatre has an essential being which transcends history, place and persons altogether.

Interpreting the Interpreters

In *Person, time, and conduct in Bali*, Geertz takes two kinds of calendar (from Goris 1933) and aspects of behaviour he characterises as 'ceremony, stage fright, and absence of climax' (1973b: 398, the last, especially, is from Bateson 1949). In other words, Geertz is working largely with interpretations of interpretations. For an analysis which claims not only to pay close attention to Balinese behaviour, but even to reveal what Balinese experience 'with excruciating intensity', curiously he offers no detailed examples of Balinese practice, still less of Balinese talking about and commenting on themselves. Geertz doubly transfixes Bali: on a sustained dramaturgical metaphor and on a pathological general description of personality. He preinterprets, because the analysis rests upon western common-sensical assumptions about the nature of both theatre and the person. Balinese have quite different, highly developed and largely incommensurable ideas (on theatre, see Hobart 1983; on the person, see Connor 1982; Duff-Cooper 1985).

The analysis hinges on the cultural associations of the word *lek*. Balinese actors waxed lyrical about stage fright, for which however they used the word *jejeh*, plain 'frightened'. Significantly, when actors talked of stage fright or when people referred to themselves or others being *lek*, they dwelt not on the inner state, but on its manifestation facially, in one's speech and body movements, which squared with their careful differentiation of the body, expressions and movements. Balinese did indeed refer to *lek* in performing, but as *sing nawang lek*, not knowing *lek*, of actors who played roles like that of the mad princess, Liku, whose part requires groping other actors' genitals on stage and blurting out the unmentionable. By imposing interpretations upon actions in the absence of – or rather, despite all – the evidence, yet again Geertz overinterprets.

In *Negara*, among innumerable asides, Geertz opposes periphery to centre, body to mind and word to meaning, as if the relationship between these were transitive. The centre:periphery opposition, upon which much of *Negara* is predicated, is a particularly fine, if now rather tarnished, stroke of orientalist genius (see e.g., Heine-Geldern 1942). For someone ostensibly so opposed to the assumptions of Dutch structuralism (1961), Geertz manages to find dual oppositions where Balinese usually use triadic or quite different schemes altogether. In fact, almost all frames of reference to the self I know of involve at least three overlapping and potentially interacting qualities (e.g., Duff-Cooper 1985: 68-71 on the *trisarira*; Hobart 1986: 148-49 on the *triguna, triwarga and tiga-jñana*). Granted Geertz's erudition, we must question whether his blithe opposition of body to mind as if it were quite self-evident is a slip born of a rhetorical flourish. It is unlikely. The whole structure of *Negara* depends upon a (Cartesian) contrast between political geography and 'symbology'.[9] An obvious point about the various Balinese schemes for relating thought and action (Hobart 1986; Wikan 1990) is that they presuppose that body and mind are not dualistically separated. In the light of these evasions, it should come as no great surprise that Geertz should treat the constitutive concept of interpretation, 'meaning', as equally unproblematic. In *Negara*, as his other writing on Bali, Geertz not only skirts round the whole issue of semantics, but also avoids inquiring into Balinese usage, which is intricate (see p.126 below). How far has Geertz created the object of his interpretations, meaning, by conflating what Balinese distinguish? It is not a promising start to establishing more probable interpretations. What is rather frightening, especially in an interpretive approach which promises to take 'us into the heart of that of which it is an interpretation' (1973a: 18), is that it may never have occurred to Geertz that Balinese might think and talk about such matters among themselves.

A remarkable feature of Geertz's interpretive approach to the (*ipse dixit*) central symbols of Balinese kingship is that it involves precious little engagement with Balinese thinking in action. It is in fact, in Raymond Williams's phrase (1983), an exercise in identifying keywords. Geertz generalises from the carefully textually circumscribed analyses of earlier Dutch scholars, such that (to quote Geertz himself in his definition of how religion works, 1966: 4, my parentheses) by 'formulating conceptions of a general order of existence and...clothing these conceptions with such an aura of factuality...[the results] seem uniquely realistic'. As with religion, the 'aura of factuality' is a product of the process itself. It requires confusing what Volosinov distinguished as theme and meaning.

> *Only an utterance taken in its full, concrete scope as a historical phenomenon possesses a theme...* Theme is the *upper, actual limit of linguistic significance;* in essence, only theme means something definite. Meaning is the *lower limit* of linguistic significance. Meaning, in essence, means nothing; it only possesses potentiality – the possibility of having a meaning within a concrete theme. (Volosinov 1973: 100-1)

The timeless phantasmagoric world of Balinese kings is not just the result of the interpretive method and its presuppositions. It is the world the hermeneuts have condemned themselves to occupy.

In the passage cited by Geertz, what he omits, significantly, is that Hooykaas was questioning this simple identification.[10] Qualifying Stutterheim (1929-30) on the link between *liṅga* and ancestor effigies, Hooykaas pointed out that

> the Sanskrit neuter word *liṅgam* in the first place means 'a mark, spot, sign, token, badge, emblem, characteristic'... The word *liṅga*, moreover alternates with *liṅgih*, staying... Those upright pointed, flat, oblong stones are marks, *liṅga*, of the ancestors, and after performances of due ritual they may become their place of descent, their seat: *paliṅgihan, liṅgih, liṅga* of their purified and deified spirits. (1964: 175-76)

One might have expected an interpretive anthropologist to have leapt at the possibilities opened up by *liṅga* being a mark, sign, token etc., terms which are constitutive of Geertz's entire project.[11] To do so would have complicated Geertz's neat symbolic closure though; to have followed so obvious a lead into Balinese semiotic categories would have vitiated the entire epistemological grounds for Geertz's endeavour. To judge from Geertz's analysis of the pivotal role of imaginary symbols in the construction of kingship, the doubtless unworthy suspicion arises that at times the interpretive anthropology of Indonesia is simply Dutch philology with the scholarly caveats, doubts and qualifications taken out.

While Geertz claims to be able to reach down to the excruciating intensity of Balinese inner states (cf. Needham's 1981 critique), Boon instead identifies Bali as a locus of the intersection of texts, which situates it firmly as an object of Western and Indonesian textuality. He rightly reminds the reader of the risks of isolating Bali as a pure object, free from preinterpretation. The cost however is high. As Johannes Fabian noticed long ago, Boon's method

> avoids calling the Knower and the Known into the same temporal arena. Like other symbolic anthropologists, Boon keeps his distance from the Other; in the end his critique amounts to posing one image of Bali against other images... The Other remains an object, albeit on a higher level than that of empiricist or positivist reification... As an ideology it may widen and deepen the gap between the West and its Other. (1983: 136-37)

Boon's concentration on the multiple textual constitution of Bali leads to a curious ahistoricity. Note in the extract how Balinese textual practices and their implications are cast throughout in the timeless present (a 'thousand years of familiarity with the art of writing' 1990: 84). In the criss-crossing of metaphors and images, where motley's the only wear, what gets lost is that many Balinese have been to school since the 1930s, now read newspapers and have been watching television since the late 1970s. What would Boon make of the delightful cartoons in the *Bali Post*, which comment scathingly on the doings of Balinese and foreigners? Are these not 'traditional', therefore dismissible? Or are they yet another manifestation of the infinitely adaptable 'Menippean satire'?

Along with this detemporalising goes a pervasive essentialising. In a few broad brush strokes Boon encapsulates the entire range of Balinese textual practices, past and present in all their diversity, and evaluates the lot as not involving exegesis 'proper' or 'in the strict sense'. As very little has been written on his one example, text-reading groups – and what has recently (e.g., Rubinstein 1992) undermines his argument – Boon is on shaky ground here. It is doubly insecure in that Balinese read and comment on a whole range of kinds of work for different purposes on different occasions (Hobart 1990; Wiener in press). Anyway, in my experience works are performed in theatre far more often than they are read. Are we to narrow the definition of text to exclude these? If not, what is Boon's evidence for his assertion? There are less than a handful of translations of performances and no detailed account of Balinese commentaries, whether by the actors or audiences. Instead of evidence, we are offered another familiar preinterpretation, with a long genealogy: Balinese are ritualistic and, if not incapable of, quite uninterested in 'neutralised', let alone critical, commentary. Were they to, not only would Boon have to take account of them, but his variety of exegesis would be dead in the water. Therefore Balinese do not. To succeed in ignoring so much of what is evidently happening suggests quite how important preinterpretation is to much anthropological analysis.

Keeping Distance

For all its claim to a radical new insight into Bali, anthropological hermeneutics reproduces earlier approaches to a surprising extent. For instance, Geertz reiterates and even makes central to his whole vision the increasingly rancid old chestnut that Balinese avoid climax (Bateson and Mead 1942; Bateson 1949). As Jensen and Suryani have pointed out (1992: 93-104), the whole argument is implausible and rests on all sorts of preconceptions.[12] We all preinterpret in varying degree. But this implies neither that our preinterpretations are of the same kind, nor that we cannot criticise them or learn better. For this reason, the excuse that all description, interpretation and translation involves 'betrayal' (Boon's reply to my criticisms, 1990: 205, fn 2) is not just limp, it is a defence against engaging with those with whom we work. Boon's texts that speak back to him do so on his terms. They produce a simulated engagement (Fabian 1991b), which distracts attention from the very real and immediate dilemmas which anthropologists face.

Boon's approach raises a final point. An interpretive analysis does not require intensive fieldwork, as one might have expected it to. Nor does it require any command of Balinese.[13] That is the extractive function of mere ethnographers like myself. Interpretive anthropology exists to explain to us and the world what we have found. What distinguishes these brands of hermeneutic anthropology it is the distance – in every sense – its practitioners keep from any engagement with the people who are producing the 'texts' and 'meanings', and the conditions under which they do so. It sheds a new light on the supremacy of the text over the people who do the writing, speaking, reading, performing, commenting, criticising and joking.

The Purposes of Interpretation

Interpretation presumes a double account of knowledge. This account must depict the nature of native knowledge, distinguish itself from this and then explain how it can understand the former. Understanding is possible through the 'intersubjectivity' the anthropologist has with the natives, by which he can appreciate their meanings and symbols. Although both sides share a common human nature, its expressions are different; and so the relationship of knower and known. The repeated refrain of Balinese ritualism – 'extraordinary ritualization'

(Geertz p.115 above), 'ritual celebrations, ritual experts, ritual registers' (Boon p.117 above) – is crucial to that differentiation. The passages purport to be descriptive. They are however commentative and evaluative. By making Balinese live in a closed and threatened world, incapable of critical reflection on themselves, they justify the intercession of the interpreter, who is more than just endowed with superior rationality. He is open, empathetic, critical, well-read and with a superior vision. The depiction of Balinese could have come straight from an Orientalist: 'ritual has a strong attraction for the Indian [read 'Balinese'] mind' (Renou 1968: 29; my parentheses). Balinese add an extra twist by being uniquely dramatistical as well.

To aspire to unchallenged authority, it is vital to preclude the suspicion that interpretive knowledge is at the whim of the hermeneut and his imagination. So the preexistence of meanings and texts must be established. Boon has to predetermine culture as being text or Text (it varies); and Geertz overdetermines its meanings. Anything less intimates the vicarious nature of the whole enterprise. Text (for Boon) or meaning (for Geertz) therefore becomes not just the object of study, but a Transcendental Agent. Consider 'the systems of ideas which animate [the organization of social activity] must be understood' (Geertz 1973b: 362, my parentheses).[14] Or, texts 'certainly speak back; they may, moreover, change their mind's message on each rereading' (Boon 1990: 52). Boon finds tongues in trees, books in running brooks. Such indulgence might be fine, except that it silences and denies the thinking of the people with whom we work in the clevernesses of intellectual fashion.[15]

Meaning or text, being transcendent, is not available for ordinary mortals to understand – certainly not the ritualistic, non-exegetical Balinese. The ontology requires there to emerge an immanent intelligence of this transcendent agent to explain what is going on, lest the uninitiated miss it. Fortunately the hermeneut is at hand to do so. What though are the subjects through whom this agent exemplifies the workings of its Will? For Boon, as you might expect, above all it is the literati of priests and puppeteers. At first sight, it is harder to see who embodies meaning in Bali for Geertz. A moment's reflection shows why he lays such stress both on anonymisation, detemporalisation and ceremonialisation and on stage fright. All Balinese are on stage: they *all* instantiate meaning, which operates through ritual symbols (hence the crucial role of symbols and ritual in kingship.) Lastly, how does the hermeneutic intelligence work? Proximately, for Geertz, it is by an intersubjective empathy: one which neither requires the anthropologist to be coeval, or even go there. It also leaves the question of 'how can a whole people share a single subjectivity?' (Crapanzano 1986: 74). Ultimately though, it is through a kind of conscious philosophical reasoning, epitomised as the reading of a novel, with its ever 'more detailed reading of episodes, texts, and institutions selected for the multiple countertypes, contradictions, and even ironies they contain' (Boon 1990: ix).

For all the talk of intersubjectivity and explicating the native Mind in its palpable, excruciating intensity, hermeneuts actually pay scant regard to people as subjects or, better, agents. It is not necessary to ask about Balinese criteria of analysis, because Balinese are preconstituted as incapable of self-reflection (except mechanical 'meta-social commentary', Geertz 1972), criticism and self-transformation. Balinese are objectified into the raw materials to be thought. Gerundively they are not merely describable, but comprehensible, and so to be comprehended. Preinterpretation is enshrined in the disciplinary practices of university courses in anthropology: to train incredulous young minds into the realities of society, culture, kinship, ancestors, ritual, rationality, taboo and what they will find when they finally get to the field. (As with all good discipline, there are lots of exclusions. The authors you are not supposed to read are numerous and far more interesting on the whole.) Postinterpreting takes up almost as much time, not just in textualising and contextualising the insights, but in defending the interpretations against criticism (e.g. Geertz 1983b; Boon 1990). Purporting to advance understanding of human action, the human condition, the nature of textuality, by claiming to engage other hearts and minds as no other approach, interpretive anthropology may enshrine a hidden political agenda (Pecora 1989). It certainly offers at once a superior form of surveillance and a reassurance that other people out there are understandable and understood, manageable, controllable. It has also proven eminently marketable back home.

In their actions if not their words, interpretivists stress the relationship of anthropologist and reader at the expense of that between anthropologist and native. They play to the sensitivity of the reader; and in so doing displace the native yet again. The anthropologist's role is double: both inquirer and author. As author, she is the conduit for the ethnographer's experience. But she reworks that experience in writing; and so anticipates the experience for her successors. Volosinov forewarned of the consequences of confusing theme and meaning: the circularities of endless signification and representationism, which have been the hallmarks of the Literary Critical cul-de-sac. In rejecting, rightly, naive realism, the hermeneuts have backed into a hall of mirrors. 'In finished anthropological writings...what we call our data are really our own constructions of other peoples' constructions of what they and their compatriots are up to' (Geertz 1973a: 9). The problem is that in the writings in question the constructions are of meta-level far beyond Sperber's nth degree. Ethnographers do not intuit other peoples' constructions. They elicit informants' representations or inferences of others' utterances, acts or representations. Only then do they get to what they write in their notebooks, or more often reconstruct afterwards. Cross-cutting this process is the imposition of technical terms, in which Sperber detected further levels of interpretation. Interpretation is not sequential abstraction: simply 'trying to rescue the "said"...from its perishing occasions and fix it in perusable terms' (Geertz 1973a: 20). There is a continual to-and-fro in which we select and direct our attention and our informants'. After all that what appears in seminar papers, then the published ethnography, is further reworked. What is more, interpretivists like Geertz and Boon largely work with other authors' constructions. In stressing the value added in western centres of learning, the effect ironically is subtly to reinscribe the extractive mode of ethnography, now you collect constructions not facts. There is no critical dialogue with those whose constructions they are: no engagement with local intellectuals or academics. As an analytical framework it is about as illuminating as Soviet production statistics and as stimulating as a sex manual for the politically correct.

However precarious the constructivist tower of babel, it rests upon familiar substantialist and realist foundations. An interpretive approach is substantialist in that it is concerned with that which is 'unchanging and consequently stands outside history' (Collingwood 1946: 43), here symbols, the 'said' not 'its perishing occasions' (Geertz 1973a: 20). It is realist in the sense that it fails critically to consider the presuppositions of those whose activities are under scrutiny. It is the anthropological equivalent of what Collingwood trenchantly described in history as 'the scissors-and-paste' method (1946: 33; on realism, see Collingwood 1940: 21-48).[16]

> The method by which it proceeds is first to decide what we want to know about, and then go in search of statements about it, oral or written, purporting to be made by actors in the events concerned, or by eyewitnesses of them, or by persons repeating what actors or eyewitnesses have told them, or have told their informants, or those who informed their informants, and so on. Having found in such a statement something relevant to his purpose, the historian excerpts it and incorporates it, translated if necessary and recast into what he considers a suitable style, in his own history. (1946: 257)

Collingwood's delineation of the scissors-and-paste method is, not coincidentally, a classic description of overinterpretation.

To conclude this discussion, how does the approach I am starting to sketch out differ from an interpretive approach? Oddly enough, in the little world of anthropology, the two approaches share quite a lot in common, not least because I have learned much from the interpretive approach. Some of the divergences emerge in the differences between guessing and questioning. Both involve preinterpretation, but of different kinds. The anthropological hermeneutic approach enshrines a very conservative sense of dialectic: modifying your questions and guesses. In the versions discussed, it excludes any consideration of the participants' categories in use or the need to revise the assumptions of the analysis in the light of these. It does not allow the possibility of attempting radically to rethink the presuppositions and purposes of the analysis. Still less does it consider the continual reworking of one set of discursive practices in the light of another. Nor can it contemplate that this reworking must be done in large part *in situ*, where people argue back, criticise the analyst at each point and suggest alternatives. Lastly the criteria for evaluating guesses, circularly, are part of the same logic of validation as those for formulating the guesses. This hermeneutics is, in the end, hermetic.

By contrast the approach I am suggesting (foreshadowed by Bakhtin/Volosinov and Collingwood among others) is one that recognises that what an anthropologist works with is the historically particular outcome of asking questions, dialectically of materials of all sorts, dialogically of people and that both change, as does the anthropologist, in the course of inquiry. The purposes and circumstances of that inquiry crucially affect the results, both for the ethnographer and those who are raising questions as part of their own lives: the two not always being separable.

> Any true understanding is dialogic in nature. Understanding is to utterance as one line of a dialogue is to the next... meaning belongs to a word in its position between speakers; that is, meaning is realized only in the process of active, responsive understanding. (Volosinov 1973: 102)

Questioning is of two contrastive kinds. One assumes the object of inquiry to be knowable and susceptible to explanation by fairly predictable sequences of questions. It is exemplified in how teachers instruct students in the appropriate moves in inquiry as part of learning a discipline, be it chemistry or law. The other assumes what you know to be conditional in part on the questions, so critically reflecting on provisional answers requires you continually to rethink the assumptions behind the question. Collingwood considered the latter to be exemplified by critical philosophical and historical thinking. I think there is a case for adding critical anthropological thinking.

Such critical thinking is certainly not exemplified in reiterating the absence of climax or the presence of stage fright decades later from the safety of your own university. That is reinventing the wheel as an octagon. It requires expending enormous effort not in critical thinking, but in ignoring what the people you are studying are doing and even trying to tell you. Unless such critical thought involves continually rethinking the questions we ask and reflecting on our own presuppositions through our emerging understanding of other peoples' questioning, it lands up like the hermeneutic circle as the sort of one-legged dialectic, a hermeneutic hop. For this reason, you cannot tidy up the problem of interpretation simply by formulating clear, falsifiable, inductive steps (although that would be a definite improvement), or splitting the process, as does Sperber, into two stages. The effect is to make your own thought stand as yet more hierarchical over those whose thinking you are studying and to deny the fact that they too are likely to be thinking and questioning in ways which the claimed hegemony of closed interpretation would make unknowable.

Some Balinese Practice

Any reader who is not terminally committed to existing brands of interpretivism will not be surprised to learn that Balinese engage in all kinds of writing, oral composition, theatre, painting and so forth, which have always been changing (Hobart 1991; Vickers 1990; Wiener in press). They have a broad range of overlapping practices, which do not easily match our categories of interpreting, commenting, criticising or re-enacting. To highlight the differences with the interpretive approach discussed above, let me begin with meaning.

Balinese usage would require a monograph (which I am writing) to do them justice. For simplicity of exposition, let me begin with my present understanding of the terms Balinese use to evaluate and understand utterances, and even actions. First, there is what is the most important, *pamekas*, in what someone says or does. Second, there is the explanation or clarification of a statement, *teges* (a definition also used by the Balinese scholar, Ktut Ginarsa 1985). Third, there is the *tetuwek*, the objective or target (*sasaran*), the point (*tuwek* is the point of a weapon) of saying something, or a person (or group) pointed to, or to be affected by what is said. Fourth, there is the purpose or the directed aim of speech, its *tetujon*. Fifth, there is *daging raos*, literally 'the meat' of what one says, the matter under discussion. Sixth, there is the *arti*, which may be translated as 'meaning', but often has connotations of 'intended reference, significance' (e.g., Ginarsa 1985: 39). Seventh, there is the *pikolih*, what results from saying something, the manifest outcome, the effect. Finally, there is a *suksema*, which is untranslatable (it suggests subtle, immaterial, fine). Provisionally I think it is something like the subtle effect on the listener after due reflection. Balinese widely make use of at least four (especially *tetuwek, tetujon, pikolih and suksema*) in analysing speech and action. Something of Balinese usage might be related to a combination of the functions of language (Jakobson 1960) or speech acts (Austin 1975). Balinese stress the purpose of the act – be it speech, dance, painting – and the effect on the listener or spectator. In Volosinov's terms, all but *teges* (which significantly is the most literary term) form part of the theme, rather than the meaning. There is a nigh unbridgeable gulf between Balinese and their interpreters' ideas about meaning. This may be in part related to differences in speech practices.[17] Balinese has an extraordinarily large vocabulary, consisting mostly of terminal words referring to very specific features, states or movements. (There are at least 22 named eye movements or positions, 46 specific terms for hand movements, 13 named sleep postures for a single person, 6 more for two people etc.) To know a word is to know what it refers to or how it is used. Treating Bali as essentially a problem of deep understanding, of unravelling in English an almost inexpressibly dense and involuted 'symbology' (Geertz 1980: 98ff.) centred on a few key words, may be to miss much of how Balinese address their own language is use. Certainly one of my most infuriating, and sadly frequent, experiences is watching theatre and suddenly losing the thread because of the use of a highly specialised word which I do not know. Not infrequently these are puns which leave the anthropologist puzzled as to why, for instance, meticulous agricultural advice on how to plant vanilla should convulse the audience in ribald laughter.[18] The proliferation of terminal, specific words is accompanied therefore by associative assonance, both conventional and extemporised, between words with quite unrelated referents.

Apart from the semantic terms already mentioned, there is also a minimal critical vocabulary which the Balinese with whom I worked insisted that I learn if I were to understand them talking about history and theatre. I apologise in advance for the indigestible litany of terms. As with body movements, Balinese often eschewed general categories which were hybrid (as is the notion of interpretation itself) in favour of more specific kinds of practice, exemplified in the widespread use of what we would call verbs. Some deal with what we would call knowing (*uning*), such as examining (*maréksa*), questioning (*nakènang*), trying out (*ngindayang*), demonstrating (*nyihnayang*) and proving (*muktiang*). These shade into the more hermeneutic operations of guessing (*nurahang*), illustrating (*ngèdèngang*), understanding (*ngaresep*), explaining (*nerangang*). These in turn linked with more obviously performative practices like embellishing (*ngiasin*), advising (*nuturin*), confirming the truth of (*ngawiaktiang*), commanding (*nganikain*), and pointing to the moral (*ngalèmèkin*).

Besides these, there are two terms which are primary candidates for glossing the English 'interpreting'. They are *ngartiang*, paraphrasing, glossing, translating; and *melutang* unpeeling, unravelling, disentangling. Both are forms of what Balinese refer to as *ngaraosang indik*, commenting, or talking about. There is another sense of interpret, exemplified by the French use of *interpreter*, as in performing a musical piece. This includes reading in general, *ngawacèn*; reading manuscripts aloud, *ngogah, kadundun* (literally 'to be woken up') which is usually succeeded by *ngartiang*, translating or paraphrasing them; *nyatwayang*, telling a story, *ngaragragang*, developing or elaborating a plot by actors, a puppeteer or story-teller. This shades into *ngaredanayang*, creating or recreating a story or text. As practices they overlap. Elaborating a plot requires telling a story, illustrating, demonstrating, explaining, embellishing and not least saying what is the moral of it all. As Balinese go to some lengths to treat not just readers and actors, but audiences as active participants in reworking and re-creating what happens (Hobart 1991), trying to split creation from interpretation is unhelpful.

Perhaps I can best make the point by an example from theatre.[19] The elder of two servants asks a question of the prince, who replies. They then *ngartiang* his words. The prince is singing in Old Javanese, the servants speak Balinese. The parentheses are mine.

Old Retainer:	To whom should one...(pray for grace)?
Young Retainer:	That's right! That's what we should ask.
Old Retainer:	That is what your servants beg, M'lord.
Prince:	Praise God.
Young Retainer:	'My dear chap! My dear chap!'[20]
Old Retainer:	What's going on?[21]
Young Retainer:	'Don't fool around when working. Don't listen to idle speech (of people who denigrate the importance of performing ceremonies). I am speaking of acts of devotion. You should never be done with them. There is none other, as you said earlier, than God.'

Note how much was left unsaid. A great deal of interpretation seems to me to be possible only, as Nigel Barley once put it, through the hovercraft effect – passing rapidly and noisily over the subject in hand, with much mistification and to no long-term effect. I needed a group of Balinese, including two actors, to argue through this exchange and fill in what *they* thought made sense not just of the gaps, but what was said. Their postinterpretation was for my benefit.

Both actors and members of the audience with whom I worked on this piece were explicit that the retainers were *ngartiang* the prince. At no point in the play did they translate the prince's words *verbatim* or anything near. Instead they paraphrased, explicated or expatiated upon them. The actors, here and in the other plays I have worked on, were not translating the essence of the speech, but elaborating and making what was said relevant to the immediate situation. As royal characters in shadow theatre speak Old Javanese, much of the play is taken up by the servants expatiating in Balinese. *Ngartiang* is also used of translating between languages and of giving an explication (*teges*) of what someone said in the same language. On the occasions I have heard Balinese read and *ngartiang* written works in Old Javanese, there was usually far more overlap of the original and the translation. Insofar as the aim of a reading may be to clarify and explicate its meaning in Volosinov's sense, apart from determining its thematic relevance, it makes sense both that this should be the occasion that Balinese used the word *teges*, which is the least situationally sensitive word in the register, and that the overlap should be greater.

One reason for spending time on *ngartiang* is that the root *arti* is the main candidate for glossing 'meaning'. I have heard Balinese use it at times especially in recent years. I cannot tell though how far this usage is affected by *arti* also being Indonesian, where it has been affected by European usage. An example of my own unwitting preinterpretation and its consequences emerged when I checked my research tapes for how Balinese used *arti*. To my chagrin I discovered that it was I who kept using the word, after which the people I was working with would use it for a few sentences, then revert to the other commentative terms for meaning outlined above.

At the risk of oversimplifying, it is possible to distinguish two modes of interpretation, 'meta-lingual redescription' and 'uncovering' or explicating.[22]

The practice of *ngartiang* overlaps with *melutang*, peeling or unravelling what is said to determine as far as possible its matter, point and purpose. The term is used particularly of two styles of speaking: mature speech, *raos wayah*, and veiled speech, *raos makulit*. These two are partly related because mature people often speak indirectly or disguise the point of what they say; and you have to be mature to pull off veiled speech successfully. In listening to mature speech it is often not obvious if you miss the point, because the words also refer, *nuding*, to another manifest or ostensible topic. Listening to the more skilled orators in public meetings and reading many kinds of manuscripts requires one to unpeel them. Some of the latter require great skill, experience and subtlety. By no means all adults have the ability. Even in popular theatre, as in the example above, my own inquiries back up seasoned commentators' views that at times many young people only think about the explicit subject matter and have little idea of there often being a further point or target (*tetuwek*), or particular purpose (*tetujon*) to what is being said. As very little has been published on these practices, it is not surprising Boon seems not to know of them. It is pretty hard though to get through an ordinary day with Balinese (and certainly not a meeting or play) without needing to unpeel what they say; or more often, if you are an innocent anthropologist, failing to note that there was anything to unravel.

The End(s) of Interpretation

As an expression 'interpretation' sits uneasily on the plethora of Balinese interpretive, commentative and performative practices. It is referentially ambiguous (*ngèmpèlin*) in significant ways. Rather than try to classify or summarise the range of practices – which would be *cara magemelan yèh*, like trying to grasp water – I outline three occasions which, by most standards, we would consider to involve interpretation in some quintessential form. These are interpreting the speech of a deity, reading a dynastic chronicle and explaining a theatre performance to an anthropologist.

One common practice is concerned with understanding the will of powerful, non-manifest agents. One of the most dangerous forms is learning about *sakti*, exceptional kinds of efficacy (often glossed as 'mystical power') by reading and unravelling (*melut*) certain manuscripts. I can say little about this, although I have been invited on a number of occasions, because to experiment would have cost me the trust of most Balinese I work with.[23] Having truck with power is always potentially dangerous, especially if it is non-manifest (*niskala*) and so even more indeterminate than usual. So it is wise to reflect on, and sift through, such evidence as you have carefully. Likewise caution is advisable when inquiring about the past, because it too is non-manifest. There are only the traces (*laad*) on the landscape, in written works, in peoples' memories. They all require inferring what is the case (*tattwa*) from the evidence available.

To try, almost certainly in vain, to lay the ghost of Balinese ritualistic proclivities, I shall consider an example of how Balinese in the research village dealt with a necessary encounter with the non-manifest. As with the reading of a royal chronicle, it was an important occasion, took place in a temple and was accompanied by what Geertz and Boon would call ritual. However, rather than invoke a class, or aspect, of actions designated 'ritual', I prefer to follow Balinese in noting simply there are different forms of propriety and action suited, from past experience, to dealing with different kinds of being. What transpired had precious little to do with hermeneutic interpretation, but dwelt at length on the purpose (*tetujon*) of the inquiry, how to go about it, what the outcome (*pikolih*) implied and what action was required, if any.

Understanding Divinity

The temple priest of the local agricultural association had become too old to continue in office. The association decided therefore to inquire about the deity's wishes (*nyanjan*) as to a successor. The first attempt had failed, because the medium of whom they had inquired had come up with a successor's name, but there was no one of that name around. (The old priest gave me a hilarious imitation afterwards of the medium's tremulous speech. What this says about unleashing power or Balinese ceremoniousness I dread to think.) A famous medium was then invited to the temple. After discussion of the purpose of the occasion, the deity duly spoke through him before an audience of thousands. It was, after all, an exciting occasion: anything could have happened. The deity excoriated the village priests for sundry failings (justified according to the onlookers I spoke to), gave a history of the priesthood of the temple, then announced the personal names (correctly) of the two sons of the old priest, as his successors to the two temples where he served. The village leaders convened a meeting to discuss the speech and agreed to implement the recommendations (and they were recommendations, as they could well have been ignored). The question of whether they needed to *melut* ('unpeel' or 'unravel') what was said was not discussed. The crucial matter was whether the deity's statements of fact about the past were true, and so whether the recommendations were believable and appropriate. The process was less to do with interpretation than a rigorous – and quite juridical – examination of evidence, motives, opportunities and so on. To evaluate what happened required, however, knowing a great deal of what had happened in the village and assessing its reliability.[24]

History For What?

The second example was about a dispute over who owned a temple with extensive ricelands (see Hobart 1990). A senior prince of a powerful dynasty had been invited to repair two ancient masks in the temple in question. On learning that there was a dispute over who should take care of the temple, he said that his family chronicle had details on how the temple was founded. A meeting of senior people in the village decided it would be useful to know what was written there to see if it were relevant. (There was a conflict of vested interests, but that is not directly germane to what follows.) The prince agreed to witness the reading and, on the appointed day, arrived with a large entourage, including the island's most famous writer of such dynastic chronicles (*babad*). A local man was enlisted to read the relevant part of the manuscript which was in Old Javanese, while the writer translated it (*ngartiang*) into high Balinese. My concern here though is not with what was read, but with its purpose. It had nothing to do with being 'another ingredient of ritual celebrations', nor with any 'play of affinities, analogies, and contradictions across social forms, performance genres, and ritual registers'. That is not to say that there was not much of interest to local intellectuals. However, according to the meeting which arranged it, the prince, the reader and translator, and the members of the audience I spoke to afterwards, the purpose was to determine the relevance of what was written to arguments about who should look after, and so had rights over the land of, the temple.

From my work subsequently with a group of interested villagers, who commented on the reading in detail for me, two points among others arose. First, there was a question whether the history, being written in Old Javanese, was opaque (*makulit*, see p. 129) and so required *ngartiang* into Balinese to see if it needed to be explicated (*melut*). In their view, much depended on the skill of the translator and how trustworthy he was: on his rendering they thought that there was little that was unclear. (To establish this obviously required checking carefully for signs, or textual evidence, that it might have been *makulit*.) A bigger problem arose, second, in that it was one thing to read and translate a passage. It was quite another to determine the relevance of that passage to the circumstances in question. The committee had failed to make this clear before the reading. The outcome (*pikolih*) of the reading was therefore uncertain, and so destined to be abortive (*gabeng*). There was no agreed basis (*taledan*) from which to judge what was said.

Foolish anthropologist that I was, I had pressed the commentators to get on with the details of the text and translation. They baulked at this and insisted on spending a whole evening discussing the prolegomenon. Conventionally this is called an 'apology' (*pangaksama*, see Zurbuchen 1987: 99-100). As I learned, a *pangaksama* is – or rather should be – much more. On such occasions, which also include inviting deities to speak and theatre performances, those responsible for the event are expected to state its purpose, the limits (*wates*) of the relevance or consequences of what is about to happen, and apologise in advance to those whose interests are likely to be affected. Readings and performances do something, or fail to. To attempt to generalise their significance to the participants is as vacuous as it is to argue Bali 'demonstrates little interpretive remove from texts that would make them partly alienated objects of exegetical reflection' (Boon p. 117 above).

So Long as They're Happy

The form in which Balinese most often encountered texts was in theatre. Theatre involves a double act of interpretation. The performers interpret a work; the spectators interpret the performance. Neither actors nor spectators treated audiences as passive. In most kinds of theatre the dialogue and scenes were largely extemporised and tailored to the audience's response. The hardest role was that of the first person on stage. They had to gauge the particular audience, while the rest of the cast listened carefully to what was going on to judge how best to play the piece. Some villages had reputations for liking slapstick, others bawdiness, others political commentary extrapolated from the story, others wanted careful exegesis.

From working with actors over the years, however, there are certain points which they often alluded to. One of these also came up repeatedly when I worked on recordings of plays with members of the audiences, whether male or female. Again it shows my tendency to preinterpret. I would keep on asking what was the *arti* of what was said (or done), only to be told there was no *arti*. When I rephrased the question to ask what the purpose was, the usual answer was: *mangda panonton seneng*, so that the audience would be happy. I take the following extracts from a commentary by ex-actors and their friends on the play excerpted above.

Once again, the commentators stressed what happens before the event. Anticipation and the uncertainty about who will be performing affect the occasion and the spectators' interest. One old actor summed it up: 'If you are not hungry, you do not enjoy your food. If it is something you have never tasted before, you are excited and afraid.' Shortly after the play began, a well known television actor, I Midep, appeared on stage. The parentheses are my additions.

Ex-actor: The reason that as soon as the play began people knew that they would enjoy themselves – isn't that so? – is because I Midep is known for playing a servant (a humorous role).
Me: Uh. Huh.
Ex-actor: What's more, when he plays a servant, he is also very funny.

Plays were far from just occasions for jokes though. The ability to induce sad feelings (*nyedihang*) in the spectators was also greatly appreciated. The best plays are *magenep*, they contain a mixture of different elements: jokes, tragedy, historical detail, advice, political criticism. They must above all be performed well; and Balinese standards of critical judgement were ferocious. I have seen troupes famous throughout the island evidently apprehensive on seeing experienced actors in the audience. To say this is all Menippean satire tells us little about the forms it takes and how it is appreciated.

Making people laugh and cry has further importance though.

Ex-actor: (If) you often listen to the meaning (*arti*), if you watch (carefully), you need to look for what it reflects.
Friend: Yes, so that it sort of fits, a little like being given advice.
Ex-actor: That is where you have to keep on searching for instruction.

Friend:	That's it.
Ex-actor:	In theatre, if you are happy, you watch.
Me:	Yes.
Ex-actor:	That's how it is.
Friend:	Yes, you have to sift it through again and again, what is suitable for you to use. What is bad you throw away immediately.

This makes the point, I trust, that the audience is not presumed to be passive. It also hardly points to exegetical indifference.

A few sentences later on the commentators came to the importance of being happy again.

Ex-actor:	There (in the play) it's like – what do you call it? – if the audience's thoughts are happy, don't they understand (*ngaresep*) quickly?

If you are enjoying the play, you pay attention. You are also able to understand much more quickly. What I know of theatre in Bali worked, as did much else, by recognising and treating people as potentially active participants in thinking about, working on and understanding what was going on. What is interesting in the passages above is the realisation that the commentators considered the state of being of the participants to be relevant to the success of the occasion. Feeling happy was centrally implicated in understanding. If you were sad, miserable, in pain, you were likely to be distracted, uninterested, unengaged. Rather than wheel out yet again the tired clichés about how ritualised Balinese are, it might be more instructive to follow through what Balinese themselves say, namely that *suka*, happiness, enjoyment and *duka*, suffering, pain are crucial aspects of human action and its consequences, not least exegesis and understanding.

The Hyperreal

To take Balinese commentaries on their own practices seriously would entail setting aside many of our deeply beloved assumptions, methods and purposes of inquiry. It would leave a large number of old, and not-so-old buffers in anthropology departments and museums bereft, if they could not opine happily on the meaning of symbols, rituals, pots and unBritish sexual activities, often among peoples who disappeared long ago or who are now more interested in television, computers and income from tourism. Interpretation is, in many ways, the core constitutive practice, without which anthropology's survival may be far less assured than that of its erstwhile subjects. If action is to be understood in terms of its purpose, as Balinese suggest, then perpetuating our practices and its practitioners looks like many anthropologists' primary concern. Likewise, who is supposed to acclaim the hermeneuts' analyses of Bali? It is not the Balinese, nor theirs' the reward. (These 'interpretations' are, incidentally, not mine but those of Balinese friends. I incline to agree with them.)

Am I then proposing a radical hermeneutics which, if nothing else, might give a facelift to anthropology's sagging jowls?[25] If, as I suspect, anthropology was a 'discipline' made possible by the conjunction of a naturalist epistemology (people and institutions as objects to be studied scientifically) and colonialism (the unreciprocal entitlement of Europeans to intrude upon and write about these objects), then no amount of transplants will help. The ideal of some meeting of free and equal sovereign minds is a delusion, which ignores the degree to which the interlocutors are differently situated. Balinese enter any such hermeneutic exchange on vastly unequal terms, economically, politically, experientially, epistemologically. Not least, we pay our research assistants and 'informants' for their attention, skills and loyalty. Many anthropologists pay lip service to these problems. In their practice, precious few ever realise it.

What makes it so hard for anthropologists, whose work is notionally to engage in precisely this lengthy, uncertain dialogue of unforeseeable outcome, to avoid a *trahison des clercs?* In the panoply of the human sciences, our appointed job is to remove the cultural limescale encrusting rationality, to polish away the blips on the cosmic mirror of philosophy, disinfect a few of the running sores on modernity and serve as a foil to postmodernisms. Sanitising Balinese and others, making them safe for democracy, is what brings the accolades, the respectability and the bucks. We have been firmly contextualised. And, as it takes torture to make a good torturer, we contextualise and textualise those we work with. Whom the hermeneuts wish to destroy they first textualise. It all requires less effort than the alternatives and the results do not threaten our peers or ourselves. A Balinese who could speak would be as unwelcome as Wittgenstein's lion.

Contextualising articulates what we write about with a world of other, existing texts. As we saw with interpretive analyses of Bali, hermeneuts confine themselves 'not only to what can be reproduced, *but that which is always already reproduced*'. Oddly enough this was Baudrillard's definition of the hyperreal (1983a: 146, original emphasis). Once you make the step of recognising, as the hermeneuts of Bali do, that the text in whatever form is the primary reality, the corollary is that you are presuming 'the *absence* of a basic reality'. The further implication is that the image created may bear 'no relation to any reality whatever: it is its own pure simulacrum' (Baudrillard 1983a: 11), so setting the conditions for the replication of hyperreality. It is of the same order as the dancer with whom I began.[26]

The difficulty of even some of the clearer postmodernist and post-structuralist writings is that, elegant and persuasive as they may sound, quite how do they translate (sic) into hard argument? To answer a question with a question: how did Bali become identified with ritual? One of the answers is through death. Cremations, especially those which involved the immolation of widows, have fascinated Europeans for centuries before they ever tamed the Balinese beast. Who actually witnessed these, and what if anything they saw through the throng and the smoke, is much less clear than the I-was-standing-right-there-on-the-cremation-pyre accounts suggest. Nonetheless these accounts have been replicated endlessly as testimony to the savage ritual essence of Bali (Connor n.d.). And who reproduces these yet again as striking images to support their interpretation of the ritualised Balinese? It is none other than our two hermeneuts (Boon 1977: 176-224; Geertz 1980: 98-120, 231-235).

It would be sad to leave Bali in the maw of Geertz, Boon and their nemesis, Baudrillard, condemned to eternal hyperreality. Despite the two million tourists a year, the Indonesian government (not unaided) making their culture a commoditisable object and the kind attentions of all the Baliologists, Balinese somehow manage to carry on much of the time resisting the pure textuality that Boon (1982, 1990), and the silence and the spectacle that Geertz (1980) and Baudrillard (e.g. 1983b: 9-11, 19-24), join in unholy alliance to foist on them. Between the texts, silences and spectacles, for the moment at least many of them carry on living and even sometimes thriving. What they do is encompassed simply neither by hyperreality, nor even reality (a noose I leave to philosophers to hang themselves). For want of a better word, I shall call it hyporeality. By the expression I am referring to that domain of underdetermined facts which are subject to continued analysts' – and in a quite different way sometimes Balinese – attempts to subdue and determine, and which usually elude them. It consists not least of that myriad of actions, speech, ruminations and their absences which make up so much of human living. Pace de Certeau (1984) we have great difficulty explaining or interpreting the ordinary. A reason, I suggest, is that our theoretical practices are overwhelmingly concerned with singling out – according to predilection – the structural, the foundational, the essential, the determinative, the limiting case, the puzzling, the unlikely, the dramatic; but very rarely the ordinary. It is what Balinese call *biasa* and regard as beyond explanation. Actions *in situ* and their unintended consequences remain sufficiently contingent as to make a mockery of theorising, even if it is not the fashion of these times. Most of what humans do remains – and I suspect will always remain to the half-honest scholar – delightfully intransigent to explanation if not to overinterpretation.

Notes

1. Felicia Hughes-Freeland, a former student of mine, uses detailed ethnography from Yogyakarta to provide a devastating critique of the habit of reading meaning into dance (1986: 1991).
2. Appositely, one of Wittgenstein's key expositions is on the confused senses of interpretation. Significantly paralleling Balinese usage, he notes that to interpret is 'to do something' (1958: 212).
3. Sontag brings out nicely the implicit connection with the New Right. 'Interpretation is a radical strategy for conserving an old text, which is thought too precious to repudiate, by revamping it' (1961: 6).
4. My argument reiterates part of Foucault's criticism of Derrida (1972: 602, translated by Spivak 1976: lxi-lxii).
5. I refer to the Lit. Crit. Mode of (Re-)Production as an industry because it is one of the major growth areas with much sub-postmodernist boilerplate writing. In the social sciences, its forms range from the New Historicism (Veeser 1989) to the work, at its best perhaps, of Spivak (e.g. 1988) and Bhabha (1990) to come full anthropological circle in the writings of people like Appadurai (1990). A more extended critique of this literary tendency will have to wait another occasion; but the discussion below of interpretive practices on Bali covers some aspects. The recidivist skull beneath the svelte postmodernist skin comes out neatly, for example, in the writings of one of its more sensitive practitioners, Homi Bhabha, for all the ironic reflexivity and self-conscious detachment he invests into rethinking the nation as an ambivalent, abstract object. Within four pages of the Introduction, the practice of narrating the nation – a self-evidently western idea of narrative, of course – reinscribes itself (significantly in the passive tense, by rounding up the usual suspect semantic and epistemological metaphors of space) into a strategy for 'a turning of boundaries and limits into the in-between spaces through which the meanings of cultural and political authority are negotiated' (1990: 4). *Plus ça change...* The scope for catachresis reaches a giddy apotheosis in Appadurai's analysis of globalization (e.g. 'global cultural flow', 1990: 301) in which an imaginary processual object is built out of a series of constitutive metaphors of knowledge (see Hobart in press).
6. They are not the only ones. Years ago I provisionally sketched out four kinds of practices which Balinese seemed to me frequently to engage in (1985; 1986). They were: essentialising, contextualising, pragmatising (a horrible neologism – I could not think of better at the time – intended to suggest having to reach a practical decision whatever the exegetical niceties), and elaborating. Some time I hope to get the time to rethink and develop the idea. As with the far more detailed account of named Balinese practices later in this chapter, they are less classificatory subspecies of interpretation (or overinterpretation), but overlapping practices. It would be possible to produce a taxonomy of kinds, and degrees, of overinterpretation, but that itself risks becoming an unnecessary act of essentialising and overinterpreting in turn.
7. There is an interesting Balinese practice of *majejangkitan*, highlighting ambiguities often in mundane statements and to the discomfiture of the original speaker. It draws attention to the textual preconditions of speech and understanding, but also to their situatedness. I was told of the following exchange with some glee:

> Misan tiangé demen tekän durän.
> Yäh! Mirib demenan ia neda padang.
> My cousin likes durian.
> I thought (she) preferred grass.

Misan is first cousin; misa is a female water buffalo, with a terminal 'n' indicating the genitive, as in 'my water buffalo'.

8. My thanks to Ron Inden for his comments on the draft of this chapter and in particular for a useful discussion on contextualising as an academic practice. Incidentally, these critical remarks make use of a Balinese rhetorical device: *negakin gedebong*, 'sitting on the stem of a banana palm'. My ostensible target is anthropologists, because I am one and I know their practices best. If anyone else reading this piece finds anything seeping through (in Bali, the image is wet sap through the underpants), then so be it.

9. Despite their claim to radical chique, the Lit. Crit. tendency remains firmly the loyal opposition within a conservative and dualist epistemology. To achieve this requires transcendent entities, especially 'meaning' to be wreathed with an aura of factuality, commonly through catachresis, involving notably conduit and spatial metaphors of knowledge (Salmond 1982), although rarely as magnificently as in the following example:

> the ambivalent, antagonistic perspective of nation as narration will establish the cultural boundaries of the nation so that they may be acknowledged as 'containing' thresholds of meaning that must be crossed, erased, and translated in the process of cultural production. (Bhabha 1990: 4)

10. For a radically different analysis, which is carefully argued from detailed accounts of Balinese themselves, see Wiener (in press). Hooykaas is quoting Krom who was in fact engaged in an argument with Bosch on the applicability of Cambodian evidence to Java. Bali gets tagged on as the tail to the hermeneutic dog.

11. Geertz writes:

> To describe the negara is to describe a constellation of enshrined ideas... Ideas are not, and have not been for some time, unobservable mental stuff. They are envehicled meanings, the vehicles being symbols (or in some usages, signs), a symbol being anything that denotes, describes, represents, exemplifies, labels, indicates, evokes, depicts, expresses – anything that somehow or other signifies. (1980: 135)

12. When Balinese are permitted to speak for themselves a quite different picture emerges. For instance, the *Gaguritan* Padem Warak (the song of killing of the rhinoceros, translated by Vickers 1991) depicts a 'ritual' in terms we would by most accounts consider to be sustained and repeated climaxes.

13. Geertz's analyses are based on seven months in Bali; Boon sadly had to leave Bali because of illness shortly after starting fieldwork. By Geertz's own admission his Balinese is minimal (1991). Boon's problems with Balinese in his writings make it evident.

14. Crapanzano's perceptive comments on how the narrative devices by which 'Geertz likens his nonpersonhood to being "a cloud or a gust of wind"' (1986: 71) attain a new significance. I have made use of ideas in an unpublished paper by Ron Inden (n.d.) in this analysis of agency.

15. In fairness to Boon, he is not the only, or even the most celebrated, scholar to get his intellectual knickers in a textual twist. Consider the following:

> alternative constituencies of peoples and oppositional analytical capacities may emerge – youth, the everyday, nostalgia, new 'ethnicities', new social movements, 'the politics of difference'. They assign new meanings and different directions to the process of historical change. (Bhabha 1990: 3)

Note the conflation of possible real complex agents (Hobart 1990; Inden 1990) such as ethnic groups with 'analytical capacities', 'nostalgia', 'the everyday' in a semantic soup. As Sontag has pointed out however of nostalgia (1977: 15), such representations are agentive and self-fulfilling.

16. Interpretive anthropologists are less obviously realist than their more positivistic colleagues, in that they recognise the engagement of mind with their object of study. It remains realist to the extent that they condense mind to text, genre and rhetorical device and ignore the presuppositions, notably the purposes, of others' actions and their own inquiries.
     Geertz and Boon may be matchless, but they are not alone, in overinterpreting Bali. I cheerfully wrote about how Balinese viewed process sometimes in cyclical terms in my thesis (1979: 24-25). When I subsequently thought to check this, to my mortification I discovered that I had imposed a spatial metaphor on what they talk about quite differently. On some future occasion I hope to consider other styles of overinterpretation in the work of anthropologists like Duff-Cooper and Howe, and area specialists like Vickers.

17. I am grateful to Ernesto Laclau for drawing the implications of Balinese usage to my attention and also for suggesting a more general difference between redescription and explication, *see below* .

18. The link follows Balinese conventions on assonance (which are sometimes quite unexpected to an English-speaker), here a well known one between panili, vanilla, and teli, vagina.

19. The play was a *prèmbon*, a historical genre in which some of the actors are masked, some not, about the prince of Nusa Penida, an island off Bali. It was performed in the research village in March 1989.

20. The word used was *Paman*, a fond but respectful expression royals use to their ministers and close retainers.

21. The old retainer acts as if it is the young retainer who is speaking to him, not as paraphrasing (*ngartiang*) his master's words.

22. The clarity of the distinction may owe more to my overdetermination than to Balinese usage. As I understand them, Balinese interpretive practices involve realising, recognising, appreciating and acting upon the implications of your reflections, to which redescription and explication are overlapping means.

23. Having worked in a celebrated centre for such writings, Lovric (1987) is informative. She died not long afterwards. Hooykaas worked on well-known texts involving *sakti* , e.g. the *Kanda 'mpat* (1974) and *Basur* (1978).

24. In subsequent talk around the village, the key issues were that the medium had not been tested with fire (*kapintonin*) to see if he was conscious (*éling*) and so play-acting (*ngaé-ngaé*); and whether anyone might have leaked details of the past history of the temple. Popular opinion was that it was unlikely (but unprovable), because it did not seem to be in the interests of the few who did know.
     My diary entry for that day is interesting. The relevant passage reads: 'It kept running through my head that this was a good case against Sperber and Wilson: whether it is mutual knowledge, shared context or whatever, it certainly isn't couched in a propositional form which permits the kind of inference they draw' (referring to Sperber and Wilson 1982).

25. I am emphatically not suggesting hermeneutics as remedial therapy. This is the view that our problems of understanding stem from a lack of adequate theoretical frameworks, intersubjective empathy or even linguistic competence which, if remedied, would suddenly render the Balinese understandable and transparent to our knowing minds. Less inadequacy on the part of outside 'expert' commentators is as devoutly to be wished as it is unlikely to come about. It would provide far less excuse for the prevailing cultural myopia (aka ethnocentrism) and would make the scale of the problems of understanding more obvious. Understanding itself however is a peculiarly flabby, frequently tautological, term which refers to no discriminable kind of thinking. It is therefore singularly appropriate to woolly hermeneutics. (If the structure of understanding resembles concentrated gelatine, then doing Interpre-

tive Anthropology waters it down into a lurid-coloured jelly.) Equally the idea of
another culture being, in any sense, 'clear' or 'transparent' indicates the prior determinations both of the kinds of 'object' presumed to be knowable (or rather the
process of re-rendering them, as collective representations, symbols, images, so
they become knowable, understandable) and of the theory of knowledge invoked.

Practices, being situational, changing, contested, often relatively unverbalised
or culturally marked, are not easily squeezed into convenient objects of knowledge
or of understanding. Therefore they are ignored. In short, I suggest that, for the
problems of society or culture being more or less wrapped up or even having any
workable ontology, we are still largely at sea. So Laclau could write of 'the impossibility of society' (1990). Reflection on practices is less the solution than a first step
away from the massive prevailing hypostatising and essentialising which has dom-
inated thinking in the human sciences.

26. 'The collapse of the real into hyperrealism' comes about by 'the meticulous reduplica-
tion of the real, preferably through another reproductive medium such as advertising
or photography' (Baudrillard 1993: 71). For Bali we have both in superabundance,
and reinterpretation too.

Bibliography

Appadurai, A. 1990. 'Disjuncture and difference in the global cultural econ-
    omy'. In M. Featherstone (ed.), *Global culture: nationalism, globalization
    and modernity.*. London: Sage.
Austin, J. L. 1975. *How to do things with words.* Oxford: Clarendon Press.
Barthes, R. 1977. 'From work to text'. In *Image-music-text.* Trans. S. Heath.
    Glasgow: Collins.
Bateson, G. 1949. 'Bali: the value system of a steady state'. In M. Fortes (ed.)
    Social structure: studies presented to A.R. Radcliffe-Brown. Oxford: Claren-
    don Press.
———. and M. Mead 1942. *Balinese character: a photographic analysis.* New
    York: Academy of Sciences.
Baudrillard, J. 1983a. *Simulations.* Trans. P. Foss, P. Patton and P. Beitchman.
    New York: Semiotext(e).
———. 1983b. *In the shadow of the silent majorities ... or the end of the social
    and other essays.* Trans. P. Foss, P. Patton and J. Johnston. New York:
    Semiotext(e).
———. 1987. *Forget Foucault.* New York: Semiotext(e).
———. 1993. *Symbolic exchange and death.* Trans. I.A. Hamilton. London: Sage.
Bhabha, H. 1990. 'Introduction: narrating the nation'. In H. Bhabha (ed.),
    Nation and narration. London: Routledge.
Boon, J.A. 1977. *The anthropological romance of Bali 1597-1972: dynamic per-
    spectives in marriage and caste, politics and religion.* Cambridge: University
    Press.
———. 1982. *Other tribes, other scribes: symbolic anthropology in the compara-
    tive study of cultures, histories, religions, and texts.* Cambridge: University
    Press.
———. 1990. *Affinities and extremities: crisscrossing the bittersweet ethnology
    of East Indies history, Hindu-Balinese culture, and Indo-European allure.*
    London: University of Chicago Press.

de Certeau, M. 1984. *The practice of everyday life*. Trans. S. Rendall, London: University of California Press.

Collingwood, R.G. 1940. *An essay on metaphysics*. Oxford: Clarendon Press.

———. 1946. *The idea of history*. Oxford: Clarendon Press.

Connor, L. 1982. 'Balinese therapy in theory and practice: the unbounded self.' In A.J. Marsella and G.M. White (eds), *Cultural conceptions of mental health and therapy*. Dordrecht: Reidel.

———. n.d. 'Contestation and transformation of Balinese ritual traditions: the case of ngaben ngirit'. Paper to conference at Princeton University, July 1992.

Crapanzano, V. 1986. 'Hermes' dilemma: the masking of subversion in ethnographic description'. In J. Clifford and G. Marcus (eds), *Writing culture: the poetics and politics of ethnography*. London: California University Press.

Davidson, D. 1973. 'On the very idea of a conceptual scheme.' Presidential address delivered before the seventieth annual eastern meeting of the American philosophical association, reprinted in J. Rajchman and C. West (eds), *Post-analytical philosophy*. New York: Columbia University Press.

Duff-Cooper, A. 1985. 'An account of the Balinese "person" from Western Lombok'. *Bijdragen* 141(1): 67-102.

Evans-Pritchard, E. E. 1956. *Nuer religion*. Oxford: University Press.

Fabian, J. 1983. *Time and the other: how anthropology makes its object*. New York: Columbia University Press.

———. 1991a. 'Culture, time and the object of anthropology'. In his *Time and the work of anthropology*. New York: Harwood.

———. 1991b. 'Dilemmas of critical anthropology'. In L. Nencel and P. Pels (eds), *Constructing knowledge: authority and critique in social science*. London: Sage.

Foucault, M. 1972. *Histoire de la folie*. Paris: Gallimard.

———. 1973. *The order of things: an archaeology of the human sciences*. New York: Vintage.

———. 1986. *The use of pleasure: volume 2 of the history of sexuality*. Transl. R. Hurley. Harmondsworth: Viking.

Geertz, C. 1961. 'Review of Bali: studies in life, thought and ritual'. *Bijdragen* 117: 498-502.

———. 1966. 'Religion as a cultural system'. In M. Banton (ed.), *Anthropological approaches to the study of religion*. London: Tavistock.

———. 1972. 'Deep play: notes on the Balinese cockfight'. *Daedalus* 101: 1-37.

———. 1973a. 'Thick description: towards an interpretive theory of culture'. In his *The interpretation of cultures*. New York: Basic Books.

———. 1973b. 'Person, time, and conduct in Bali'. In his *The interpretation of cultures*. New York: Basic Books; reprinted from 'Person,time and conduct in Bali: an essay in cultural analysis'. Yale Southeast Asia Program, Cultural Report Series No. 14, 1966.

———. 1980. *Negara: the theatre state in nineteenth-century Bali*. Princeton, N.J.: Princeton University Press.

———. 1983a. 'From the native's point of view': on the nature of anthropological understanding'. In his *Local knowledge: further essays in interpretive anthropology*. New York: Basic Books.

————. 1983b. *Local knowledge: further essays in interpretive anthropology.* New York: Basic Books.

————. 1988. *Works and lives: the anthropologist as author.* Cambridge: Polity Press.

————. 1991. 'An interview with Clifford Geertz'. *Current Anthropology* 32, 5: 603-613.

Ginarsa, K. 1985. *Paribasa Bali.* Bali: Kayumas.

Goodman, N. 1968. *Languages of art.* Indianapolis: Bobbs-Merrill.

Goris, R. 1933. 'Bali's hoogtijden'. *Tijdschrift voor Indische Taal, Land- en Volkenkunde* 73: 436-52; Trans. 1960 as 'Holidays and holy days'. In W.F. Wertheim (ed.), *Bali: studies in life, thought and ritual..* The Hague: van Hoeve.

Hall, S. 1980. 'Encoding/decoding'. In S. Hall et al. (eds) *Culture, media, language: working papers in cultural studies, 1972-79.* London: Unwin Hyman.

Heine-Geldern, R. 1942. 'Conceptions of state and kingship in Southeast Asia'. *Far Eastern Quarterly* 2: 15-30.

Hobart, M. 1979. *A Balinese village and its field of social relations.* unpublished Ph.D. thesis, University of London.

————. 1983. 'Review of Geertz, C. Negara: the theatre state in nineteenth-century Bali'. *Journal of the Royal Asiatic Society* , part 1.

————. 1985. 'Anthropos through the looking-glass: or how to teach the Balinese to bark'. In J. Overing (ed.), *Reason and morality. ASA Monographs in Social Anthropology* 24: 103-34. London: Tavistock.

————. 1986. 'Thinker, thespian, soldier, slave? assumptions about human nature in the study of Balinese society'. In M. Hobart and R.H. Taylor (eds), *Context, meaning, and power in Southeast Asia:* 131-56. Ithaca, New York: Cornell Southeast Asia Program.

————. 1990. 'The patience of plants: a note on agency in Bali'. *Review of Indonesian and Malaysian Affairs* 24, 2: 90-135.

————. 1991. 'Criticizing genres: Bakhtin and Bali.' In P. Baxter and R. Fardon (eds), *Voice, genre, text – anthropological essays in Africa and beyond:* 195-216. Manchester: Bulletin of the John Ryland Library, University of Manchester 73: 3.

————. 1995. 'As I lay laughing: encountering global knowledge in Bali'. In R. Fardon (ed.), *Counterwork: managing diverse knowledges:* 49-72. ASA Decennial Series, London: Routledge.

————. forthcoming. 'Cabbages or kings? Balinese rulers as articulators of worlds'. In J. Bousfield and J. Kemp (eds), *The Magical state.* EIDOS Series, London: Routledge.

Hooykaas, C. 1964. 'Śiva-Liṅga, the mark of the Lord'. In *Āgama tīrtha: five studies in Hindu-Balinese religion.* Verhandlingen der Koninklijke Nederlandse Akademie van Wetenschappen, afd. Letterkunde. Amsterdam: Noord Hollandsche Uitgevers Maatscahappij.

————. 1974. 'Cosmogony and creation in Balinese tradition'. *Bibliotheca Indonesica* 9, The Hague: Nijhoff.

————. 1978. 'The Balinese poem Basur: an introduction to magic'. *Bibliotheca Indonesica* 17, The Hague: Nijhoff.

————. 1980. *Drawings of Balinese sorcery.* Leiden: Brill.

Hughes-Freeland, F. 1986. *The search for sense: dance in Yogyakarta.* Ph.D. thesis, University of London.

———. 1991. 'Classification and communication in Javanese palace performance.' *Visual Anthropology* 4: 345-66.

Inden, R. 1986. 'Orientalist constructions of India'. *Modern Asian Studies* 20(1): 401-46.

———. 1990. *Imagining India.* Oxford: Blackwell.

———. n.d. 'Social scientific thinking; or four ideas (and more) of human nature'. Unpublished paper.

Jakobson, R. 1960. Concluding statement: linguistics and poetics'. In T. Sebeok (ed.), *Style in language.* Cambridge, M.A.: M.I.T. Press.

Jensen, G. D. and L. K. Suryani, 1992. *The Balinese people: a reinvestigation of character.* Singapore: Oxford University Press.

Krom, N. J. 1931. *Hindoe-Javaansche geschiedenis.* The Hague: Nijhoff.

Laclau, E. 1990. 'The impossibility of society'. In *New reflections on the revolution of our time.* London: Verso; originally published in the *Canadian Journal of Political and Social Theory* 7: 1-2.

Lovric, B. J. A. 1987. *Rhetoric and reality: the hidden nightmare. Myth and magic as representations and reverberations of morbid realities.* Unpublished Ph.D. thesis, University of Sydney.

Needham, R. 1975. 'Polythetic classification: convergence and consequences.' *Man* 10(3): 349-69.

———. 1981. 'Inner states as universals: sceptical reflections on human nature'. In P. Heelas and A. Lock (eds), *Indigenous psychologies.* London: Academic Press.

Pecora, V. 1989. 'The limits of local knowledge'. In H.A. Veeser (ed.), *The new historicism.* London: Routledge.

Quine, W.V.O. 1953. 'Two dogmas of empiricism'. In *From a logical point of view: nine logico-philosophical essays.* Cambridge, Mass.: Harvard University Press.

———. 1960. *Word and object.* Cambridge, M.A.: M.I.T. Press.

Reddy, M. 1979. 'The conduit metaphor – a case of frame conflict in our language about language'. In A. Ortony (ed.). *Metaphor and thought.* Cambridge: University Press.

Renou, L. 1968. *Religions of ancient India.* New York: Schocken Books.

Ricoeur, P. 1976. *Interpretation theory: discourse and the surplus of meaning.* Fort Worth: Texas Christian University Press.

———. 1981a. 'The model of the text: meaningful action considered as a text'. In J. B. Thompson (ed. and trans.), *Hermeneutics and the human sciences.* Cambridge: University Press.

———. 1981b. 'The task of hermeneutics'. In J.B. Thompson (ed. and transl.), *Hermeneutics and the human sciences.* Cambridge: University Press.

Rubinstein, R. 1992. 'Pepaosan: challenges and change'. In *Balinese music in context: a sixty-fifth birthday tribute to Hans Oesch. Amadeus, Forum Ethnomusicologicum* 4: 85-113.

Salmond, A. 1982. 'Theoretical landscapes. On a cross-cultural conception of knowledge'. In D.J. Parkin (ed.), *Semantic anthropology.* London: Academic Press.

Sontag, S. 1961. 'Against interpretation'. In *Against interpretation and other essays*. New York: Octagon.

——. 1977. *On photography*. Harmondsworth: Penguin.

Spencer, J. 1989. 'Anthropology as a kind of writing'. *Man* 24(1): 145-64.

Sperber, D. 1985. 'Interpretive ethnography and theoretical anthropology'. In his *On anthropological knowledge*. Cambridge Studies in Social Anthropology 54, Cambridge: University Press.

Sperber, D. and D. Wilson. 1982. 'Mutual knowledge and relevance in theories of comprehension'. In N. V. Smith (ed.), *Mutual knowledge*. London: Academic Press.

Spivak, G. C. 1976. 'Translator's preface', to *Of grammatology*. London: Johns Hopkins University Press.

——. 1988. 'Can the subaltern speak?' In C. Nelson and L. Grossberg (eds), *Marxism and the interpretation of culture*. Basingstoke: Macmillan Education.

Stutterheim, W. F. 1929-30. *Oudheden van Bali I, het oude rijk van Pèdjèng*. Singaraja: Publicaties der Kirtya.

Veeser, H. A. (ed.) 1989. *The new historicism*. London: Routledge.

Vickers, A. 1990. 'Balinese texts and historiography'. *History and Theory* 29: 158-78.

——. 1991. 'Ritual written: the song of the Ligya, or the killing of the rhinoceros'. In H. Geertz (ed.), *State and society in Bali: historical, textual and anthropological approaches*. Leiden: K.I.T.L.V.

Volosinov, V. N. 1973. *Marxism and the Philosophy of Language*. Transl. L. Matejka and I. R. Titunik. Cambridge, Mass: Harvard University Press.

Wiener, M.J. in press. *Visible and invisible realms: the royal house of Klungkung and the Dutch conquest of Bali*. Chicago: University Press.

Wikan, U. 1990. *Managing turbulent hearts: a Balinese formula for living*. London: Chicago University Press.

Williams, R. 1983. *Keywords: a vocabulary of culture and society*. London: Flamingo.

Wittgenstein. L. 1958. *Philosophical investigations*. Trans. G.E.M. Anscombe, 2nd. edn. Oxford: Blackwell.

Zurbuchen, M. S. 1987. *The language of Balinese shadow theatre*. Princeton, N.J.: University Press.

Chapter 6

CONTEXT AND INTERPRETATION

REFLECTIONS ON NYAU RITUALS IN MALAWI

Brian Morris

Introduction

Aristotle begins his *Metaphysics* with his famous observation that all humans[1] are by nature actuated with the desire for knowledge. Such knowledge goes beyond that of utility, and is concerned to understand the 'causes' of a phenomenon – its form, materiality, origin or efficient cause, and purpose or end. It would be too simple to suggest that these four causes relate to four analytic strategies – formalist/interpretative, materialist, causal/historical and teleological – but clearly for Aristotle knowledge of any phenomena implies looking at it in four different ways, each implying a varying degree of context. Scharfstein has indeed defined context as 'that which environs the object of our interest and helps by its relevance to *explain* it', and notes that the environing may relate to a wide fan of referents – historical, ecological, social, cultural, psychological (1989:1). Context in this sense goes beyond meaning in its ordinary sense. It would also seem to break down the familiar demarcation, derived from Neo-Kantian scholars, between interpretation (with its emphasis on semiotics and meaning) and sociological explanation or analysis (with its emphasis on function, causality or analysis).

In a sense, explanation is seen as a kind of interpretation: it simply puts the phenomena to be interpreted into a wider frame of reference than that which simply focuses on socially-established 'structures of

meaning' (Geertz 1975). But Scharfstein also suggests a polarity
between an approach that focuses on 'context' – implying an extreme
cultural relativism and a focus on the 'absolute individuality' of the
phenomenon, and a universalist approach that divorces the phenomenon entirely from its context. The phenomenon Scharfstein has in
mind of course is a specific 'culture'. Scharfstein suggests a position
between these two extremes. Essentially, this has been the strategy of
all the classical historical sociologists – Marx, Dilthey, Weber, Mauss,
Evans-Pritchard – even inspite of himself, Geertz – who have
attempted to go beyond the Neo-Kantian dualistic paradigm and com-
bine interpretative understanding with sociological analysis. Many
recent scholars have followed this same tradition. Pierre Bourdieu
(1990) for example, has stressed the need to go beyond both social phenomenology and 'objectivist' social science (structuralism, functionalist analysis, some variants of Marxism), while preserving the gains of
each of them. Similarly, Collier and Yanagisako (1987) have suggested
an 'analytic programme' that consists of three aspects or strategies – a
cultural analysis of meaning, an analysis of 'structures of inequality'
and a 'historical' perspective that highlights the interaction of ideas
and practices in an ongoing dialectical process. This would suggest a
form of analysis that examines social phenomena in terms of several
interpretative contexts, with the implication that an historical perspective incorporates and transcends the analytical dichotomy between cultural interpretations and materialist analysis (1987: 47-48).

The suggestion here, then, is that each analytical context – interpretative, materialist and historical – imply distinct theoretical strategies, and that the historical approach encapsulates both the semiotic
and the material 'domains'. The historical perspective is thus envisaged as providing a wider, more integrative context, without oblating
the other two interpretative strategies.

Two points of interest emerge from the above analyses. The first is
that the three contexts invoked do not suggest a universalist approach,
the situating of the phenomena in a trans-cultural context, although
the 'comparative method' and a universalist strategy has a long history in anthropology. Secondly, these approaches tend to prioritise historical understanding, although many scholars, from Lévi-Strauss to
Foucault have been wary of privileging history, given its Eurocentric
bias and 'modernist' origins.[2]

The important question, of course, is which phenomenon is being
contextualised or framed for the purposes of analysis. Within anthropology, and the social sciences more generally, it may relate to a variety of phenomena: an event, a text, a myth, a ritual complex, a
particular cultural phenomena such as totemism or shamanism, a
social institution, or the culture or society itself may be conceptualised

as the unit of study. How the phenomenon is contextualised is equally varied – and besides the interpretative contexts discussed above – each suggesting a differing research strategy – anthropology has long contextualised phenomena within a universalist perspective, in adopting a comparative method. What phenomenon is contextualised and what interpretative strategy is adopted would appear to depend on many factors – the personal biography and interests of the scholar, and the historical trajectory of a particular research discipline or tradition both being important.

In this paper I want to explore the interpretation of *nyau* rituals in Malawi, and to look specifically at four interpretative contexts that have been suggested by earlier anthropologists. These relate to historical, mythological and sociological contexts, and to an interpretation in terms of an immanent logic that is seen to underlie all rituals. Although there is some validity in each of these approaches, I suggest that the empirical data does not fully support them. I conclude by tentatively suggesting that *nyau* rituals are intrinsically related to gender, and to the cultural 'creation' of the male affine.

Nyau: Introductory Note

Cullen Young and Banda long ago described the *nyau* as a 'primitive masonic brotherhood' with its special vocabulary, rigid restrictions to initiates only and its similarities to the carnivals of the Mediterranean region. Its essential purpose, they argued, was a 'coming-of-age' ceremony, and no Chewa man was deemed to have the full status of an adult male if he had not been through the *nyau* initiation (1946: 25).

At the time they wrote, however, given the long influence of the Christian churches, many Chewa men had not been initiated into the *nyau*, and this is still very much the case. More recently, Isaac Lamba wrote that as a secret society the *nyau* 'constitutes the pith of Chewa traditional life' (1985: 68).[3]

The *nyau* is an ancient fraternity of men that is specifically associated with the Maravi peoples (Chewa, Nsenga, Nyanja, Chipeta, Nthumba, Mang'anja, Mbo). But the kind of masked dance associated with the *nyau* usually referred to as *gulewamkulu*, the big dance, or *masewero* (play or dance) is by no means restricted to the Maravi peoples for it has clear affinities to the masked dances found throughout central and eastern Africa known variously as *chinyago* (Yao), *isinyago* (Makua), *midimu* (Makonde) and *makishi* (Ndembu) (cf. Turner 1967: 239-44; Wembah-Rashid 1975: 123-37; Binkley 1987).

The term *nyau* has diverse meanings. It is the name given to the secret male societies as well as to the masked dance itself, while the esoteric masked dancers and theriomorphic structures are also described as *chinyau* (plural *vinyau* or *zinyau*). Both Rita-Ferreira (1968) and Mlenga (1982) stress its role as the initiation into adulthood; but the *nyau* masked dancers also play a crucial role at funeral ceremonies (*maliro*), at commemorative rituals for the dead (*mpalo* or *bona*), and during the initiation of girls (*chinamwali*). In recent years *nyau* dancers have also performed at national celebrations and at cultural performances arranged by the Museums of Malawi. There are variations, however, in the degree to which *nyau* is associated with funeral rites.

The origins of the *nyau* is clouded in mystery, and is clearly of great antiquity. Rangeley, in his pioneering study of the *nyau* of Nkhotakota (1949), suggested, probably correctly, that the Chewa brought the ceremonial dances with them when they migrated from the Congo heartland, for the use of ceremonial masks is widespread throughout west and central Africa (Laude 1971).[4]

All writers confirm that the *nyau* dancers consist essentially of two types, although both are referred to by participants as *zirombo* – wild animals. In the first category are the masked dancers who imitate human beings and whose enactments are treated as 'exemplary models', as they usually depict certain human traits or characteristics. They are regarded as spirits of dead ancestors who come back in the form of *nyau* and they are usually associated with the day. Early writers spoke of them generally as *visudzo* .

The second category consists of theriomorphic structures or figures which represent animals. Rangeley (1949) suggested that there was no general term for these, but early writers describe them as *mikhwala* derived from the verb *ku-khwala*, to seek or look for. They are usually associated with the night ceremonies. These are only rough categories, some do not belong to either class, and some theriomorphic figures do perform during the daytime (Hodgson 1933: 146-51; Jackson 1929, Rangeley 1949: 42).

In the construction of the theriomorphic figures, a variety of plant materials are used such as bamboo, grass, branches, banana leaves, maize husks as well as skins or cloth. The common *kasiyamaliro* (antelope) is usually impressively made from woven bamboo much like the traditional maize store (*nkhokwe*) and this constitutes a woven basketwork figure. But the larger structures, such as *njobvu* (elephant) and *mkango* (lion) – which may be several metres in length – are motivated by several *nyau* members. The *nyau* structures are moved around with tremendous speed and agility, often spinning around in a cloud of dust accompanied by rhythmic drumming. Significantly, whereas the masks are kept for future use – and are increasingly being sold as tourist items – the theriomorphic structures are ritually burnt at the end of the *nyau* performance, and their ashes scattered in a stream.

When the structures are burnt the *nyau* members must not look back at the animal figures, otherwise this is seen as giving rise to the condition *chirope*.

In an important sense the masks and the theriomorphic structures have a different function relating to the different conceptions of time. The masked dancers encapsulate historical time, and often depict historical figures – *kenyoni* for example relates to a past colonial administrator Kenyon Slaney – while the theriomorphic figures imply a cosmological conception of time. The latter figures thus return to the woodland, the domain of the spirits.

Although in some areas women are beginning to participate as *nyau* performers, in the past only men were allowed to wear masks and carry the theriomorphic structures. For the simple reason that the *nyau* society is essentially a male organisation. Schoffeleers refers to it as a 'kind of men's club' (1976: 60).

Within a given locality there are a limited number of animal structures associated with a specific *nyau* 'club'. Each *nyau* image having its own name, songs and drum beats. But throughout Malawi, the number of masks and structures run into several hundred, even though names of specific masks may vary from district to district. Father Boucher has recorded around 300 different masks from the Mua and Dedza districts alone.

The masked dancers and theriomorphic figures make their appearance, as earlier noted, on three different occasions: at intervals (both night and day) during the girls' *chimwali* ceremonies, at funerals (*maliro*) and at commemorative rites for the dead (*mpalo*). Both Hodgson (1933: 132-33) and Mvula (1992) have given useful accounts of typical *nyau* performances on these occasions. Essentially, the masks and the theriomorphic figures are secretly brought by the *nyau* members from the *dambwe* (situated in the wooded graveyard) where they are usually hidden, to the *liunde* at the edge of the village. The *bwalo* is cleared and prepared by the *mkulu wakumudzi* (*chiwinda*) and various helpers and the stage set for the performance. The people of the village gather at the *bwalo*, the women and children usually forming a compact group with the senior women (*anamkungwi*) nearest the dancers and facing the drummers across the *bwalo*. The *nyau* members usually feast before commencing the dance. At the appropriate time drumming begins, and the women and various *nyau* begin the singing, usually in the form of the rhythmical chants. The calls of the *nkhandwe* (jackal) and *mkango* (lion) are usually made during the night ceremonies, giving a tense atmosphere to the proceedings. The *bwalo*, as Mvula witnessed, has the form of an open-air theatre, and there is much audience participation. Drumming, singing and hand-clapping eventually reaches a crescendo, and responding to the songs, the *chinyau* make their appearance in turn. At most *nyau* performances it is the *kalulu* (hare) who opens the ceremony – and the animal (*chirombo*) is described as *nthenga obwalo*, messenger of the village. The *chinyau* figures, the *visudzo* (masked dancers) and *mikhwala* (theriomorphic structures) usually alternate with each other. There is continuous interaction between the *chinyau* usually addressed by the women as *zirombo* (wild beasts) and the women themselves, both in songs and gestures. These invariably have sexual connotations.[5]

The Interpretation of Nyau Rites

A number of interpretations of *nyau* rituals have been made, none of them fully convincing. Each interpretation situates the *nyau* within a specific context. I shall discuss four such interpretative contexts, namely,

1. HISTORICAL, the suggestion being that the *nyau* represent a 'survival of stone-age hunting rites';
2. MYTHOLOGICAL (CULTURAL) – that they constitute a ritual re-enactment of the Chewa primal myth;
3. SOCIOLOGICAL, that *nyau* rites have a cathartic function for the solidarity of male affines in a matrilineal society, or alternatively, constitute the formal incorporation of the boy into the matrilineal kin-group; and, finally,
4. an ESSENTIALIST context, namely that the *nyau* reflects an immanent logic characteristic of rituals universally.[6]

I shall consider each of these interpretative contexts in turn.

Historical Context

The notion that the *nyau* rituals represent a survival of the hunting rituals of earlier foraging societies has been expressed by several scholars. Basing himself on the researches of Matthew Schoffeleers (1968) in the Lower Shire, Ian Linden thus suggests that the *nyau* societies 'were taken by the Bantu from the hunting rituals of the bushmen-type culture in Malawi or the Congo. Similar figures of men wearing animal structures occur in bushman cave paintings in South Africa' (1974: 133). That animals play a fundamental role in *nyau* rituals is evident, that the hunting of animals plays an important part in the life of foraging societies is also evident; and animals such as the eland and antelopes were also significant in the religious life of the Khoisan peoples of southern Africa. But there is very little to connect the two social situations. Although hunting mimicry is performed in the *nyau* ceremonies, particularly with respect to the *njobvu* (elephant), and the Ajere

hunters, there is very little evidence of any 'hunting magic' being practised by the *nyau*. No medicines are used with regard to hunting, and
none of the rituals are aimed at hunting success. A close identification
is, indeed, made between the men as members of the *nyau* society and
wild animals, but this identification emphasises their role as outsiders
or affines. It does not effect success in hunting. It is also important to
note that theriomorphic structures have little significance in the social
and religious life of the foraging peoples of Africa or of foragers elsewhere (cf. Turnbull 1965; Marshall 1976; Lee 1979; Barnard 1992
with respect to the African hunter–gatherers).

For African foragers, hunting is something that a boy needs to be
initiated into, in the sense that it marks the primary identity of an
adult male, and the first animal killed is usually ritually celebrated.
But among Khoisan foragers like the !Kung and G/wi and forest
hunter–gatherers like the Mbuti of Zaire, there is very little evidence of
any masked dances resembling that of the *nyau*. As Laude (1971) indicated, such rituals tend to be developed not among foragers and pas-
toralists, but among subsistence cultivators. Paradoxically, it is among
agriculturists that rituals around hunting are most elaborated (*see*
Douglas 1954 on the Lele), and theriomorphic structures are most
commonly found. The only rituals found among foragers in Africa that
resemble the *nyau* ceremonies is the Eland Bull Dance, performed in
the occasion of a girls' first menstruation among many Kalahari
hunter–gatherers. According to Alan Barnard, it was most elaborate
among the Nharo. The girls in the menstrual hut could not be
approached by any man, apart from a man who represented the eland
bull. Wearing horns and mimicking this animal in his steps, he would
chase the women around the fire. They would lift up their skirts
provocatively as they danced and according to Barnard, they represent
female sexuality in opposition to the powerful 'medicine' of the eland
bull. The man, representing the bull, although elderly, is always an
affinal category (Barnard 1992: 60). Earlier, Doke (1936) had
described the highly stylised baboon dance among the Khomani foragers, the man imitating the behaviour of baboons with 'obvious sexual movements' in relation to the women dancers. These obviously
have similarities to the *nyau* rituals, the male dancers representing animals in the girl's initiation ceremony – but they are not elaborated
among such hunter–gatherers. The wearing of animal skins by
dancers, particularly by male dancers, which is evident in the rock
paintings in southern Africa and elsewhere, is clearly associated with
shamanistic rituals. But taking the outward form of an animal, while
also being the medium of a spirit, is by no means restricted to shamans
and *nyau* dancers. In Malawi it is also a common practice among
herbalist-diviners (*asing'anga*) and circumcisers (*ngaliba*), as well as

among spirit mediums. There is, therefore, no strong evidence to suggest that the *nyau* ritual is simply a form of 'hunting magic' derived from the early hunter–gatherers – the Akafula. The rites associated with Chewa and Mang'anja initiations, both boys' and girls' – and with the Chinyau, seems to be more elaborate and more complex than anything found among African foragers.

The connection made between *nyau* and the early foraging communities of Malawi via the paintings on rock shelters hinted by Schoffeleers (1976: 66-67; cf. also Lindgren and Schoffeleers 1978) also seems untenable. The earlier red schematic paintings which are clearly associated with the early inhabitants of the country have no connection with *nyau* – or at least none have yet been established – and people do not know who drew these paintings. The white paintings or the charcoal drawings, on the other hand, which do depict *nyau* figures, on such rock shelters as Namzeze and Chencherere, are clearly of fairly recent origin.

Mythological Context

A second interpretation of the *nyau* is to suggest that their rituals have a religious function, namely, the re-enactment of the Chewa primal myth of creation. This myth suggests that the earth always existed, but that it was waterless and lifeless. God (Chiuta) lived in the sky. Then one day, a storm built up, the skies opened and it poured with rain. Down to earth came Chiuta, the first man and woman and all the animals. They landed on a small, flat-topped hill, Kaphirintiwa, in the mountains of Dzalanyama. The soft ground where they landed turned to rock and the footprints of the first humans and animals can still be seen there. For a period Chiuta, humans and the animals lived together peacefully and food was plentiful, until one day, quite by accident, man discovered fire. Everyone warned him of the problems that might ensue but the man did not listen. This event caused great commotion among the animals. The goat and the dog ran to the humans for safety, but all the rest of the animals ran away into the woodland. Chiuta, helped by the chameleon and the spider, escaped by ascending into the sky. Thus God was driven from the earth by the 'wickedness' of humans (Werner 1906: 70-74; Schoffeleers 1968: 196-98; Schoffeleers and Roscoe 1985: 19).

Schoffeleers, among others, has seen this creation myth as providing a charter for the *nyau* brotherhoods, a style of analysis reminiscent of Mircea Eliade. For Eliade essentially saw all rituals as evoking primordial events. As he put it: 'Myths serve as models for ceremonies that periodically re-actualise the tremendous events that occurred at the beginning of time' (1954: xiv).

But the source of Schoffeleers's thesis was a more immediate one, and seems to have stemmed from a reading of Foa's rather romanticised account of a *nyau* ritual. For Foa, the *nyau* represented the spirits of the dead who periodically returned to the village 'to the sound of drums and to the light of the nocturnal luminary'. He writes of the 'spirit of the forest' sending to the village his 'subjects' and suggests a temporary reconciliation between humans and animals (1900: 40). Schoffeleers suggests that this was a brilliant intuition and that the Chewa creation myths provide a 'script for the *nyau* drama' (1976: 63). With Linden, he spells out the thesis clearly and succinctly. They write that in cosmic terms the *nyau* performances, 'may be interpreted as a re-enactment of the primal coexistence of three categories of men, animals and spirits in friendship and their subsequent division by fire. Fundamental to the religious significance of the cult is the belief that underneath his mask the dancer has undergone what might be called a 'spiritual transubstantiation' to become a spirit. The spirits and animals come in from the bush and a temporary reconciliation with man is enacted as they associate with the people in the village around pots of beer' (Schoffeleers and Linden 1972: 257).

The thesis as Boucher suggests (1976: 2) sounds convincing. The animals symbolised by the theriomorphic structures, and the spirits represented by the masked dancers are temporarily reconciled with men (or rather women) through the sharing of communal beer at the funeral or at the initiation festivities. And at the end of the rite, the animals structures are burnt. However, the creation myth alludes to Chiuta (God) living with humans and animals, not the spirits, in the primeval days, for the spirits – such as death – had yet to come into the world. Death was to come later, from Chiuta with messages brought by the lizard and chameleon (Werner 1906: 72).

God and spirits of the dead (*mizimu*), for the Chewa, are distinct beings. But Chiuta seems hardly to play a role at the *nyau* rituals – focused as these are on animals, sexuality and human fertility. A pregnant woman is thus not supposed to attend a *nyau* performance. Whereas the spirits of the dead are fundamentally concerned with kinship, with the human life cycle and fertility (Van Breugel [1976: 191] called the *nyau* dances ritual petitions for fertility) Chiuta is associated with the agricultural cycle and with rain. Water and fire are two creative transformations. Both are associated with important processes – the social and the ecological cyclic processes. Essentially, however, the *nyau* and the spirits are connected with the first process – and thus human fertility – while Chiuta and the primal myth are linked to ecological processes.

Although there are symbolic analogies between these two cyclic processes, this is not to suggest that the *nyau* rites simply enact the primal unity between humans and animals and their subsequent separation.

Both Boucher and Van Breugel indicate that they could find no evidence from the ethnographic material on the *nyau* to support Schoffeleer's interpretation. Boucher, who collated almost 600 *nyau* songs from the Mua area, could not find any songs suggesting the idea of reconciliation or relating to the creation myth – although there were several obscure allusions to fire and hunting (1976: 2). Van Breugel likewise noted that he could find no reference to the symbols of the 'primeval myth' in the 300 *nyau* songs that he analysed, and he remarked that this religious interpretation seems to disregard the more obvious references to fertility (1976:199).

As to the ritual performances themselves, what seems clearly evident is that they do not enact a reconciliation or friendship between humans and animals prior to the ritual burning of the theriomorphic structures at the end of the rite. On the contrary, they enact a fundamental but complementary opposition between animals – with respect to which the men are identified – and women.

Both Schoffeleers and Boucher make a clear distinction between the masked dancers associated with the day – which are seen as representing the ancestral spirits – and the theriomorphic structures which are associated with the night and are seen as animals. The distinction, as I earlier intimated, is by no means clear cut, as many of the masks clearly have animal features and are universally referred to as *zirombo* (wild animals). Clearly, both the masked figures and the theriomorphic structures represent the spirits of the dead taking the form of animals and – to varying degrees – both are associated with woodland, as they come from outside the village domain. But as the theriomorphic structures are often, in the *nyau* rites, associated with menstrual blood (*nkhole*), and as an analogy is drawn at times between sexual intercourse and hunting – a familiar theme throughout the world – both scholars suggest that whereas the masked dancers are male, the theriomorphic structures are female (Schoffeleers, 1968: 256, Boucher 1976: 23-29).

Yet there is no identification at all between women and the animal structures: the identification made – which both scholars emphasise – is that between men and the *nyau*, whether masked dancers or the theriomorphic structures. Moreover, the dominant feature in the *nyau* rituals is that they are opposed to the women – and like wild animals they are fierce, aggressive and sexual. The actions of the *nyau* – in chasing women, in being wild and amoral, in deporting themselves in a highly provocative way – suggests not that they are to be identified with women, but rather with men as affines. Many of the *nyau* carry a penis, sometimes painted a vivid red, and the horns of the theriomorphic structures (and the masked dancers) and the trunk of the elephant are often displayed in a manner that is sexually suggestive. The content of *nyau* songs are explicitly sexual, and Van Breugel remarked that in most of the *nyau* songs he collected there is some mention of the male or female organs. But rather than seeing these as utterly obscene, as did the early missionaries, what they celebrate is the powers of life, the positive aspects of sexuality, and the importance of human fertility (1976: 191). The association of menstruation with animal structures has therefore less to do with gender and the supposed 'femininity' of the theriomorphic structures, than with the powers of blood. Both menstrual blood and animal blood have dangers and harmful consequences for men, both can harm by entering the body. The first leads to *kanyera*, a wasting disease, the second to the condition *chirope*. Both these conditions can be fatal to men.

Although not explicitly emphasising the fertility aspect of the *nyau* – though he does in terms of Mang'anja culture more generally – Schoffeleers does stress the fact that in *nyau* rituals men are equated with animals. He also puts a focal emphasis on gender roles and on 'sexual polarity' which he indicates is a preoccupation of the *nyau*. But it seems to me that the crucial distinction expressed in the *nyau* rites and songs is not of gender but of the opposition between women as a kin group and men as an affinal category. The meaning of the initiation is very different for boys and girls in both Chewa and Mang'anja communities: for the boy it means a cultural identification with the woodland, with the spirits, with wild animals and with their role as affines. This leads me to the third form of interpretation of the *nyau*, namely, as stated by Rita-Ferreira, that it is a 'reaction of the males against female predominance characteristic of the matrilineal and uxorilocal societies' (1968: 20).

Sociological Context

My own immediate response to this interpretation is to suggest that *nyau* is not a 'reaction' to the matriliny but rather is intrinsic to it. This interpretation of the *nyau* has been clearly and lucidly expressed by both Schoffeleers (1968: 296-400) and Boucher (1976: 9). The gist of the thesis is that in a matrilineal society, the bond between brother and sister is emphasised at the expense of the marriage tie, and given that marriage is uxorilocal, the position of the husband is tenuous; his authority within the village and over his children very limited, and that his loyalties are divided – between his wife (affines) and sister (kin). As Max Marwick put it: among the Chewa there is a 'tendency for the conjugal link frequently to be sacrificed on the altar of the consanguineal matrilineage' (1965: 180). A consequence of this is the loss of authority by the in-marrying spouse. They are frequently alluded to as strangers and outsiders – and their function within the village is simply to be hard-working and to provide his wife and her kin group with children.

The *mkamwini* is often described in terms of his purely sexual function – as a male goat (*tonde*), a cock (*tambala*) or hyena (*fisi*). Additionally, as succession to the village headmanship is within the 'sororate group', competition and tension often arises between a man and his sister's son. The lot of the in-marrying spouse is therefore seen as insecure, full of conflict and tension and, with regard to his wife and her kin, lacking in authority.

Although Marwick (1965: 181) had noted that cross-cousin marriage was seen by the Chewa as a way of alleviating the conflicts – that a man's father-in-law would be his mother's brother – both Schoffeleers and Boucher emphasise that *nyau* in a sense is a way that men solve what Audrey Richards long ago called the 'matrilineal puzzle' (1950: 246). Thus through *nyau* performances men are able to reverse their normal position, which is one of having no control or authority in their wife's village. They are able to assert their superiority over women. Since they are also strangers in the village, the *nyau* provides the men with a way of banding together for mutual support. It provides them with, as Schoffeleers writes (1976: 60) – a kind of 'men's club' which can on occasion also act as a pressure group. Seen as a vehicle for the expression of male frustration within a matrilineal society, *nyau* thus has a cathartic function, acting as a 'safety valve' for the tension and conflicts that are generated within the village. As Kings Phiri (1983) wrote, the *nyau* societies may have given married men a 'sense of solidarity' and even considerable influence within the matrilineal context. More recently, Nurse in a review of Kubik's (1987) study has affirmed the role of *nyau* in upholding the dignity of men in a matrilineal society, 'tolerated and encouraged by the women in the interest of social stability' (1988: 39). If *nyau* is simply concerned with asserting male dominance, it is however difficult to understand why *nyau* is tolerated, and obviously much enjoyed by the women.

Although there is clearly some validity in this interpretation of the *nyau*, the analysis tends to assume a male perception, and views the emphasis on masked dancers and affinity as a 'response' by men to the matrilineal situation, rather than as being intrinsic to it. *Nyau* in a sense, is a means whereby affines are created, rather than being simply a response by them. In the past cross-cousin marriage was the ideal and was probably more widely practised than it is nowadays. In addition, the Chewa/Manganja kinship system implies a 'moiety' system, whereby cross-cousins (*chisuwani*) and affines (*alamu*) are equated. And, as Phiri perceptively notes, a more widespread practice than cross-cousin marriage is that of marrying within one's own neighbourhood. Even today, he remarks, as a Chewa himself, the majority of Chewa men, in rural areas at least, marry within a five kilometre radius of their own matrikin (1983: 262). In other words, the boy to be initiated into *nyau* is not a stranger within the village, he is a member of a matrilineal group, the *mbumba* of which his mother's brother is a nominal guardian (*mwini*). He has been initiated into his mother's group at birth, through the *kutenga mwana* ceremony. The essence of the *nyau* ceremony, therefore, is to symbolically separate the boy from his kin group, and to make him into an affine, into (symbolically) an outsider. From boyhood he has been on intimate terms with both his kin and 'affines' and will be throughout his life, so he will not – empirically – be an outsider. Moreover, in any given neighbourhood, villages or kin groups are closely related to each other through marriage exchanges. These are affirmed on all ritual occasions when 'affines' play an important role. The *nyau* ceremonies, therefore, are not specifically concerned with gender per se, even though, on the surface, there seems to be almost institutional rivalry between men and women. As a brother, a male kin, the initiate is already a member of his own kin group and will nominally have his own separate group (*mbumba*), his sisters and their children. What is involved in *nyau* is to make the boy into an affine. This is done by identifying him with the spirits and the animals associated with the woodland (*thengo*). He is symbolically marginalised from the village (kin group), and the emphasis is put on sexuality and on his role as an affine. *Nyau* does not so much make him into a man, as into a male affine. When Rangeley suggested that the spirits are the concerns of men (1949: 38), it was only partly true – for men do become spirits in the form either of animals or of anthropomorphic figures. But spirits are even more closely associated with women, for at the *nyau* performance women (as a kin group) articulate a relationship with the spirits, especially the theriomorphic figures, whose sexuality is affinal and responded to collectively by the women. The *nyau* dances do not symbolise so much the reconciliation of humans and animals as express a dialectical relationship between women (as a group) and spirits in the form of animals. And it is from the spirits, ultimately, via affinal males, that the kin group derives its fertility and reproduces itself through time. Semen from the male fertilises the kin group in the same way as water fertilised the earth. And the continuing reproduction and fertility of both the human group and the earth (agriculture) is derived symbolically from outside the village – from the Brachysteria woodland.

Simply put, the relationship of men to animals is one of kinship (which is why the killing of animals is fraught with danger), the relationship of women to animals is one of affinity.

However, although the dominant motif expressed in the *nyau* rites suggests that the theriomorphic figures (spirits/animals) are outsiders, of the woodlands, fierce, wild and sexual, and thus symbolically affines – and with these figures *nyau* members identify – the rites do express the complexity of *nyau* relationships with animals. As Boucher (1976) has written; the relationship of humans to animals is essentially an ambivalent one; as embodied in the contrasting meanings of the two concepts, *nyama* and *chirombo*. Both terms are frequently used to describe the *nyau* theriomorphic figures and even outside the ritual context, the terms can be applied interchangeably to the same mammal.

As a hunted species or meat, the *gwape* (grey duiker) and *ngoma* (kudu) are *nyama* ; as a wild animal associated with the woodland and potentially harmful to crops they are *chirombo*. But *nyama* is also linked with the 'power of vengeance', which is why hunting is hedged with ritual. Consequently, as Boucher writes, animals have for humans a paradoxical meaning; of edible meat, nourishment, power, well-being; and of danger, fear, hostility, vengeance (1976: 3). Both sexuality and the hunting of animals are important for human life; but because they generate 'heat' both have to be kept within bounds, otherwise they lead to madness. Sex, the hunting of animals and madness are closely linked by both the Chewa and Mang'anja. This ambivalence towards animals comes out very clearly in the *nyau* rites, for the theriomorphic figures frighten and punish and may even destroy valued things in the village, but they are called by the women, cheered by the women and as playful characters they also comfort, teach and entertain.

It is, of course, worth noting that male secret fraternities and masked dancers similar to those of the *nyau* are widespread through-out Africa and are by no means restricted to matrilineal/uxorilocal contexts. They are found also among societies with a patrilineal kinship and in matrilineal societies like the Ndembu who practice viri-local marriage.[7]

From the foregoing, it seems evident that the *nyau* rites are not specifically concerned with the initiation of boys into matrilineal kin groups. This was suggested by Mary Douglas (Tew) who felt that because the father was not allowed to be present at the initiation of his son, and the fact that the boy was presented to his sponsors by his mother, then this signified that the *nyau* rite involved his 'formal incor-poration' into the matrilineage (1950: 47). But, as earlier suggested, the boy is already initiated into the kin group, and the *nyau* rite has the opposite function, namely, to separate the boy from his matrikin. It implies that he becomes a member of the *nyau* society, a group that is in structural opposition to the *mbumba* group.

Essentialist Context

The fourth interpretation of *nyau* ritual would situate them in a very different context, namely as an emanation of an immanent logic inherent in all ritual forms. The context here is universalist. This kind of interpretation has recently been suggested by Maurice Bloch. In his study *Prey into Hunter* (1992), Bloch develops a strategy similar to that of Eliade and Turner, in that he postulates that underlying all rituals is a minimal structure or 'core' that constitutes the archetypical essence of this kind of phenomena. Although unlike Turner and Eliade, Bloch offers a more materialist interpretation, his analysis is equally ahistoric and dualistic, with neo-Platonic overtones. It is an elaboration of a theme earlier noted by Eliade, with respect to African initiation ceremonies. Eliade suggested that the masters of the boys' ceremonies, dressed as they were in animal skins, represented the divinities in animal form. By means of circumcision, the initiate is symbolically killed. He is then resuscitated by becoming a full member of the male fraternity and, putting on the skin of the animal, he himself becomes a beast of prey, a hunter. In the end, Eliade concludes, the novice 'becomes both the victim and the murderer' (1958: 24).

This is the essential theme that is elaborated by Bloch in his stimulating but highly speculative study. Like Van Gennep (1960), he views all rituals as consisting of three essential phases. In the first, the initiate is symbolically killed by an act of violence, such as in the Orokaiva boys' initiation, when the boys are conceived as pigs and ritually hunted and killed. This is seen by Bloch as a process whereby the vital processes of material life are negated, the 'mortal' or 'life' aspects of the initiate being fundamentally eradicated. Thus in the second phase of the ritual, the initiate enters a 'world beyond process'. He becomes, in being identified with the spirits of the dead, an entity that is pure spirit, beyond the material life processes. He becomes something permanent, immortal, part of a transcendental realm that is beyond time and process. The third phase of the ritual Bloch calls a form of 'rebounding violence' which entails the 'conquest' of the here-and-now by the 'transcendental'. As spirits – hunters – the initiates reincorporate vitality from the outside by, usually, the hunting of animals. Thus, simply put, the ritual process – universally consists of: i) the violent elimination in the initiates of ordinary vitality; ii) a stage when the initiate is pure immaterial spirit; and, iii) the introjection of vitality from external sources into the initiate by the consumption of food. The initiate has now become at the end of the ritual a dual being: part vital, living, changing, chaotic, mortal; part transcendental, superior, spiritual, unchanging and immortal. The latter aspect of the person, Bloch contends, is seen as a constitutive part of a transcendent order, an 'institutional framework' that is unchanging, and which transcends the material processes of life and existence' (1992: 1-23).

In its emphasis on violence, in seeing hunting as implying the 'conquest' of the natural world, and in the radical antithesis that is postulated between spirit and life processes, Bloch's analysis has a very masculinist and neo-Platonic ring to it. He sometimes writes of death as a reverse 'process' and suggests that 'spirits do not die', without sensing that 'permanence' might be conceived in terms of an ongoing cyclic process rather than in terms of an unchanging spiritual realm. With a little imagination one could easily fit some of the Malawian ethnographic material into the schema of 're-bounding violence', particularly with respect to the boys' initiation. The novices are conceived of as animals and are placed in the bush. They are ritually 'killed' by the *ngaliba* at the *jando* (Yao) circumcision rite, at which the circumcisers are dressed in the skins of beasts of prey. They symbolically become spirits of the dead when they don the theriomorphic structures. They ritually imbibe medicated meat, usually in the form of a chicken, in order to get strength and vitality.

Yet there is also much in the Malawian ethnography that does not resonate well with Bloch's analysis. Death is not seen as necessarily violent, it represents the end of the natural human cycle. Nor is death seen as the antithesis of life, in fact, almost by definition, death is part of this world, for without death how could humans be mortal. But the *mizimu*, the spirits of the dead ancestors *(makolo)* are not, for the Malawian, in reality 'dead' and they may speak of the *mizimu*, like earth and water, as having *moyo*, life. They do not of course die, but they are reborn – as living human beings. The spirits then do not belong to a 'world beyond process' as Bloch suggests, but are simply an aspect of the cyclic process that includes humans and spirits. Humans *(anthu)* are associated with the villages and with cultivation; the spirits *(mizimu)* are associated with the woodland and with animals. Human life has no beginning or end, it constitutes a cycle, an ongoing process, and birth and death are simply transitions in this cyclic process. Moreover, the Malawian conception of change is one of the transformation. It is essentially metamorphic, for they do not have a dualistic conception of humans, consisting of a body/mortal frame, and a spiritual essence. And the emphasis on killing and violence in Bloch's account does not invoke an echo in Malawian initiation ceremonies, particularly in the *chiputu* ceremony of the girls.[8]

Malawians make a clear distinction between killing *(ku-pha)* and dying *(ku-mwalira)* and the initiates are spoken of as dying, not being killed. in fact the initiates are referred to as *mwali* (from *ku-mwala* , 'to be lost or dispersed').

Malawians, as most other peoples, do recognise a 'duality of existence'. *Mizimu* and *munthu* do constitute distinct and contrasting modes of being. However, these do not represent a radical dualism between a static transcendental order and a mundane realm (as in Plato) but rather they are two aspects of a cyclic process. The *mizimu* or spirits of the dead are not beyond process, they are an essential part of it; they do not constitute a negation of life, but rather reflect its essence, as a permanent ongoing process. The kin group – as Bloch, following Durkheim, perceptively suggests – has a kind of mystical permanence. But this 'immortality' in Malawi, is grounded not in some transcendental spiritual realm (as in Platonic idealism) but on the acknowledged permanency of the life processes themselves. Organic life itself, as an ongoing process, has permanence, and is in a sense 'immortal', an idea that would be difficult to directly translate into Chewa as they have a dynamic conception of being. Thus Malawian conceptions are biocentric, rather than theocentric.

Initiation rites in Malawi are essentially maturity rites that occur between birth and death. They are not, therefore, so much transition rites – inspite of the symbolism of death and rebirth – as rites of transformation (cf. Heald 1982).

They do not, however, as Bloch would hold, make the individual into a dualistic being, part organic, part spiritual, with the latter dimension equated, in Durkheimian fashion, with the social order (1992: 21). Malawians do tend to view, as Bloch writes, their social groups as quasi-mystical entities that transcend the individual. But the 'illusion' is not of some static spiritual order but rather of an ongoing cyclic process. And a person's initiation into the process takes place shortly after the birth in the *kutenga mwana* ceremony, when the child is ritually 'warmed' – cooked – by sex. It involves no violence at all. The transformation that occurs at initiation is similar: the initiate is symbolically 'cooked'. Initiation, however, does not involve incorporation into the kin group. This takes place much earlier.

Bloch (1989: 43) writes that circumcision rites do not make adults out of little boys, drawing on the authority of Van Gennep. Van Gennep was keen to stress that initiation rites were not closely tied to physiological puberty, but it is difficult to find where he expresses the views that Bloch credits him with. On the contrary, he emphasised that initiation rites were focused on 'social puberty' and were fundamentally concerned with gender identity (1960: 67). This was essentially confirmed by Audrey Richard's classic study (1956) of the girls' initiation ceremony among the Bemba, and has been emphasised by La Fontaine. In both her introduction to Richard's text and in her more general study of initiation, La Fontaine stressed that maturity rites proclaim the fundamental distinction between men and women. Gender identity and maturity, then, are key aspects of initiation rites (1985: 117-38).

In Malawi, both of these aspects are stressed. The essence of the rituals is to strengthen and aid the growth of the child. For both boys and girls, this is all embodied in the notion of *ku-khwima*, which has a wide fan of meaning. It means to be strong, and firm, to be mature, to be able to understand harmful forces, to grow and to be ripe. The senior women of the *litiwo* rites are called *mtelesi*, which is derived from the verb *ku-teleka ,*' to put on the fire or brew beer'. The elders of the Chewa and Mang'anja ceremonies referred to as *anamkungwi* from the verb *ku-kungwa*, 'to make firm'. The initiation process for both boys and girls is therefore to be conceived in the following images: to 'cook' them, to see that they are properly fermented, like beer or mature like a fruit, or to strengthen them by medicines – all organic metaphors. To die, to become a spirit or an animal, is not therefore seen as a process of devitalisation; to the contrary, the vitality of the child is strengthened by the contact with the forces of nature. Vitality, as Bloch suggests, is derived from external forces, from the woodland in the Malawian context. There is however, no prelude or phase of devitalisation in this context. Symbolic death or identification with the animal/spirit world does not imply a devitalised state, it suggests contact with the sources of power and vitality – the woodland.

For boys and girls in Malawi, initiation does not entail incorporation into the matrilineal kin group. It does, however, imply the separation of the initiate from their parents/immediate kin. The implications of initiation are very different for each gender.

For the girl it separates her from her mother, and the emphasis is placed upon her fertility and the setting up of her own home – or potential village. At the same time, she is incorporated into the wide kin group of women and the solidarity of women is stressed throughout the rites. For the boys, a fundamental emphasis is placed on symbolically separating him from his mother and kin group and making him not so much a man, as an affinal male. The boy is identified with the spirits and animals, with the woodlands. He is made through the ritual into an affine, an outsider. And a crucial emphasis is placed on his sexuality, his potency, his strength and his courage.[9]

The relationship between humans and animals, expressed in the rituals, is also quite different with respect to gender. A fundamental opposition is expressed between women and animals: while women are associated, indeed identified, with the village, agriculture and the kin group; animals are associated with the woodland, hunting and the male affine, as well as with spirits of the dead. Women entice the animals from the woodland but the relationship between them is always one of dialectical opposition. For women, animals represent fierceness, aggression, sexuality and the male affine – her husband, her father and her brother's son. For men, on the other hand, an essential identity – kinship – is expressed between them and animals. The young initiates become animals and as both Schoffeleers and Boucher suggest with respect to the *nyau*, there is a strong sense of identification between animals and men established during the initiation ceremony. This means that hunting does not imply an opposition or hostility between men and the animals world, to the contrary, it evokes kinship. Killing of an animal is likened to killing a kin-person and may have serious consequences if proper ritual precautions are not taken.

In her study of the girls' initiation among the Bemba, Audrey Richards suggested that while empirically in the village, a man as an outsider must be submissive, quiet, and respect his in-laws; in the ritual, however, he is depicted as an animal – a lion, crocodile or hyena – or as an hunter, and that his virility is emphasised throughout the *chisungu* rites. Many of the songs sung during the ceremony, and the pottery figurines made of clay, relate to or depict animals: the lion, bat, crocodile, hyena, porcupine, monkey, tortoise, all of which have salience also in the Malawian context (1956: 158, 187-212 cf. also on the role of the hyena in the Mkang'a ceremony of the Ndembu [Turner 1968:225]).

Conclusions

In this paper I have focused on – and thus problematised – *nyau* rituals in Malawi, and have explored four interpretative contexts whereby scholars have sought to explicate such phenomena. Although each interpretation has a certain validity, I expressed some dissatisfaction with each of these interpretative approaches. I, like some of the anthropologists discussed in the first part of the paper, thus came to situate the analysis between two 'extremes'. On the one hand, I expressed dissatisfaction with the narrow contextual approach: the interpretation of *nyau* – either as a cultural survival of earlier 'hunting magic' of foragers, or as a simple ritual re-enactment of the Chewa creation myth. On the other hand, I expressed dissatisfaction with the universalist interpretation of Bloch, which attempts to explicate all rituals – but specifically initiation rites – with reference to an essential archetypal pattern. In this regard I emphasised the specificity of *nyau* rituals with respect to the Malawian cultural context. I therefore came to develop and expand upon the sociological approach, tentatively suggesting that *nyau* rites are intrinsically associated with gender and kinship, and with the cultural construction, through ritual, of the male affine – hence the emphasis on sexuality and fertility noted by all observers.

Notes

1. In his political writing Aristotle essentially argued that only aristocratic males are fully rational and are thus able to apprehend knowledge. In contrasting humans with animals in his *Metaphysics*, however, he implies that all humans have the powers of reason.
2. For recent discussions of the prioritising of time and historical understanding in Western scholarship see Soja (1993) and Casey (1993). It is of interest and ironic that the figure who is seen as the main pre-cursor of post-modernism, Nietzsche, was a keen advocate of historical understanding.

3. Writers like Lamba and Schoffeleers and more recently Kaspin (1993) tend to see *nyau* as the key ritual in Chewa cultural life. Indeed, Kaspin virtually equates the *nyau* with Chewa cosmology, unaware that this cosmology is implicit and co-present among all the matrilineal peoples of Malawi. It is well to keep in mind that the *nyau* initiation takes secondary place to the complex initiation rituals associated with women, that many Chewa men are not initiated into the cult and that the *nyau* dance is only one aspect of the Chinamwali complex.

4. Kaspin (1993) suggests that the *nyau* dance was originally a 'royal ritual' of the Mar- avi chieftanship, and that during the colonial period it was transformed into a 'ritual of resistance' among the Chewa, surviving today only in the rural areas as a 'ritual of the underclass'. This interpretation runs completely counter to the interpretation that *nyau* rituals have their origin in an earlier hunter-gathering culture discussed below. It seems to me that the resistance to colonialism expressed through *nyau* ritu- als – emphasised by Schoffeleers, Linden and Kaspin – was in essence a defence of the subsistence economy and local Africa culture, rather than being an expression of Chewa ethnicity. The conflation of the Maravi state with the Chewa as a dialectical group, and the latter with a single 'cosmological order' that is somehow unique to the Chewa – as Kaspin implies – seems to me highly misleading.

5. Although I was initiated into the Chinyago rites of the neighbouring Yao – rites which have close affinities to those of the *nyau* – and have had long discussions with *nyau* members on *nyau* rituals and animal structures, I deliberately refrained from joining a local *nyau* fraternity, given the emphasis among the Chewa on secrecy. Data for this paper is thus mainly drawn from the published and archival material on the *nyau* – which is voluminous.

6. I have not in this paper examined the interpretative approach that has a long tradition in anthropology, namely to interpret rituals within a closed ethnic context, and to see them as giving expression to a single cosmological system that unites all aspects of a particular culture. Such a hermeneutic approach has recently been suggested by Kaspin (1993) who sees *nyau* as a 'totalizing ritual system' that expresses a 'sublimal order', a cosmological order, or 'universe of meaning' that forms the implicit frame- work of the Chewa 'social universe'. However, such a cosmology is neither specific to *nyau* rituals, nor to the Chewa – it is found among matrilineal peoples throughout Malawi – nor is it totalising. The limitations of this kind of analysis has been high- lighted by both Bloch (1989) and Bourdieu (1990), and was discussed in my work on the anthropology of religion (Morris 1987).

7. See, for example, the interesting study by Fardon (1990) on the Chamba of the Cameroon, where spirits of the dead are conceptualised as masculine, and the masked figures may be of either gender.

8. Although the focus of this paper is on the *nyau* ritual, it is well to bear in mind that this is only a part of the Chinamwali (initiation) complex – one centred on boys' ini- tiation, although unlike the Yao, the Chewa do not practice circumcision. It is also important to note that the Chewa share a common cultural heritage with the other matrilineal people of Malawi.

9. It is important to recognise that in the Malawian context a fundamental distinction is made between the territorial chief *Mwini Dziko*, 'the guardian of the land', and the affinal male, who are both conceptualised as outsiders, sexual, aggressive hunters, and, by contrast, the village headman *Mwini Mbumba*, 'guardian of the matrikin', who, as a brother, is identified with the collectivity of women who constitute the matrilineal core of the village community. Ideally he should be a male mother.

Bibliography

Aristotle. 1991. *Metaphysics.* Trans. J. H. McMahon. Buffalo, N.Y.: Prometheus Books.

Barnard, A. 1992. *Hunters and herders of southern Africa.* Cambridge: University Press.

Binkley, D. A. 1987. 'Avatar of power: Southern Kuba masquerade figures'. *Africa* 57; 7 5-97.

Bloch, M. 1989. *Ritual, history and power.* London: Athlone Press.

———. 1992. *Prey into hunter.* Cambridge: University Press.

Boucher, C. 1976. 'The Nyau secret society'. Unpublished paper. Mua.

Bourdieu, P. 1990. *The logic of practice.* Cambridge: Polity Press.

Casey, E. S. 1993. *Getting back into place.* Bloomington: Indiana University Press.

Collier, J. F. and J. Yanagisako (eds) 1987. *Gender and kinship.* Stanford: University Press.

Cullen Young, T. and H. K. Banda. 1946. (eds). *Our African Way of Life.* London: United Society for Christian Literature.

Doke, C. M. 1936. 'Games, plays and dances of the Khomani Bushmen' *Bantu Studies* 10: 461-71.

Douglas, M. (née Tew). 1950. *Peoples of the Lake Nyasa Region.* London: International Africa Institute.

Douglas, M. 1954. 'The Lele of the Kasai'. In D. Forde (ed.), *African worlds.* Oxford: Oxford University Press, for the International Africa Institute.

Eliade, M. 1954. *The myth of the eternal return.* Princeton: University Press.

———. 1958. *Rites and myths of initiation.* New York; Harper.

Fardon, R. 1990. *Between god, the dead and the wild.* Edinburgh: University Press.

Foa, E. 1900. *La travesée de l'Afrique.* Paris: Cie.

Geertz, C. 1975. *The interpretation of cultures.* London: Hutchinson.

Heald, S. 1982. 'The making of men'. *Africa* 52: 15-35.

Hodgson, A. G. O. 1933. 'Notes on the Achewa and Angoni of the Dowa District.' *J. R. Anthr. Inst.* 63: 123-65.

Jackson J. 1929. *Description of the Chinyao dance.* Mss. Afr. 556 Rhodes House Library, Oxford.

Kaspin, D. 1993. 'Chewa visions and revisions of power: transformations of the Nyau dance in central Malawi'. In Jean and John Comaroff (eds.), *Modernity and its malcontents*: 34-57. Chicago: University of Chicago Press.

Kubik, G. 1987. *Nyau: Maskenbunde im Sulichen Malawi.* Vienna: Osterreichishen Academie.

La Fontaine, J. 1985. *Initiation.* Harmondsworth: Penguin

Lamba, I. C. 1985. 'The missionary and ethnography in Malawi'. *Society of Malawi Journal* 38: 62-79.

Laude, J. 1971. *The arts of black Africa.* Berkeley: University of California Press.

Lee, R. B. 1979. *The !Kung San.* Cambridge University Press.

Linden, I. 1974. *Catholics, peasants and Chewa resistance in Nyasaland.* London: Heinemann

Lindgren, N. E. and J. M. Schoffeleers 1978. *Rock art and Nyau symbolism in Malawi.* Lilongwe: Antiquities Publ. 18.

Marshall L. 1976. *The !Kung of Nyae Nyae*. Cambridge, M.A.: Harvard University Press.

Marwick, M. 1965. *Sorcery in its social setting*. Manchester: University Press.

Mlenga, D.K. 1982. *Nyawa initiation rites in Dowa district Zomba*. Chancellor College: Seminar Papers in Traditional Religion.

Morris, B. 1987. *Anthropological studies of religion*. Cambridge: University Press.

Mvula, E.S.T. 1992. 'The performance of Gule Wamkulu'. In C. Kamlongera (ed.) *Kubvina: dance and theatre in Malawi Zomba*: 34-57. University of Malawi.

Nurse, G.T. 1988. 'Review of Kubik (1987)'. *Man* 23: 391.

Phiri, K.M. 1983. 'Some changes in the matrilineal family system among the Chewa of Malawi since the 19th. century'. *Journal of African History* 24: 257-74.

Rangeley, W. H. J. 1949. 'Nyau in Kota Kota district ' *Nyasaland Journal* 2: 35-49.

Richards, A. 1950. 'Some types of family structure amongst the central Bantu'. In A.R. Radcliffe-Brown and C.D. Forde (eds) *African systems of kinship and marriage*: 207-51. Oxford: University Press.

———. 1956. *Chisungu*. London: Tavistock.

Rita-Ferreira A. 1968. 'The Nyau brotherhood among Mozambique Chewa'. *S. Afr. J. Sc.* 64: 20-24.

Scharfstein B. 1989. *The dilemma of context*. New York: University Press.

Schoffeleers J.M. 1968. *Symbolic and social aspects of spirit worship among the Mang'anja*. D.Phil. Thesis. Oxford University.

———. 1976. The Nyau societies: our present understanding. *Society of Malawi Journal* 29: 59-68.

——— and I. Linden. 1972. 'The resistance of the Nyau societies to the R.C. missions'. in T. Ranger and I. Kimambo (eds), *Historical study of African religion*: 252-76. London: Heinemann.

——— and A. A. Roscoe. 1985. *Land of fire: oral literature from Malawi*. Limbe: Popular Publ.

Soja E. 1993. 'History: geography: modernity'. In S. During (ed.) *The cultural studies reader*: 135-50. London: Routledge.

Tew M. 1950. *Peoples of the Lake Nyasa region*. Oxford: University Press.

Turnbull C. 1965. *Wayward servants*. New York: Natural History Press.

Turner V. W. 1967. *The forest of symbols*. Ithaca: Cornell University Press.

———. 1968. *The drums of affliction*. Oxford: Clarendon Press.

Van Gennep A. 1960. *The rites of passage*. London: Routledge and Kegan Paul.

Van Breugel J. 1976. *Some traditional Chewa religious beliefs and practices*. Unpublished Mss: Lilongwe Missionaries Africa.

Wembah-Rashid J. 1975. *The ethnohistory of the matrilineal peoples of southeast Tanzania*. Vienna: Acta Ethnol. et Linguistica 9.

Werner A.1906. *The natives of Bntish Central Africa*. London: Constable.

Chapter 7

THE HOLISTIC INDIVIDUAL

CONTEXT AS POLITICAL PROCESS IN THE NEW AGE MOVEMENT

Ruth Prince and David Riches

Introduction

The New Age movement as a way of life may be characterised in terms of a paradoxical juxtaposition of certain basic values. On the one hand, individualistic values predominate with regard to ongoing matters of daily living (education, health, work, religious observation, forging relationships). The New Ager expects to proceed largely free from other people's demands, impositions or constraints – as it is often colloquially put, the New Ager should be permitted to do his or her 'own thing'. On the other hand, concerning the reflective side of human existence, New Age cosmology is strikingly holistic. Thus most New Agers uphold the notion of Gaia, or spiritually ordered universe, whose transcendent power subsumes all things, organic and inorganic. Correspondingly, at the level of the human person, the New Age movement, with its non-dualistic conceptions, upholds the physical, the spiritual, the mental and the emotional in the human being as indissolubly one.

We shall argue that this paradoxical juxtaposition may be explicated in terms of the analytical notion of context, whereby the holistic in the New Age functions as context for the individualistic. The relationship between the New Age movement and the broader Western main-stream[1] is the basis for this explication, specifically that the New Age (in our view) is counter-cultural vis-à-vis the mainstream. If a religious movement is to be counter-cultural then its values must be utterly distinctive, yet certainly with regard to matters of everyday living, there is, between the New Age and the Western mainstream, ostensible similarity – individualism characterises both. The salience of New Age holism as context is in rendering New Age individualism different from mainstream individualism. In this regard the mediating factor, between context (holistic cosmology) and contextualised (individualistic practices), seems to be the New Age *individual* – who is construed *holistically*. All this said, it may be noted that our exposition, grounded in interpretative anthropology, reverses the priorities more normally assigned to context and contextualised, arguing that the former is dependent on the latter. In the next section we articulate this theoretically.

Theoretical

Dumont's account of the relationship between holism and individualism is a useful point of departure (Dumont 1980, 1986). In this account holistic principles constitute the foundation of human society everywhere, for a 'society as conceived by individualism has never existed anywhere for the reason...that the individual lives on social ideas' (1980: 44). Dumont famously exemplifies this with reference to India where, according to him, religious notions of purity constitute the bedrock on the basis of which political and economic differentiation (between individuals and groups) flourishes. But, Dumont insists, holistic principles inform the constitution of Western society as well, notwithstanding the much-vaunted 'Western individualism': Western individualism, its roots in the development of Christianity, must, he argues, be understood as an ideological construction. Thus holistic fundamentality is 'embedded in commonsense' in societies like India (1986: 102-3), but in the West it is mystified.

Allied to such thinking is Dumont's notion of encompassment which implies, within a society, the existence of social phenomena at different 'levels', whereby phenomena at the 'superior' level 'transcends' those at the 'inferior' level, differentiation within the latter level manifesting itself as an expression of opposition, or 'contrary', to the phenomenon at the higher level (1980: 242-43). In general, the superior, encompassing level may be expected to have holistic qualities. Thus in India purity encompasses power (1986: 252). As to the New Age, a Dumontian reading would readily see New Age holistic values as encompassing individualistic ones. However, in this chapter we will not follow Dumont's approach, and indeed would reverse his priorities. Our disavowal of Dumont's position is that it question-begs the source of the so-called encompassing notions, or 'social ideas which individuals live on', and more specifically on the matter of how and why these notions/ideas are socially constructed. Here discussion on the idea of context is helpful.

The idea of context, implying a domain which both contains and bounds upon a phenomenon at issue, is clearly included in the idea of encompassment. This is reinforced by the fact that context generally bears implications for meaning: its specific context makes a difference to what the phenomenon at issue actually means.[2] Our disagreement with Dumont arises when one asks, in any particular instance, firstly, who the meaning-maker here is (anthropologist or informant), and, secondly, whether or not the relation between context and contextualised is a deterministic one. To say that its 'context makes a difference to what the phenomenon means' certainly sounds deterministic, i.e. it implies that context *controls* meaning, and this squares with Dumont's declarations relating to the matter of encompassment (the phenomena – the contraries – that are encompassed are ontologically dependent upon the phenomenon that encompasses). There may be no objection if such determinism is something construed by the anthropologist in the guise of a privileged interpreter of how 'society really works'. However, if anthropological enquiry orientates itself epistemologically to informants' meanings it is another matter. Then, that which is context (encompassing) has to be understood as something individual human agents have constructed. And, in this regard, an important aspect of what is constructed must be the rhetorical attribution such that 'that which is context' is *represented* as controlling, determining, making a difference. Such a rhetorical attribution is instructive. Rhetoric, along the lines of 'that which is context...controls, determines', suggests that, as a social construction, context is essentially a political process. In short, we argue, within the standpoint of interpretative anthropology, that context is socially constructed as a means to legitimise the contextualised. This means, in accordance with the discussion so far, that holistic (commonly cosmological) notions exist so that individualistic notions (commonly relating to day to day practice) may be defended. Taking India as the example, far from being a bedrock of the system, the value relating to purity may be seen as existing thanks to certain economic and power relations (obtaining among definable social groups) which it is summoned to justify.

A non-Dumontian position rings true in the case of the New Age movement. For a start, the term 'holism' is very much part of New Age rhetoric: against the mainstream New Agers assert their identity by celebrating what they call the 'holistic vision', 'holistic living', 'holistic health'. Secondly, New Agers uphold their way of life as morally superior to the mainstream, and this being so the legitimisation of this way of life will, for them, be of vital political moment. Thirdly, New Agers uphold their superiority vis-à-vis the mainstream especially in terms of the conduct of everyday life. Here the importance of legitimacy is underlined since, even though (as we shall show) New Agers regard their individualistic everyday practices as different from so-called mainstream individualism, they are individualistic nonetheless. As has been intimated, we claim that New Age holistic notions function in this regard to defend the distinctiveness of New Age individualism, and maintain that such notions may be understood as having been socially constructed to this end. In the final section of this article we shall justify this interpretation of New Age culture, but beforehand we shall outline in three sections the relevant ethnography. These cover, firstly, New Age individualistic practices, secondly, the New Age holistic cosmology, and lastly the distinctive New Age conception of the human person – whose existence, we shall argue, permits the holistic cosmology to sustain the validity of individualistic practice.

New Age Individualism

The sociological theories of the New Age movement advanced by virtually all key commentators very prominently attend to its individualism, mostly in the context of seeing the emergence of the movement, in early 1970s' America and Europe, as a particular manifestation of cultural themes or trajectories more generally pervasive in the West and from much earlier times. The particularity of the New Age movement in this regard is that it provides, for the individual, the experience of personal transformation (Melton 1990: xiii), a 'self-spirituality' liberating the inner, or higher, being (Heelas 1996: 15-19). The various commentators capture the Western cultural trajectory in different ways. Thus David Hess, upholding the emergence, in the present-day West, of a broad, transcending para-culture, embracing both orthodox science and the New Age, asserts that the New Age movement reflects the restless optimism and individualism of wider American society (in which, judging by the social profile of the typical New Ager, middle-class baby-boomers find particular appeal) (Hess 1993: 14, 174). For his part, Paul Heelas attends to 'detraditionalisation', the release of the individual from institutional controls which for him defines the condition of late modernity, arguing that New Age spirituality reflects its radical and sacralised variant (Heelas 1996). Yet other writers, such as Michael York, explore the proposition that the West in the late twentieth century manifests postmodernity, wherein the West is construed as exhibiting enormous cultural fragmentation (highly appropriate to the prevailing consumerist ethic) where truths and orthodoxies no longer hold sway (York 1994). Such writers focus on the New Age movement's doctrinal tolerance, with its individual members free to draw inspiration from, and eclectically participate in, cultural material originating from a wide range of sources (e.g. Buddhism, Celtic, pagan, tribal, etc.). The New Age movement, for these writers, both exemplifies and is an inherent part of contemporary postmodernity.

This chapter, written from the perspective of one New Age community – the 700 or so New Agers settled in and around the English market town of Glastonbury in 1987 and 1990 (the period of fieldwork) – takes a quite different perspective. Though a dispersed, unorganised and culturally quite heterogeneous body of people, arrived in the town from all parts of the world mostly within the previous ten years, these New Agers held in common an identity relating to their having rejected (in whole or in part) the social circumstances of the wider mainstream Euro-American society, and to having been drawn to Glastonbury because of the town's famous mystical associations. This being the Glastonbury New Agers perception of things, we consider that an anthropologically focused theory of the New Age movement should take, as its point of departure, the fact of radical difference between the New Age and the mainstream, and not basic cultural similarity. One should, then, identify how New Age individualism is different from mainstream individualism.

In Glastonbury many New Agers rejected the mainstream on the grounds that its individualism is, in fact, both a sham and inhumane – that it is a highly constraining individualism and not the 'freedom' which mainstream apologists uphold it to represent. New Agers saw their own individualism/freedom as far more thoroughgoing and pervasive, yet at the same time they often tempered it with a concern for what might be called community justice. Mainstream individualism, in short, they regarded as being delineated by the requirements of capitalism. The New Agers, then, would have approved of Macpherson's observation, referring to the capitalist West '...that individuals defined as choice makers in the market are [in fact] managed and manipulated – the choices they make are those which the producers wish them to make' (Macpherson 1964: 496). That New Age individualism embraces different values is especially evident in New Age ideas about work, which uphold the importance of an individual man or woman's self-reliance, and about children, which celebrate the child's self-determination. These values are hardly those that a 'producer' would wish people to take. This may be illustrated with the Glastonbury material, turning first to the matter of work.

Among New Agers in Glastonbury the need to support oneself resulted in their following a variety of economic strategies, ranging from holding down a full-time job in the mainstream (for example, in

computer programming) to improvising a living independent of the
mainstream (such as living on a patch of land and farming it by
permacultural principles). By and large, however, there was a general
concern to not be caught up in mainstream capitalist enterprises
(which treat people as human fodder rather than as real individuals),
to reject the 'false distinction' between work and play, and to infuse
one's economic life with spirituality. In particular New Agers articulated these general principles by appeal to Schumacher's notion of
Buddhist Economics and to the idea of the 'informal economy'. These
imply both a pervasive and a humane individualism.

Schumacher's articles and lectures over twenty years and more
have inspired and influenced those in the West interested in pursuing
'alternative lifestyles' to the degree that a college devoted to the pursuit
of 'environmental' thinking has been opened in his name, and 'small
is beautiful' – Schumacher's aphorism, which captures the advocacy
of small-scale technology in economic development – has entered
common parlance. Familiar to virtually everyone in Glastonbury,
Schumacher's economic ideas have entered the standing of holy grail
among New Agers in the town. Schumacher's attitude towards work
and earning a living is outlined in his chapter entitled 'Buddhist Economics'; the author begins by explaining the title:

> Right Livelihood is one of the requirements of the Buddha's Noble Eightfold
> Path. It is clear, therefore, that there must be such a thing as Buddhist Eco-
> nomics. (1973: 44)

For Schumacher the logic of the modern mainstream economy is
the minimisation of labour, the maximisation of short-term production, and the use of people as tools; in this economy, moreover, consumption is the sole end purpose of economic activity. Right
Livelihood, Schumacher argues, should in contrast be based on small-
scale enterprises where 'the aim should be to obtain the maximum of
well-being with the minimum of consumption.' (ibid.: 48) An intrinsic
element of Right Livelihood is what Schumacher calls the Buddhist
approach to work:

> The Buddhist point of view takes the function of work to be at least three-
> fold; to give a man a chance to use and develop his faculties; to enable him
> to overcome his ego-centeredness by joining with other people in a com-
> mon task; and to bring forward the goods and services needed for a becom-
> ing existence ... To organize work in such a manner that it becomes
> meaningless, boring, stultifying, or nerve-wracking for the worker would be
> little short of criminal; it would indicate a greater concern with goods than
> with people, an evil lack of compassion and a soul destroying degree of
> attachment to the most primitive side of this worldly existence. (ibid.: 45)

This three-pronged position on work is replicated in many of the attitudes that one would hear expressed in Glastonbury. Firstly, people in the town were looking for work which was creatively satisfying – for themselves. Thus 'conventional job roles' were often distrusted because they suppressed the individually innate and creative spirit. For this reason, a flexible attitude to work – an attitude careful not to inhibit the human spirit – was favoured, and prevailed. Ruth Prince's experiences in working with New Age enterprises and events in Glastonbury confirm this. Epitomising them was the advice she received, in 1987, when helping in an office to prepare for the Harmonic Convergence, a global New Age ritual[3] in which Glastonbury figured prominently, where she was told to come in 'when you feel moved to' or 'with the flow'. Schumacher's second observation – about overcoming 'ego-centeredness' – is particularly interesting in relation to Glastonbury, for it highlights the complementary relationship between individualism and community in the values of the New Age movement. In the New Age community in the town the notion of community and working together was very strong, and yet work was a highly individualistic matter, with, for example, New Age enterprises (such as running a vegan restaurant or setting up as a healer) mostly being owned and managed by just one or two people, though sometimes casually employing one or two others. The salient point here was that the New Age community considered itself to be a caring community, which demanded that New Age enterprises be, in a humane way, considerate in respect of their impact on other members of the community. The third prong of Buddhist economics – bringing forward the goods for a becoming existence – is highly pertinent, for it underpins the stance against materialism and consumerism that was strongly emphasised in Glastonbury, and also the recognition, which many New Agers in the town clearly expressed, of the need to develop an economic infrastructure that is 'sound', and not based upon ecological or human exploitation.

In Glastonbury the 'informal economy' refers to a body of economic practices that have gradually evolved as increasing numbers of newcomers have swelled the ranks of New Agers in the town. As occurs in many areas of Britain where low-income populations are concentrated, people in the New Age community would stretch out their incomes by taking on and combining, concealed from the surveillance of mainstream fiscal institutions, different forms of work and economic support. Ullrich Kockel, writing about New Agers on the west coast of Ireland, maintains that the idea of informal economy in such a context should be understood as encompassing more than matters of tax evasion, to include the following positive features: non-monetarised exchange [barter], occupational pluralism, lack of commercialisation and market orientation, and primary goals other than utility or profit (Kockel 1989:4). These features ring true for the basic economy of the New Age community in Glastonbury, although, that said, in relation to certain New Age luxury goods shops, such as those selling items like 'alternative' ornaments and handmade shoes at high prices, some mainstream ideas, not excluding the profit motive, were becoming increasingly accepted. Thus barter – the swapping of goods and services in a strategic way according to need – occurred frequently. For example, in one office the main tenant allocated half the space to a man running a word processing and accountancy service, and in return received two days per week free word processing. Occupational pluralism, where individuals work part-time in a variety of occupations requiring different skills, was also common. Thus a person might work in a bar (or a cafe, or a shop) and perhaps also make a small income as a musician, gardener or healer. This was something many people applauded, for the reason that it gives a person the chance to explore, and take full advantage of, different aspects of his or her personality. The further dimensions of informal economy were evident more in the recently established High Street shops and other, properly constituted businesses. In an intriguing way, these enterprises' goals were invariably a little less than solely commercial.

The various types of New Age business enterprise in Glastonbury, each one developed through shared discussion and the exchange of ideas as well as on the strength of individual initiatives, constituted the growth point in the New Age economic infrastructure in the town in 1990. The ideological context of these enterprises was submitting oneself to work that nurtured the inner self, which implied a commitment to throw oneself as far as possible to the mercy of one's own personal resources. However an interesting fact here is that to set up their businesses, not a few people had taken advantage of the Enterprise Allowance Scheme set up by Margaret Thatcher's government in the 1980s. With the consequence of small businesses, free market basic wages and the ethos of individualism one might be forgiven for seeing the bottom of Glastonbury High Street as a perfect exemplification of the Thatcherite dream! Yet these were not standard capitalist enterprises. Their rationale would appear to revolve more around making a living than making a profit, for they commonly incorporate strongly informal and even overtly spiritual dimensions which seem to nullify capitalistic ideology and logic. Above all, flexibility informs the organisation of these enterprises: there is over-generosity, and there is apparent stinginess; there is ingenious self-reliance, and there is concern for providing opportunities for others; there is interest in accumulating money and material resources, and there is ideology which states that the means by which money and material resources accumulate should avoid the need directly to exploit others.

Turning now to New Age values relating to children, the notion of individualism captures very well the capacities attributed to the younger generation in the New Age community in Glastonbury. The essence of the child, in New Age thinking, is as an autonomous being, with an existing personality that only needs nourishment to develop. In Glastonbury such autonomy and individuality was recognised as existing even from before birth. As part of the 'birthing process', it was common, in the town, to hold a small ritual during labour to welcome the person entering the world. This ranged from the simple saying of prayers, to the lighting of incense and to chanting and playing drums. Correspondingly, the New Age community was quick to criticise the seen and not heard philosophy of the larger British society – the ethos that children's opinions are unimportant, and not sufficiently worthy of 'adult airspace' to be expressed publicly. As one mother said:

> I had a child five years ago when I was forty so I've had plenty of experience of being an adult and not having a child, but I find British people in general seem to hate children. They send them off to bed as early as possible and seem to avoid contact with them, not like other countries where the children are running around the cafes at 11pm at night. We don't have to be strict disciplinarians as parents, there are ways of getting our point across creatively without being dogmatic. Some of my friends always let their child interrupt them when they are having a conversation because they believe everything that the child has to say is important and needs to be recognised.

Interestingly, in response to this statement, a man who was not a parent observed:

> I understand what you mean, don't get me wrong, I love having children around, it's just that if a child keeps interrupting I find the energy channels around adults get blocked.

Children in Glastonbury, then, were generally treated as independent agents who, no differently from adults, are capable of making choices to suit themselves, from bed-time to matters of schooling. The child's rights in this regard were clearly expressed. One person commented:

> I think children should be able to choose whether they want to go to school or not. If they don't, why should they be forced into doing it? They can learn as much from a tutor, or even listening to other people and spending time in nature. Not that they even teach them the really important things at school anyway, like how to make a fire with only wet wood.

Likewise, an adolescent in Glastonbury, in an interview published in *Glastonbury Times* (the town's alternative newspaper), confirmed the fact that the desire for autonomy, and the power to determine one's choices, was well articulated by the young people themselves:

> I think that everyone should get a year off from school when they get to about 14. It's just a break in the conditioning and it's just when you start finding out about life, and it's good to give the system a break. (Bloom 1990: 16)

The relationship between New Age parents and children in Glastonbury was normally marked by amicability, consistently with the quality of the social relations which obtain more generally in the New Age community. Parental discipline was understated and adults would explain to their children that it 'would be a good thing' if they did or did not do a certain thing, rather than directly commanding them ('do this' or 'do that'). Only when a parent was severely fraught would they ever consider hitting a child. In the home, a child's education mostly took the form of negotiation. For example, a request to the child that he or she play outside might be presented as, 'Adam, how would you feel about being outside while I meditate. I really need the space in the creativity room.'

The setting up, near Glastonbury in 1989, of an independent primary school, in the name of 'alternative', non-mainstream principles, exemplifies these values very well. The children in this school came from a variety of backgrounds, and from an area up to ten miles around. Some had been unhappy in state schools, and their parents had worried about them and looked for an alternative. At the beginning of the school year there had been eighteen pupils but the numbers had dropped. Ruth Prince was told by a man who was both a teacher in the school and a parent that children were encouraged to share toys, and other resources, and that many of the teaching sessions were held with both children and teachers sitting cross-legged in a circle. When asked about gender roles he said that they endeavoured to reduce them; inevitably the 'usual differences' emerged, but they tried not to encourage them. He also said they aimed to make teaching an interactive task, with the distinction between the teachers and pupils lowered. The children were to be viewed with respect, particularly out of regard for their sensitive spiritual awareness. As for recreation, they played no competitive games.

A mode of teaching long out of fashion in mainstream education informed the methods to bring about these sorts of ideals and practices: small classes, teaching by topic rather than by subject discipline, and an emphasis on extensive contact with nature. The school was one big classroom, with only the infants separated from the rest, and the teacher/pupil ratio was high; it was felt easiest, by such organisation, to respond to individual needs, and also to ensure that the children were not restricted to interacting with one age group. Teaching by topic meant that a single theme was looked at from a number of different angles. The Native Americans were a favourite theme: by looking at the structure of the *tipi* the children were taught geometry, by finding out where the people live they learned geography, and they learned music by singing Native American chants – sitting in a circle. Another exercise initiated by the school was looking at things from other people's perspectives. A teapot was placed in the centre of a circle, and everybody was told to draw it. Two teachers sitting in different positions in the circle got up and looked at each other's pictures. Then they enacted a small drama in which they asked one another why they had not drawn the same picture. This was intended to show that different people look at things in different ways. As to the importance of having a close relationship with nature this was borne out in weekly visits to a plot of ground where there were a group of New Agers living without water or electricity; there the children were given the opportunity to learn that people can and do live without modern conveniences. These occasions also provide children with the chance of running wild in the woods, and for leadership roles to emerge different from those of the classroom.

In 1990 the long-term future of the school was uncertain. The parents had decided not to apply for it to be granted official status, nor to follow the demands of the National Curriculum. One problem was that the school only catered for pupils up to the age of eleven, and so most children would have to be streamed off into the state school system. However the parents, at this time, were more preoccupied simply with how to keep the present school going.

Holism

There are a number of important holistic tenets in New Age thinking, of which those that are unequivocally holistic have mainly to do with the nature of the universe (Gaia) and the notion of a transcendent spiritual essence. We shall examine these in turn.

Gaia

The result of this more single-minded approach was the development of the hypothesis that the entire range of living matter on earth, from whales to viruses, and from oaks to algae, could be regarded as constituting a single living entity, capable of manipulating the Earth's atmosphere to suit its overall needs and endowed with faculties and powers far beyond those of its constituent parts. (Lovelock 1991: 166)

James Lovelock's scientific hypothesis, quoted here, implies that the planet Earth may be viewed as an independent living organism (Lovelock 1979). Naming this hypothesis Gaia, after the Greek Earth Goddess, Lovelock drew an unexpected body of supporters – the New Age movement. With its comparison of the elements of the earth with a nervous or communication system, many people in the movement hailed it as science recognising the integral interconnectedness of all things: New Agers have adopted the Gaia hypothesis as the symbol of the holistic vision.

Many people in Glastonbury, embracing the idea of wholeness, interdependence and interconnectedness in nature, construed the Gaia hypothesis as acknowledging the earth as having a consciousness – as being alive. At a night-time vigil on the Tor[4] during the Harmonic Convergence of 1987, one man, who lived in a tent in nearby woods, explained how he felt about Gaia:

> When I look up at the sky now and see the stars twinkling, I feel the aliveness of the earth, I can feel her breathing. We are part of it all, we are the communication system of Gaia's body. When I realised that I knew it didn't matter who I was or where I was, I knew I could never feel lonely.

Others in Glastonbury attributed to nature a corresponding moral quality of 'goodness'. Following a violent storm in which a number of trees were blown down, one woman said, 'it's a message, she's expelling herself at the roots, the fallen trees are there to teach us a lesson.'

Many New Age commentators concord with this view, that the problems facing the 'human race' today are caused by our misplaced arrogance towards the earth. Thus, Sahtouris, in her article, 'Gaia's dance', states:

> Our ability to be objective, to see ourselves as the 'I' or 'eye' of our cosmos, as beings independent of nature, has inflated our egos – 'ego' being the Greek word for 'I'. We came to separate the 'I' from the 'it' and to believe that 'it' – the world 'out there' – was ours to do as we pleased, telling ourselves we were either God's favoured children or the smartest and most powerful naturally evolved creatures on Earth. This egotistic attitude has been very much a factor in bringing us to adolescent crisis. And so an attitude of greater humility and willingness to accept some guidance from our parent planet will be an important factor in reaching our species maturity. (Sahtouris 1991: 167)

But not that Lovelock himself attributed a consciousness to the earth as an intelligent being. Such an interpretation of his ideas is strictly misleading:

> Sentience, the possession of senses, suggests some level of awareness, and awareness suggests consciousness. Gaia begins to resemble an intelligent

being. It is hardly surprising, therefore, that given a very brief and simplified outline of this new view of the way the planet works, together with a name to attach to it, that some people may come to regard Gaia as a god. Not only is this incorrect, it is potentially harmful. The apparently persuasive line of reasoning that leads to this interpretation is false. Gaia, or the Earth, is not intelligent, does not think, and most emphatically is not a god. To this extent the name Gaia is perhaps unfortunate. (Allaby 1989: 111; *see also* Milton 1996)

To New Agers in Glastonbury, however, this is beside the point. For them, the Earth, the one giant living organism, includes human beings as an integral part. As people in Glastonbury explained it, this serves to further the idea that human beings have a place and connection in relation to each other, beyond individual needs and perceptions.

Notion of Common Essence

Linked to the ideas incorporated in Gaia is a parallel sense, in New Age thinking, of a common essence among all living forms, particularly among human beings. Most usually spoken of as a common 'spirit', this is sometimes expressed in terms of a common divinity, and at other times in terms of a higher or common self which the individual is usually suppressing. At this higher level, the idea of separation (of individuals from one another) is illusory, and a movement away from the 'truth' or 'spirit':

A mind that conceives of itself as fundamentally separate from all that it perceives is an instrument of division. It can do nothing but divide, analyse, compartmentalise, and dissect. Everything on which it turns its attention is reduced to disconnected segments, while the spirit, the life of the whole, is forgotten. With the fictitious premise that it is fundamentally distinct from both 'others' and nature lying at the root of its thinking, the ego is not capable of reason, for its premise is a lie. (Carey 1991)

The author of this quotation maintains that the 'lonely ego' is something isolated, and lacks the strength and power of the spirit, or truth. His statistic is that 'without the spirit, the ego is capable of using only about ten percent of the brain's capacity'. The spirit is what is common to all, and what links all to all.

One of the most ardent, and famous, proponents of such a theory was Sir George Trevelyan (who died in 1996), the founder of the Wrekin Trust. Sir George was a regular visitor to Glastonbury and had close contacts with people there, and he participated in many local events, as well as giving lectures in the town. When Ruth Prince was in Glastonbury during the Harmonic Convergence, she met Sir George a number of times; a tall, craggy man with piercing and bright blue eyes, his agility, charisma and vivid, sweeping gestures belied his older years. The thrust of his teaching lies in people becoming more aware of the oneness of life, to realise that each human being is part of a wider life-force: to their detriment, human beings are divided each one from the other – similarly to the Ancient Mariner ('and no one told pity on my soul in misery'). Through knowing the oneness of all life it is possible to move beyond the transitory states of personality. He wrote:

> This consciousness includes the capacity to be one with any other human being. Normally you and I experience separation: we are separate beings, which is the essence of Newtonian thinking. When I look into your eyes, however, I realise that it isn't just two chaps. The divinity in me is the same as the divinity in you. Obviously: the holistic viewpoint implies it. I can look through your eyes and it is the divinity in me looking at itself through you. In this sense we are one. (Trevelyan 1986: 15-16)

To exemplify these ideas, Sir George practised a ritual, which he describes as an experiment. As one of the helpers during the Harmonic Convergence Ruth participated in it. He told each person to stare into someone's eyes and look beyond the outer faces of personality so one didn't feel the need to visually respond to that level of communication. At that point what you saw in someone's eyes was the same thing and part of the same whole as yourself: that which you see and that which is in yourself is a little droplet of divinity. When Ruth participated in the ritual it was to welcome the 'energies' of Sun Ray as they came down to earth. As Ruth describes it:

> *Firstly ten of us stood round an oak tree holding hands to give thanks, some of us with flowers to celebrate nature. Then we moved to a circular rose garden to 'appreciate the beauty of creation'. At that point we branched into pairs and I, the participating observer, found myself staring into the eyes of Sir George himself. We were to look into the soul in each other, and then say, 'I wish you the beauty of the rose and the strength of the oak'. Then he gave me the Essene blessing by putting his hand on my cheek and saying 'Blessings be with you', and I replied, 'And with you'. Then we exchanged a hug.*

The Holistic Individual

The New Age 'person' very basically includes four inseparable and mutually affecting elements: the physical, the emotional, the mental and the spiritual (there is also a fifth, social element which we shall consider shortly). The spiritual element requires special comment since in New Age thinking 'spirituality' commands many meanings and this makes the 'spiritual in the human' a demanding notion. A metaphor drawn from New Age ethics, spirituality specifies two key ideas in daily thought and practice. It evokes the idea of a personalised, non-institutionalised religion, and it refers to the non-material aspect of any thought or activity. Through spirituality the New Age constitutes two key domains: firstly the cosmos, the broadest possible domain of existence, in respect of which every human being is merged; secondly the holistic person. In relation to the human person, spirituality signals not just the presence of something over and above the purely physical, but that this something is equally, if not more, fundamental. 'Energy', in New Age thinking, functions to express these ideas. A metaphor drawn from the notion of interconnectedness, particularly with respect to the cosmos as an holistic domain, 'energy' in its most elementary sense refers to any enhanced level of 'activity'. Energy may be used to describe an atmosphere in a room, or the appeal of a painting, or the quality of interaction between two people. With regard to a particular entity (as a whole) the discourse of energy therefore conveys the idea that this is something which is animated. In the case of the human person, energy combined with the idea of spirituality delineates a *being* with sacred properties.

The multi-dimensional nature of the human person has a central bearing on New Age ideas about health and illness. Wellness, in New Age thinking, implies a proper balance among the various elements (physical, emotional, mental and spiritual) which constitute the human being, and illness that such a balance is lacking. Indeed people in Glastonbury would criticise different social groups or individuals in these terms. Thus academics were deemed to place too much emphasis on the mental and not enough on the emotional or intuitive, and people who became wrapped up in the spiritual and paid little attention to the physical and the mental were accused of being 'ungrounded'. It follows that healing, and the maintenance of wellbeing, consisted of restoring or sustaining the correct balance. This contrasts with Western biomedicine which, focusing solely on the physical, must speak of health and illness (employing metaphors of violence) in terms of the invasion of the physical body from the outside and of the concern that such contaminating elements be expelled.

Such New Age holistic interpretations were summoned in relation to Ruth Prince's experience towards the end of summer 1990, as she recalls.

> *I developed a virus which came and went over a period of a month and left me feeling faint and nauseous. I went to my own [National Health Service] doctor, but she said there was very little she or I could do except that I should look after myself and wait until it left my system. At the same time I was helping with the 'alternative' newspaper in the town. My relations with the woman running it were deteriorating, the newspaper seemed to be going through a period of unpopularity and there were few helpers to put together the autumn issue. When I*

became sick I phoned up and said I would have to stay at home for the day. But aware of the pressures of getting the newspaper ready to go to print, I returned the following day, not feeling completely better. After a few hours I began to feel physically very drained and decided to go home again. The woman I was helping said to me:

"I'm rarely ill, perhaps the odd cold but that's all. It's because I let my emotions in and out freely, when I'm angry I scream and so I don't get any blockages. The reason why you are ill is because you suppress things. This is your chance now you are here in Glastonbury to let go. You are trying to hold down a job and career, have a monogamous relationship, trying to please others. Now you are in Glastonbury you have a chance to throw it all off and to really experience yourself. All the resentment and frustration you have is manifesting itself on a physical level."

There is a further, crucially important sense in which the New Age individual is a holistic individual and this is being deemed to be inherently social: according to New Agers in Glastonbury, a human being is a person because he or she inherently, and elementarily, relates with others. In this sense the New Ager is less individualistic than the Western mainstreamer who, thanks to the experience of the industrial process, considers him- or herself as individuated vis-à-vis fellow humans (Strathern 1987: 281-82). New Agers in Glastonbury, in keeping with a fiercely egalitarian ethos, express such relating without recourse to formal roles, in an essentially affective idiom: New Agers in the town, by virtue of being there, mutually relate through the notion of 'love'.

Truly a dominant symbol, love, in the New Age, has various meanings, and, in Glastonbury, was summoned on many different types of occasion. In the first place, as an ideal to which people aspire, love evokes a perfect way of being, in which aggression finds no place. For New Agers 'unconditional love' therefore implies deep affection, positiveness and altruism; from the object of love nothing is expected in return, nor is there any desire for it (or he, or she) to be anything other than it is. As well as this, in Glastonbury love was considered to be unlimited. Thus it was thought possible to love many others at the same time, and this meant, on a practical level, that the traditional confines of the family unit might be played down, with people becoming involved in one another's nuclear families, taking additional lovers, and so on.

There are further meanings. Love refers to oneself, underlining the fresh awareness and the raising of consciousness inherent in participating in the New Age movement. Love may also be applied to a task. On another level altogether, love applies to the world: accepting the world as it is is seen as a true expression of love. (Critics of the New Age movement cite this as evidence of its political passivity.) Lastly, it was said in Glastonbury, the 'world beyond' (e.g. the mainstream world) is devoid of love, from the point of view of both relations among people and one's veneration of oneself as a divine being. Significantly, for New Agers in Glastonbury, the opposite of love is fear.

Mutuality in the human person is, through love's properties, provided with an ideal moral and emotional substance. Love, it is evident, expresses an inherent capacity in the human being, as well as the intensity of sharing existing between any two people by virtue of their common humanity. Thus, in Glastonbury, love connotes an awareness of *being* a New Ager and an unqualified acceptance of *others who are* New Age.

Holism as Constructed Context

New Age individualism is, for New Agers, a politically sensitive matter. It is different from mainstream individualism, as has been described: mainstream individualism, as New Agers see things, is more constraining and less humane than New Age individualism. Yet New Age individualism is individualism for all that, and this may partly be why many academic commentators have come to argue that the New Age and the Western mainstream are culturally all of apiece. Perhaps more to the point, New Age practices, in their pervasive individualism, are laid open to criticism from politically-attuned mainstreamers. New Age individualism, complain the movement's critics, equals New Age self-indulgence. That the New Ager sees his or her personal transformation, relating to proper individualistic practice (in work, relationships, health care, religious observance) as presaging the transformation (for the better) of the wider society becomes, in the face of accusations of narcissism, invisible.

Through notions of holism, New Agers clearly assert a radical cultural distinctiveness from the mainstream. For example, New Age ideas of a holistic, spiritually-attuned environment within which human beings and all other entities are humbly subsumed make for the compelling expression of difference, with the mainstream easily being represented as heading, in its arrogant treatment of the environment, for ecological ruin. But holism, if it is to address the political vulnerability of the New Age movement around the matter of individualism, must clearly link into such individualism. That this plainly occurs is evident in the New Age conception both of the holistic person and of the existence of mutual, though highly unformalised and egalitarian, relations (of love) in which all New Agers are suspended.

We argue that, in New Age understanding, holism permits meanings to be constructed in relation to individualism such that New Age individualism is expressed as different from mainstream individualism, and that it does so in a politically highly potent way, in particular by rendering the human agent of individualistic practice as different – i.e., as holistic. In this respect holism clearly functions as context to individualism, both abutting it as a separate domain and also containing it (the holistic individual). Moreover in the New Age representation of things the holistic is clearly seen as controlling and informing the individualistic: the holistic is what gives the individual agent his or her distinctive (non-mainstream) cultural qualities. Meanwhile more general holistic notions (e.g., ecological holism) assert the veracity of holism as a separate domain. But we use the term representation advisedly. The idea of 'context determination', we argued at the beginning of this chapter, is part of context construction as a political process. Such construction involves the elaboration of a domain external to a phenomenon at issue, with the rhetorical claim that such an external domain is somehow responsible for the phenomenon at issue being as it is. But in the process of construction, it is the phenomenon at issue – where political contentiousness lies – that is primary, its contextualisation a political gambit in its support. In this way, we contend, New Agers produce and reproduce holistic ideas – so that their individualistic practices, subtly different from the mainstream (less constraining, more humane), secure legitimation through being expressed (via the holistic individual) as entirely different from the mainstream.

Such a reading of the relation between New Age holism and individualism we contend makes better sense than any other. Suppose, in the construction process, holistic ideas were primary and determining then one would expect to find (which one does not) New Age practices as the highly institutionalised object of an embracing social structure. Moreover the primacy of individualistic practices is supported in the fact that New Agers in Glastonbury have arrived (from widely scattered parts) in the town mostly separately as individuals having made the decision that the constraining mainstream was not for them. For them to sustain a viable lifestyle as long-term residents in Glastonbury one would expect them to attend in the first instance to ongoing daily practice, and not to the intellectual realm of holistic cosmology. Thus individualistic practice must be treated – as has been the case in this chapter – as analytically primary, and cosmological reflection secondary.

Notes

1. The 'broader Western mainstream' is our label for the social world that most New Agers see themselves as having, in total or in part, turned their backs on. It is hardly a homogeneous category, of course. But for present purposes it may be treated as referring to the milieu of the White, urban, middle class.
2. Thus the common complaint, frequently voiced by politicians, that one has been misunderstood, having been 'taken out of context'.

3. Based on Mayan prophecy, the ritual, timed for 16 and 17 August 1987, marked a galactic synchronisation presaging global transformation, and featured a renewal in the recognition of the mystical power of light and the sun (York 1995: 83-85).
4. The Tor is the remarkable conical hill, with long-term mystical associations, which rises spectacularly above Glastonbury and the surrounding countryside.

Bibliography

Allaby, M. 1989. *Thinking green*. London: Barrie and Jenkins.

Bloom, J. 1990. 'A voice of youth'. *Glastonbury Times*. Spring Equinox Issue.

Carey, K. 1991. 'Instinctual living – the path beyond language'. In *Global Link-up*. April/May.

Dumont, L. 1980. *Homo hierarchicus* (rev. edn). Chicago: University of Chicago Press.

————. 1986. *Essays on Individualism*. Chicago: University of Chicago Press.

Heelas, P. 1996. *The New Age movement*. Oxford: Blackwell.

Hess, D. 1993. *Science and the New Age*. Madison: Wisconsin University Press.

Kockel, U. 1989. 'The West is learning, the North is war: reflections on Irish identity between New Age and postmodernity'. An unpublished paper.

Lovelock, J. 1979. *Gaia: a new look at life on Earth*. Oxford: Oxford University Press.

————. 1991. 'Gaia', in W. Bloom (ed.), *The New Age: an anthology of essential writings*. London: Channel 4 Books.

Macpherson, C.B. 1964. 'Post-Liberal democracy', *Canadian Journal of Economics and Political Science* , 30 (4): 485-98.

Melton, J.G. 1990. 'Introduction', in, J. G. Melton et al. (eds), *New Age encyclopedia*. Detroit: Gale Research.

Milton, K. 1996. *Environmentalism*. London: Routledge.

Sahtouris, E. 1991. 'Gaia's Dance', in W. Bloom (ed.), *The New Age: an anthology of essential writings*. London: Channel 4 Books.

Schumacher, E. 1973. *Small is beautiful: economics as if people mattered*. London: Abacus.

Strathern, M. 1987. 'Conclusion', in M. Strathern (ed.), *Dealing with inequality*. Cambridge: Cambridge University Press.

Trevelyan, G. 1986. *Summons to a high crusade*. Flores: The Findhorn Press.

York, M. 1994. 'New Age in Britain: an overview'. *Religion Today* , 9 (3): 14-21.

————. 1995. *The emerging network: the sociology of the New Age and Neo-Pagan movements*. London: Rowman and Littlefield.

Chapter 8

CONTEXT AS AN ACT OF PERSONAL EXTERNALISATION

GREGORY BATESON AND THE HARVEY FAMILY IN THE ENGLISH VILLAGE OF WANET

Nigel Rapport

> The concept of reality is slippery because, always, truth is relative to context, and context is determined by the questions which we ask of events.
>
> Gregory Bateson
> *Communication*

Prelude

An Humanistic Beginning

In Fernandez's persuasive theory of tropes (1977, 1982, 1986), symbolic forms represent an externalisation of internal, individual senses of self. The elemental vectors of human existence are simple, Fernandez claims: we tropically project what are initially psychosomatic experiences out into the world, and these individual projections then ramify, via cultural codes, into social strategies of boundary and identity. Thus, it is with private and individual meanings that public and conventional symbolic forms are fundamentally imbued – meanings which may be 'problematic and not precisely defined', in a word 'inchoate', for the individuals themselves (1982: 544). Employing symbolic forms in cultural codes is a means by which individuals attempt to make more concrete, graspable and thus resolvable what is incomprehensible to themselves in their experience and relations with the world; the codification of their experience represents a kind of hypothesis which they bring to bear in an effort to try to figure out what their lives are and are like. Our conversational exchanges – tropic narratives of analogy, metaphor, metonymy, simile, synecdoche and the like – then represent attempts to express and compare our compositions of experiences alongside others' experiences.

However, the problem of meaning, of the fundamental solipsism of incomprehensible individual lives, is thereby compounded. For, others' access to the symbolic forms which an individual employs are at best a second-order interpretation: an interpretation of the individual's own. In attempting to approach another's phenomenological subjectivity, the experiential 'sensorium' in which another mind is enmeshed (Fernandez 1992: 135), one empathetically engages with their narrative, hoping to accede to an appropriate understanding of their tropes. Even at best, however, this may reveal what another's life is *like* more than what it *is*; knowing him [or her] in terms of the metaphorical associations he [or she] brings into play, even an individual's closest consociates more usually learn *from* him than *of* him.

In sum, Fernandez's theory reformulates a basic (existential) truth, and a sociological conundrum, to which an humanistic anthropology has been wont periodically to return:

> The paradox [is] that cultures do exist, and societies do survive, despite the diversity of the interests and motivations of their members, the practical impossibility of complete interpersonal understanding and communication, and the unavoidable residuum of loneliness that dwells in every man. (Wallace 1961: 131)
>
> The true locus of culture is in the interactions of specific individuals, and, on the subjective side, in the world of meanings which each one of these individuals may unconsciously abstract for himself from his participation in these interactions. (...) [T]he friendly ambiguities of language conspire to reinterpret for each individual all behaviour which he has under observation in terms of those meanings which are relevant to his own life. (Sapir 1956: 151, 153)
>
> [The subjective] continually challenges human beings with the contingency, and ofttimes the utter hopelessness of communicating, eliciting, or in any way doing justice to internal self-perception with external means. (Wagner 1991: 39)

A Post-Structuralist Beginning

Interestingly, this existential truth also has its post-structuralist resonances. Replacing a theory of tropes with one of technology, then, Cooper would have us understand the latter as a re-presentation of human being (its parts, capacities and needs) in such a way as to overcome human, bodily contingencies. At the same time, technology is a transformation of the inanimateness, the 'otherness', of the external world because of its becoming converted into a 'bio-technical' shape, imbued with a bio-technical nature (Cooper 1993: 280). On this view, human being is an area of precariousness, of chance and variability, and the body an arena of multiple and unstable effects: 'a volume in perpetual disintegration', where desires, failings and errors engage and efface one another in insurmountable conflict (Foucault 1977: 148). In response, human being re-presents itself to itself in terms of more durable external structures. It translates an entropic inside into a secure, objective outside, and so becomes a centre of calculation and technique in a world of material forms. Thus the body enters the world as 'technology', where this is understood, from the Greek *techne*, to be an art of making-present, of giving clear form to and hence realising, what was previously absent or remote.[1] Technology represents an 'arte-factualisation' of the body. Here is a separating out and objectifying of bodily attributes – making the latter objects-in-the-world, seemingly autonomous and distinct – in order for their possible re-appropriation, recovery and control (artefacts being more easily modified than the body they have come to represent).

In short, human being and its objectified world prefigure each other. The orderliness of human life (such as it is) takes the form of networks of relations between supposedly distinct 'subjects' and 'objects' which in fact reflect and contain each other. Here is body and world existing in dialectical process.

Context

Whether conceived of in humanistic or in post-structuralist terms, the a priori nature of human 'externalisation' in the process of individual knowledge would seem existentially highly significant (cf. Berger 1969: 3-4). Human beings create iconic forms (languages; techniques and technical relations) whereby experiences which are originally sub-jective and personal become objective and conventional. The transla-tion, however, (from feeling to felt meaning to intended meaning to elicited meaning (Wagner 1991: 39-40)) remains not only perennially uncertain but inherently ambiguous and diverse, for the externalisa-tion of subjective content as objective form has no necessary singular-ity or consistency to it even in the usage of one individual.

This truth would also seem to have important implications for an anthropological appreciation of context – as I wish to demonstrate in this chapter (cf. Rapport 1995). A sense of 'context' – understood as 'domain or arena of significance' – is what may be seen to be provided or assured the individual via an externalisation of his bodily sense of (inchoate) self. Externalisation gives onto context. For once the body's sense of itself is externalised – whether as trope or as technology – the body is afforded a ground (a landscape and a set of landmarks) against which to measure its own existence and movement, and a space in which to know and act.

Context is determined by the questions which people ask of events, Bateson claimed in the epigraph to this chapter (Bateson and Reusch 1951: 238), signalling an important link between context, perception and intention, between context, knowledge and desire. Just as many questions can be asked of events, so there will be many contexts; just as different people can ask different questions of events, so different people will determine different contexts; just as people can ask a number of different questions of events at the same time, questions of which other people may or may not be aware, so different people can simultaneously create and inhabit multiple contexts, contexts whose commonality is (literally) questionable. It is against a background of such Batesonian phrasings – employing them as context – that I shall develop my own thoughts on context in this chapter. The chapter takes the form of a 'fantasia' on certain ideas borrowed from Gregory Bateson, and his attempts, in particular, to treat the subjectivity of the objective world, its originary subjectivation, in non-idealistic terms. 'Man-environment' is one unit of becoming, as Bateson put it, so that an individual's knowledge of the world, and of himself, and the nature of the world as such, are inextricably tied.[2] When an individual secures a context for his action he is also assured a self and a world.

More precisely, I explore the contexts, the domains of significance, inhabited by a family of farmers in a small rural village in northern England. I show that Doris and Fred Harvey's knowledge of Wanet village and beyond, of people and events in their social world, is constituted by externalising, objectifying and then internalising the multiple and instable effects of their own bodily selves. Their knowing takes place within, is contextualised by, a framework of fundamental assumptions, 'prejudices' (Gadamer 1976: 9) concerning the world; and the conditions of this knowing, the processes of their knowing, are inextricably tied to their own bodily perceptions. The 'tropology' or 'technology' of the Harvey family on Cedar High Farm in Wanet consists of people and events around them which make external, other, secure and malleable, their own wishes, fears, temptations and changes of mind.

The following is in three parts. In the first, 'Theme', I outline Bateson's ideas (Bateson 1936, 1958, 1959, 1972 1980; Bateson and Reusch 1951; Bateson et al. 1974,) as they pertain to my topic. In the second, 'Fantasia', I describe an episode in the life of the Harvey family, in Wanet, in Batesonian terms. In the third, 'Coda', I return to some more general conclusions concerning the intrinsic individuality of context.

Theme

'Maps are not territories'

There is a discontinuity between a class and its members, according to Russell's theory of logical types, such that the term used for the class belongs to a different level of abstraction to the terms used for members. The class cannot be a member of itself, furthermore, and a member cannot be the class, for different logical types cannot thus meet or 'know' one another directly. Bateson cites this Russellian proof (1974: 32), and makes it central to his understanding of the universe of human behaviour. Logical types and levels, for Bateson, characterise, differentiate, hierarchicalise and interrelate world, biosphere, society, body and mind; and there is an infinite regress of such contexts of existence. For example, there is a world of material objects, of things-in-themselves, which is distinct from (which is known differently to) the world of human bodies, of metabolic supplies and channels, which is in turn distinct from the world of the mind, of narratives, thoughts and ideas.[3] The mind can thus be said to be made of parts and processes which are not themselves mental but metabolic. Consciousness represents a transformation of unconscious metabolic processes, and each human body represents an 'energy source' whose metabolism underlies a possible conscious perception of the external world (1972: 126).

Linking one logical level or context to another is a complex network of meta-relations. Moving from the world of one logical type or level to another always entails, for Bateson, a transformation of knowledge: a re-codification of how and what is known. Between distinct logical types or levels, to repeat, there can be no direct knowledge and no 'complete' communication. Hence, the metabolic processes which give rise to the rich content of consciousness are not themselves subject to direct introspection or voluntary control.

Similarly, maps are not territories; the worlds of human experience are distinct from a noumenal world of external things, of things-in-themselves. There are no rocks, trees, or even people in the human mind, Bateson is fond of saying, there are only ideas of rocks, trees and people. Things enter the human world of experience, of meaning and communication, by our ideas of them – whatever else they may be in their thingish world. Ideas are the only things human beings can know and we cannot otherwise imagine the world 'as it is'.

Ideation, the processes of perceiving and thinking and communicating about perceiving and thinking, involves a transformation or codification (translation or substitution) which might variously be described as symbolic classification, naming or mapping. We attribute names and qualities to things and so 'produce' them by reproducing them in a world of human experience. Ideation Bateson describes as itself an operation of logical typing; but since direct communication between logical types remains impossible, the 'things' that enter our minds as ideas are at best guesses at the things-in-themselves. For the mind as such is a no-thing, existing only in ideas, while ideas are also no-things; they are not the things they refer to. What occupies the mind, in short, is an abstract account of a concrete external world which otherwise remains itself, distinct and mysterious.

What ideas do involve are differences.

'Information is difference which makes a difference'

The mind operates with and upon differences; differences are the unit of psychological input. So that if minds are aggregates of ideas, then what minds contain are differences: ideas and differences are synony-mous. For to perceive something, to recognise a thing, is to recognise a difference between it and some other thing or some other perception. Things are thus defined by and through their differences. To the extent that things enter the world of human experience they do so as aggre-gates of their differences.

Another way of saying this is that human thought is relational. We perceive and think in terms of relationships – difference is a relation-ship – and not in terms of things-in-themselves. Things enter the world of human experience (are seen as separate and real) only through their inter-relations; they are epiphenomena of the relations to which we perceive them to be a party: relations to ourselves, to other things, and to themselves in other contexts.

Information about the world Bateson then defines as differences which make a difference in a particular context: differences seen as rel-evant at a particular time. Information is 'news of difference' (1980: 37), while maps are organisations of news of difference.

'All phenomena are appearances'

Since the mental worlds of human beings concern maps, and maps of maps, and not things-in-themselves, all human phenomena can be said to be abstractions, their truth-value turning upon appearances. The Berkeleyian motto, 'To be is to be perceived', therefore applies to all human behaviour, for the human universe has no objective features. Even so-called natural-scientific knowledge shares this character; Euclidean geometry, for example, is not about space as it exists but as it is defined by a human perceiver or imaginer.[4] There is an infinite num-ber of potential or latent differences and relations between and within things in the external world but only some of these become 'effective', meaningful or manifest in the world of human ideation – differences which have made a difference and become information. Hence, we cre-ate the world we perceive, editing and selecting from the noumenal universe so that it conforms with our beliefs, with our vision of 'order': of the orderly relations between objects.

To this extent, objects (and not only their experiencing) are subjective creations. In fact, all thinking and all human experience can be said to be subjective: a matter of the images our brains make about the 'external world', a matter of the mediation of our sense organs and neural pathways. Even pain is a created image. And while nineteenth-century science founded itself on the claim that this subjectivity was 'really' objective, it was the latter which was only apparent. Human knowledge and conditions of knowledge are always, and inevitably, personal; knowledge is a relationship in the eye of the beholder. Hence, 'man lives by those propositions whose validity is a function of his belief in them' (Bateson 1951: 212); they are not true or false in any simple 'objective' sense.

In this way, the subjective viewer and the personal world which he or she creates can be seen as one; since *Dinge-an-Sich* ('things-in-themselves') never enter the mind, only complex transformations of these, there is a oneness between the perceiver and the things perceived. Rather than subjects and objects there exist subject-objects and perceiver-perceiveds: always the purposive organism in interaction with its created environment; always the territory of things and objects filtered into a mental world of subjective images and maps. Bateson talks of the 'mental determinism' immanent in the universe (1972: 441).

In this way too, worlds are multiple. If order is defined as the privileging of one or more of an *infinite* number of possible relations between objects and events, between things in the world, then the perception of any two viewers, or the same viewer at different times, need not overlap. Even two individuals in interaction have a freedom regarding how they interpret: both how they codify the world and how they act upon their codifications. And differences multiply. Because to assert one thing, privilege one pattern of relations, is to deny something else.

Finally, visions of order are self-fulfilling. Human individuals live in worlds of their own perceiving, codifying, creating, imagining, because they set out to establish a correspondence between what is in their heads and what is outside them, and in large measure they succeed. They see what they want to see and want to see what they see. Or as Bateson puts it, value is a determinant of perception, and perception a determinant of value; evaluation and codification are aspects of the same central mental phenomenon. We must wish things to be as we see them, and vice-versa, or our actions will bring us frustration and pain instead of success. In short, in the perception of a particular set of relations between things, a particular order in the external world, value and information meet.

'Patterns connect'

While there are discontinuities between logical types and levels, between classes and members, Bateson also posits the existence of corresponding patterns between the components of particular types and levels which connect those types and levels. Similar relations between parts evince meta-patterns: shapes and forms of an aesthetic kind. The process of recognising connecting patterns between logical types and levels, Bateson calls 'abduction'. He finds it in metaphor, in dream, parable, allegory, poetry, totemism, and comparative anatomy, and he believes that what he calls 'abductive systems' characterise great regions of nature and human life, linking the body and the ecosystem (1980: 158).

For example, stereoscopic vision, provided by two eyes which are logically discrete but perceive corresponding patterns between the component parts of the worlds they perceive, amounts to an abductive system. Similarly, a routine relationship of exchange between two people is an abductive system; a relationship Bateson describes as a double view of something or a double description. Not internal to a single person, a relationship is based on the recognition by parties concerned of corresponding patterns of behaviour and response on each side. Or again, an abductive system characterises the process of perceiving an environment. A difference between a standing and falling tree is transformed into a difference between neurons in the human brain; the physical event is translated into an idea, a piece of information, which bears a commensurate pattern between component parts. The mental process entails a sequence of interactions between neuronal parts, which is a coded version, a transformation, of events perceived in the external world; there is a relationship of difference which connects the two.

'Mental processes are recursive'

A clear emphasis in Bateson's understanding of how we come to perceive both difference and sameness is upon the movement inherent in mental processes. We come to know difference by cognitively moving between two or more things, or moving ourselves relative to a thing, or moving between two of our cognitions of a thing. And we come to know sameness by abducting, by moving between patterns of relations between things and appreciating the metapatterns that they share. Knowing entails cognitive movement.

And we remember these movements, Bateson next argues. If we value the information which they provide us, then the cognitive movement is reinforced and comes to be habitual: an habitual pattern or pathway between neurons in the brain, an habitual association of ideas in the mind. These remembered, habitual movements, Bateson calls a 'cybernetic circuit' or 'system': a pathway, and network of pathways, along which information and transformations are transmitted

(1972: 434). He also calls them 'circular (or more complex) chains of determination': a dynamic processing of information in recursive patterns of relations between neuronal components of the brain and ideational components of the mind (1980: 102). Even the simplest cybernetic circuit possesses such memory, Bateson insists, based upon the travel of information; and as the mind matures, so it comes to consist of habituated loops of thought and networks of such loops: a total completed circuitry. Hence, an appreciation of this circuitry is essential for an understanding of human behaviour, for this is how we think, this gives onto what we know.

This also reveals how we know that we know, how we become self-conscious. It is recursive circuitry which produces an organism's autonomy and its self-control. For by getting messages about messages an organism comes to know itself. It can correct itself and make choices – to change or stay the same.[5] Through the process of recursion it is *as if* the differences between certain parts of the brain and mind – 'transmitters' – caused other parts to become 'receivers' (a 'sensory end organ'), responding to the differences between them (1980: 106). In fact there is no 'ghost in the machine' of this kind, no *res cogitans*, it being simply an effect of recursion: of a level of complexity (and hierarchy) of circuitry which causes the organism to perceive its own prior perceptions.[6]

'Knowledge is both evolutionary and tautological'

The notion of memory, of habit and reinforcement, which Bateson introduces to explain the process of recursion, whereby a maturing body and mind will contain an increasing number of cybernetic circuits – habitual pathways between neurons in the brain, between ideas in the mind – also introduces the equally important notions of development, stasis and change over time. The knowledge which the organism possesses is not fixed. Being a matter of recursion, of cybernetic circuitry, movement is indeed inherent in its nature. But more than this, the circuitry of the brain and the mind is not fixed. Habit is certainly a fixing process, but not everything in human life is habit, and habits themselves change. As individual organisms die and are replaced in a population, whole networks of habits die and come to be replaced too.

Habits are not everything and habits change, Bateson now explains, because new relations between things in the world, new pathways between neurons in the brain and new associations between ideas in the head, are always being created by the individual. Each individual human body is an 'energy source' after all, and the energy of its metabolic processes translates as a constant perception of possible new relations in the world, and hence new objects and contexts of action.[7] In his quest to see the metapatterns between logical types, Bateson refers here too to the Second Law of Thermodynamics, the law of entropy: the randomness of probability will always eat up order and pattern in the world. That is, while each purposive organism will have created an order for itself by selecting a set of possible relations between possible things in the world (and defining it as 'order', or 'law' or 'custom' or 'norm'), still its world will tend towards entropy because any number of other possible permutations of relations is likely to occur to it in future. Order and pattern in the world are eaten up by the organism shuffling and recombining the relations between components of circuits and networks of circuits in its body and mind – ideas and neurons – and shuffling and recombining the relations between components of its external world – objects and events. In short, proceeding alongside the habituation of life is a degree of entropy: relations between the components of an aggregate being mixed up, unsorted, random, unpredictable, unorderly.

The organism deals with entropy in two contrasting ways. Bateson calls them evolutionary versus tautological: an embracing of the implications and ramifications of possible change versus a homeostatic eschewing of them. The watchwords of the latter tautological process (also to be known as 'epigenetic' and 'embryological') are: coherence, steady state, rigour and compatibility. The process acts as a critical filter, demanding certain standards of conformity in the perceiving and thinking individual. Left to itself it proceeds towards tautology: towards nothing being added once the initial arbitrary axioms and definitions of order have been laid down. Hence, the first test of a new idea is: is it consistent with the *status quo ante?* is it entirely latent in the original axioms which supply the 'proof' of its correctness. In the tautological procedure, in short, every 'becoming' is tied back to the *status quo ante.*

Contrastively, the evolutionary process is exploratory, creative and stochastic, feeding on the random to make new designations of order. From the steady supply of random perceptions, from 'no-things', new information is made, new 'some-things' by a non-random selection process which causes some mutations of prior order to survive longer than others and so be maintained and taken into the future. Here is an ongoing, endless trial and error with new things and relations, setting off down new, randomly presented pathways, some of which are then chosen as components of a new order. Collecting new mutations, new imaginations, evolutionary thought gathers new 'solutions' to the problems of meaning in the world, empirically testing these solutions according to new cybernetic circuiting.[8]

If the tautological process is seen in terms of the DNA of an embryo which will determine how that organism will develop over time only in accord with latent, originary genetic terms, then the evolutionary process is one of genetic mutation where random changes will continually throw up potential alternative pathways of adaption. And Bateson deliberately juxtaposes the patterns of these different logical levels. Tautology operates alike at the logical level of the individual organism and at that of thought in his cranium, at the level of cultural patterns and again in terms of ecological systems. Evolution occurs in the mind as in the brain as in the gene pool of the population.

'Evolution and Tautology are dialectically linked'

If there are two realms, that of tautology (whose essence is predictable repetition and replication) and that of evolution (whose essence is creativity, exploration and change), then life entails an alternation of a dialectical kind between the two. As mental processes and phenomenal happenings the two may be adversarial, but a zigzag between them whereby each determines the other would appear to be necessary for the continuation of life. Homeostasis and adaption, structure and process, form and function, status and learning, conservatism and radicalism, quantity and pattern, homology and analogy, calibration and feedback... these are 'dialectical plural necessities of the living world' (Bateson 1980: 237). The survival of life involves the marriage of random mutation (independent of existing ordered environments) and environmental demands, the regularities of functioning systems (minds, bodies, social systems, eco-systems). The procedure of life runs continuously between disruption and self-healing consistency, between new existential contexts and old.

Fantasia

A Conversation in Wanet Village

Doris: Someone's reported you, Nigel, to the Kendal DHSS office. An inspector is coming tomorrow to see all our PAYE and National Insurance returns on all the people employed here on the farm or self-employed. Someone is making trouble for us... Actually it could be someone making trouble for Sid – boasting about all the work he's doing here at the moment. Because he does have a big mouth... Maybe someone like Eddie Shaw, because they don't get on at the moment. Or how about Steven Webster because we are using Sid here on the JCB; and Karen did see a Land Rover come and go out of the farmyard on Saturday without stopping, so Steven could have seen Sid's van and gone again? It wouldn't have been Hesketh in the Land Rover or he would have stopped... Or does it mean someone making trouble for Chris Noble, Fred? Could he get done?

Fred: No. We don't hire Chris as often as we could or pay him as much as he could earn; although all his different employers together could push him over the limit. We certainly don't want to make trouble for him, or mean he's paying more taxes. As for Sid, he's paid for each little job as he goes on – like the digger job... And I'm not sure that he keeps all the cards from his different jobs anyway.

Doris: So who's reported us? Could it be Glover? Or Tyler, making a fuss?

Fred: No it wouldn't be Tyler. He's not the kind of bloke to do this sort of thing – whatever else he is. Nor Glover: he'd not complain like this... There always seem to be complaints like this, you always seem to get people complaining. Like against Old Bainesy who used to work a little extra in the evenings after work. Folks don't like you to get on and be a bit better and richer than you were... These offcomers in the city get lots of pay for a few hours work a week: forty-hour weeks! And then two days off completely at weekends. I'd like that PAYE man to try working here for a day – never mind a year – and see how he likes it – how tired he gets! Then maybe he and the rest would go away and stop bothering us.

Doris: When the PAYE man comes tomorrow, Nigel, 3.15, you be here, and you too Keith. And say nowt unless you're asked. I may get stroppy if the PAYE man does... And I may ask if its a complaint or simply a spot-check... Maybe you drive a tractor up and down the yard outside, Keith...

The Conversation Contextualised

The Harveys, Doris and Fred, and children Keith and Karen, Craig and Jessica, live on Cedar High Farm in the village and dale of Wanet, in north-west England (cf. Rapport 1993). Wanet is a small rural valley, hill-farming country, and Cedar High Farm is a family farm with a dairy herd and a flock of sheep. Wanet is also a tourist destination and, in the summers in particular, the 650 inhabitants of the dale and the 200 inhabitants of the village can be outnumbered by visitors: fell-walkers, campers, caravaners, pot-holers, second-home owners and retired day-trippers. Hence, Cedar High Farm also runs a camping ground and caravan site to take advantage of the seasonal influx.

Doris and Fred were born in Wanet, and have lived here all their lives (apart from a spell in the Navy for Fred). Notwithstanding, Doris and Fred find themselves rather unsettled at present with a number of worries. They are worried about the future livelihoods of their elder children, Keith (19) and Karen (15), soon having financially to fend for themselves beyond the family home. They are worried for their younger children and for themselves who must still depend on the family farm.

Expanding the latter, its acreage (60 acres now rented and owned) and its livestock (80 cows – 40 in milk – and 100 sheep) has been one tactic they have employed to take advantage of an economy of scale (along with hiring more occasional labour, and renting more land) and modernising the farm has been another (through building a new cowshed and grass silo). But then the farm must now compete against those Wanet neighbours equally eager to remain viable by whatever means. Finally, there are worries which accrue from an ongoing influx of residential newcomers to Wanet (as in other rural areas of Britain) – many entering retirement, but some of working age and most having come from urban environments and in search of a 'country' lifestyle. In their wake, the character, the work and age profiles of Wanet, as village and dale, have become uncertain. In short, Doris and Fred have worries over their relations with their farming neighbours, with their new non-farming neighbours, and with their adolescent children. All of which also adds up to a certain amount of tension between Doris and Fred themselves. Will they cope, and will their chosen financial, social and parental strategies prevail?

This is to provide some broad contextualisation to the above conversation. For a number of months, I have been resident on Cedar High Farm in the role of apprentice farm labourer – temporarily away from college so as to learn the practice of hill-farming (I am in my early-twenties). But it is not that long after my arrival that Doris finds herself threatened by the imminent visitation of a tax-inspector, wishing to check the farm's records and returns. Let me now, then, add a more proximate (if still brief) contextualisation to her and Fred's words.

Doris opens the letter from the Government tax office as she is about to set out in the car on her milk-round. She is in the kitchen of Cedar High farmhouse, with husband Fred having recently come in from his morning's milking and now sitting eating the breakfast that their elder daughter Karen has prepared for him. The letter shocks Doris; she reads it through to herself, then sits down at the table again and reads it to Fred.

At that point, son Keith and farm-lad Nigel come in from mucking out the milking shippon and sweeping the yard, and Doris tells them the news. Some 'little Hitler' has been cooking up trouble for them. One of those bureaucrats who sit in warm offices sharpening pencils all day and thinking up schemes to hinder the prospects of working people – small businessmen who slave all hours to keep their independent enterprises alive – wants to come and check they have been properly filling out (in triplicate) their income tax (Pay As You Earn) and national insurance returns. The event, sadly, is all too familiar. Even small farmers, in a small village like Wanet, are subject these days to the increased 'dictation' of officialdom. It is a symptom of the sick country Britain has become. Rather than assisting in the survival of small businesses, governments interfere to the extent that the likes of Fred and Doris, and those they employ part-time as extra labour – Nigel, Sid, Chris Noble – may go out of business.

What is also sad – if similarly expectable these days – is that it is likely that the Harveys were reported to the tax-man by someone local, probably one of their farming neighbours. While, by rights, neighbours should be standing firm and united against this interference by outsiders, there are so many outsiders living in Wanet these days that local people come to be increasingly divided against themselves. They take on the characters of the outsiders, becoming fickle in their friendships, scheming and competitive, anxious to hinder one another's prospects at getting on in the world and being secure, or being a bit richer and better than they were.

So Doris sets about reckoning who is likely to be behind the incident. Is it someone getting at Nigel, at Sid, at Chris, she wonders aloud, or someone getting at her and Fred through them? Doris knows that Sid has a big mouth and can be boastful – fatal qualities in Wanet nowadays. People get to know your business and thus how to reverse your good fortunes. For the sake of business survival, these days, you must be careful not to express an opinion around Wanet, never mind revealing any actual business news. So, Sid has probably antagonised someone. Eddie Shaw and he don't get on – too much alike in terms of temperament – while Steven Webster could be annoyed that she and Fred are currently employing Sid (and not his firm) on the mechanical digger. In fact, if it were Steven, that would explain the incident the other day when a Land Rover drove into the farmyard and straight out again without stopping. Karen was in the kitchen, but couldn't see who was driving. It could have been Steven Webster checking up on Sid, or just arriving by accident, seeing Sid at work and guessing that he would put the cash straight into his back-pocket and not admit it to the tax people. The only other Land Rover Doris can think of at that time of day would be Richard Hesketh's, come to buy some eggs, but he would have stopped and stayed for a chat. Unless Fred thinks it is someone trying to make trouble for Chris Noble?

Chris Noble is a small tenant farmer, and Fred knows that any extra work he undertakes as a 'second job' must be limited in hours and income. But he and Chris are careful to keep his employment on Cedar High Farm within those limits. However, Chris also works occasionally for other farmers. Maybe someone has got wind that altogether this income pushes him up into another tax bracket? As for Sid, Fred doesn't see how even the tax people could keep track of all the little jobs that he does for different people in and around Wanet. As Sid says of himself, he stays tricky and hard to catch!

If it is not their employees, then, Doris continues, maybe the targets are her and Fred. Like them, Tom Glover has a milk-round and some caravans, and all he seems to think about is how to undercut Doris's prices. There is enough custom for both of them to prosper in Wanet but Glover insists on competing and trying to drive her and Fred out of business. Reporting them like this would be another ploy of his. Or else it's Tim Tyler. He sits inside his house on his back-

side all day, instead of getting out on the land (looking pasty-faced because his wife Meg underfeeds him), but he's still had it in for her and Fred ever since they started making a go of it on Cedar High Farm and expanding their operation. All he manages to come up with when you actually meet him in the pub is something snide and sarcastic about their success.

Fred doesn't think that Glover or Tyler would stoop to reporting them like this, however, whatever else they would do and say against them. But then it seems to Fred almost a general condition of life that there always will be other people trying to hold you back – keeping you small and pitiable, making you dependent, coveting your land and your stock, envying your success, even your hard work. There are always stories around of neighbours picking on each other out of sheer spite. Fred remembers how, way back, someone even had it in for Old Man Baines, an innocuous and mild bachelor who did a bit of walling on the side (when he finished working on the railways in the evening). What makes it worse these days is that outsiders are getting mixed up in it too; locals are using outsiders to get at one another. And these outsiders just don't understand how life is in Wanet: what it takes to eke out a living on the land. They sit in plush city offices, work short hours, are assured of their pay, and then saunter out to Wanet and have the nerve to tell people what they can and cannot do to earn their livelihoods. As if it were not Wanet folk who had been bred on the land! As if soft and lazy city folk also had what it takes to work without tiring or stopping.

Finally, getting up from the table again and putting on her coat, Doris considers the practical implications. She will do the talking, when the inspector comes tomorrow, and lead him into the kitchen. There, she'll find out as much as she can from him about what lies behind the incident; she'll get aggressive with him if he is with her. Fred will be there too, to lend moral support, while Nigel and Keith are to look busy, but say nothing, outside. As youngsters they shouldn't be expected to have anything to say, and Doris can thereby keep guard on what information leaves Cedar High and ensure the family's reputation. If this is a Harvey matter then they will remain united. After all, they have done nothing wrong, merely providing for their offspring, and for strays like Nigel too.

The actual visit of the inspector, the following day, lasts about twenty minutes. Nigel and Keith chop up an old tree stump in the farmyard as Doris and Fred meet with him in the kitchen. Afterwards, as they emerge from the farmhouse, Doris smiles and bids the inspector farewell in his car. 'It was no alarm!' she explains with relief, to Nigel and Keith, eager for news:

> It was just a routine check! And he said he was on his way to two more places updale afterwards... Probably to Shorts' cos I doubt his two lads are written up right. It seemed like Fred and I only saw him for a few minutes

in the kitchen... And the Inspector was very nice. He just asked Fred for his National Insurance number. 'No', Fred said [she puts on a gruff voice], 'I don't know it', so the man said – very helpful and posh – 'That's no trouble: I can easily find it out from your name and date of birth', and that was it!

Chuckling, Doris goes back into the house.

Later in the day, Sid calls to do a spot of digging, and Nigel finds Fred and Doris, in the kitchen, recounting the episode with the inspector, now far more relaxed and jocular:

Fred: ...Aye, so the inspector said, 'Who's that guy outside with the glasses and the moustache?' [i.e. Nigel]
Doris: Aye! I'm surprised he didn't ask about you, Nigel. If I'd come here, you'd have looked the most suspicious to me.
Sid: He says, 'Who's that guy outside with the glasses and the moustache?' And I say, 'He's just some loony we're taking care of for a while!'

In the denouement of the incident, then, prior expectations again come to be fulfilled. Of course it was nothing to worry about, Doris can report, just routine; because nice posh people like the inspector – upper class – can see that middle class folks like her and Fred are doing their best. She and Fred are trying hard to better themselves, working within the law, and their efforts should be respected. Fred might not have all his tax details to hand (such as his N.I. registration), but that is understandable given their circumstances, and the inspector is pleased to help by not putting them to any more trouble. This is a very different reception to what some others can expect, however, such as the lower class Shorts. The inspector will no doubt find much to keep him busy on their farm – with their rebellious attitudes to proper standards of book-keeping, their general laziness and deliberate flouting of the ethic of self-reliance and endeavour. His visit to Shorts farm will be far from routine or short-lived.

And when they think about it, Doris and Fred find themselves lucky that the inspector didn't suddenly take against Nigel. Because he stands out as obviously not part of the local, hard-working effort on Cedar High Farm. There he is, a student, wearing glasses and with hair on his face, looking distinctly out of place in Wanet – even up to no good. No wonder they used to call Nigel a 'mystery man' when he first arrived in the dale. Having come from nowhere, without a family or name, claiming to be British and yet behaving so oddly, being so ignorant and naive, it was little wonder that some people joked he could be a spy – or else part of the Baader-Meinhof gang, the boyfriend of that Astrid Proll who was meant to have passed through Wanet a few years back! Sid used to tease Nigel with the nicknames 'Professor', and 'Joshua', and 'Whiskers', and Sid still found him rather suspect. But then he seemed harmless enough to Doris; he might be a nothing, a waif, even a bit simple, but the Harveys would take care of him for a while before seeing him out of the dale again and on his way.

The Conversation Fantasised

Conversation, Berger and Luckmann have contended (1966: 140), is our most important vehicle of reality-maintenance. What I now intend is to identify in the above conversation a number of those notions which Bateson introduces concerning our human reality, its perceptual construction, orderly interpretation and creative maintenance:

i)   The conversation reveals a mental map (or maps) of their village and social environment which Doris and Fred cognitively and verbally draw. The maps serve as existential contexts of their lives.

ii)   Doris and Fred's efforts are towards first delineating and then detailing the landscape and the landmarks of these maps, and then entering the spaces they have created by taking action in terms of them. Here, then, is a business landscape, with such landmarks as 'tax returns', 'tax inspectors', 'neighbours' and 'employees', 'outsiders' and 'locals', 'city folk' and 'farmers'. Here is also a local rural landscape with landmarks called 'Eddie Shaw', 'Sid', 'Hesketh's Land Rover', 'Shorts' lads', 'complaints against Old Bainesy'. Entering these spaces, Doris and Fred cogitate on the likelihood of 'Glover', 'Tyler', 'the inspector' acting in certain ways, and plan their own actions in response: 'getting stroppy', 'having tractors driven up and down', and so on.

iii) These maps are not the territory of Wanet or of England, or of the economic climate, or of the government tax regime in a recession. These remain ineffable things. All we have are Doris and Fred's perceptual constructions of these things, as I interpret them. And these constructions do not rely on exterior or independent validation. They are true for Doris and Fred because they continue to believe them to be true: because this is how they perceive and codify the world; because they explain the world in terms of tautologies whose proof is circular, returning to axioms and principles inherent from the beginning; and because the axioms and principles derive from their own individual processes of ideation, their self-stimulations, which need not accord with the distinct things-in-themselves of which they are intended codifications. Nor need their constructions accord with the constructions of purposive others who figure in Doris and Fred's own mapping: their maps are not the territory of Sid or Tom Glover or the tax inspector either. The maps represent simply Doris and Fred's ongoing decisions and achievements in perceiving and codifying their environment in ways which continue to make sense to them and to secure certain goals.

iv)   Doris and Fred construct landscapes and landmarks by differentiating themselves from them: by perceiving a host of differences which make a difference to them. Moreover they construct a sameness between themselves (as a married couple) by claiming to share corresponding relations of difference. Hence, Fred and Doris are not Nigel or Sid or Chris Noble, or Eddie Shaw or Steven Webster, or the tax inspector, or 'offcomers', or complaining locals. And equally, it is as a couple that they are not these other people; they are alike, then, in being the focus of others' malign intentions. By conversing together, Doris and Fred express jointly their common experience and they realise jointly their mutual experiencing. With a common outlook on the environment and a common location within it, by treating other objects and events and being treated alike by them in return, they have a shared reality, a type of context for their knowing and acting, over and above their logical, bodily separation.

v)   Indeed, the more otherness in the landscape in front of them, the more surely Doris and Fred provide themselves with their own distinct identities. The more differences, and of different kinds, the more detailed and full and complex their own selves, and the more samenesses between them as a married couple.

vi)   Moreover, the more implicated they are in a certain context of action, in a certain landscape and set of landmarks, not only the more the evidence of their own existence, but also the evidence of their power. Doris and Fred become centres of orientation of the actions of others and they are centres of action in the affecting of others. Hence, Eddie Shaw, Steven Webster, Richard Hesketh, the tax inspector, outsiders in the city, Glover and Tyler, Keith and Nigel, all represent part of the context of Doris and Fred's actions, significant to Doris and Fred, and vice-versa.

vii) Once Doris and Fred have expressed it, the truth-value of the maps of their environment appears indubitable to them. Of course, tax inspectors, city folk, fickle neighbours, Sid and the Shorts, upper class and lower class individuals, will behave like this; of course, Glover and Tyler, Hesketh and Doris and Fred themselves would not behave like this. Prior expectations fulfil themselves, being not merely expressed but also realised through the medium of the conversation.

viii) Furthermore, even when prior expectations bring bad news, at least Doris and Fred have met these situations before and know how to react. Finding their expectations fulfilled is better than not understanding what is happening or not knowing what to do. It shows Doris and Fred that their maps have been and continue to be accurate; it shows them they are still successful in working out what is what. In fact, there is a certain satisfaction in finding the world to be the same old place it always was – even if that place is one of animosity rather than harmony. Hence, Doris and Fred want to find what they know they will find: their informations coincide with their evaluation.

ix) In a way, then, Doris and Fred's conversation is not simply a real-isation of a mapping of the world and their contexts of action within it, but also an ostentatious guarding and maintaining of that world. Speaking before their children, and then before Sid, Doris and Fred show others and convince themselves of their ability to cope, to survive. They are alive and they are self-sufficient, party to relations in a social and physical environment which they are able to maintain in equilibrium or homeostasis.

x) Finally, there is the invention and evolution of maps here too. This is seen in the humour with which Fred and Sid come to dismantle the episode of the visit, inventing new words and character for the inspector and the interaction, and he and it become means to tease Nigel, to make him the only outsider figure in a social milieu in which they and the inspector are now friendly equals. And Doris does the same, in less light-hearted fashion. For her, the visit of the inspector becomes part of an evolution in her map-making whereby she is able gradually to construct a new identity for Fred, herself and her family, as middle class and upwardly mobile farmer-landowners. This is most obvious in the difference between the attitudes she adopts before and after the inspector's visit. Indeed, during my time in Wanet there were a number of occurrences of this kind in Doris's (and her family's) perceptions, evidencing I suggest a cumulative habituation of a new cognitive pathway as Doris and Fred's confidence grew. Their 'middle class codifications' satisfied their senses of self, were reinforced by their thus being valued, and hence became embodied in a new mapping of the world, its objects and relations.

xi) This may be identified more clearly by focusing on the way in which Doris and her family's construction of the notion of 'posh-ness' – as a marker of upward mobility – and its relation to themselves, changed over time. The incident with the tax inspector took place at the end of April. At the beginning of February, Doris and Fred had travelled to Aldershot, where their son Keith had recently enrolled in the army, so as to witness the induction ceremony. On their return, Doris described the 'posh' accents they had met:

> The Major spoke to Fred and his wife spoke to me. I didn't realise at first who she was! Then I did, and I put on a posh voice too, and we discussed the weather and the Dales and how army life would be a big change for Keith.

Doris seemed pleased with herself on this occasion, willing and able to adapt to the situation of also being posh. In the context of Wanet, however, it was often a derogatory comment if Doris or Fred described a neighbour who 'talked posh', and a few days before the visit of the inspector, Doris had explained to me:

> Sorry, Nigel, but our manners and our table aren't posh like some folks' are. Farmers don't have time for posh manners.

But then the following week, Doris had admitted:

> I like your refined accent, Nigel. It sounds nicer than my flatter dialect... Are your parents posh? If they're not, why don't they come and stay in a caravan here in the summer?

Here is an ambiguity and an uncertainty, but not a hostility towards poshness. It is something to which Doris would aspire, even if she still finds it hard to reconcile it with their lifestyle as farmers in Wanet. Three weeks later, however, while the ambiguity is still present and the intonation regarding poshness remains wry (but not derogatory), poshness, even in Wanet, becomes something in terms of which Doris can now imagine measuring her and Fred's own, changing status:

> Webster will not be with some common bank; he'll be with Lloyds – posh – not common old Nat-West like us. And the same with his newspapers: he'll read the Times or the Observer, won't he Fred? And he eats at Hattie's restaurant too. But see, Nigel, Fred and me don't like the sort of food she serves up at the 'Rural Hearth'. We've got sort of half-way tastes, Fred and me.

Finally, some months later, Doris delivers the following verdict in which life in Wanet and life in Britain as a whole find accommodation in the same picture. She is describing difficult financial circumstances for herself and Fred, and yet there is a confidence that she is right to consider her and Fred in relation to those 'posh' people who have made a success out of social mobility:

> Wherever you go in British society there are class differences, Nigel. Like you may think all the women working on factory machines are the same class, but you find one has six kids and a dirty house, and messy, while another owns her house – its not a council house – and she does okay for herself. So, classes are there after all... And its the same among farmers, like in Wanet. We are middle class now. But there are also people in Wanet who don't try – lower class – and there are also one or two upper class... The upper class farmers are those who people know are upper class cos of how they go, how they act. They act bigger: they got more money... And its harder for the middle classes in a recession, of course. Like for us. There's the mortgage to pay for, and farm tools and what have you. Whereas the upper class come into their farm by inheriting, and everything is paid for: the house and tools, all the extras... Fred and me are now in the process of

moving up another... of moving ahead. So its a hard time and we may not make it; we may have to sell out in the end. But you must move with the times, and change, to survive. Ooh look! Our new printed adverts for Cedar High Farm! How posh we're getting.

What these snippets of conversation reveal, I suggest, is the gradual perceiving by Doris of a new mapping of the new world, a new context, in which to situate herself and her family. She relates herself to old landmarks differently; she makes new landmarks. She delineates a different landscape, one linking Wanet to what lies beyond it, linking farmers to army officers, bankers and government inspectors. In this landscape, status is flexible; it is not, here, a question of being either born in Wanet (and hence a local) or not (and hence an outsider), for instance. Now she can imagine her and Fred's relations with certain foods, newspapers, banks, and accents changing with time, and she comes to judge others and herself in terms of new criteria: land-ownership, house mortgage, inherited property. She can imagine her and Fred meeting new people and seeing less of those they have known who are less willing to try hard, learn and change. From a state of surprise, of not recognising or being nonplussed by poshness, Doris comes to recognise it in those immediately around her, and to expect it universally.

Coda

The creativity of Doris and Fred's perceptions – their achievement of tautology and of evolution in their codification and evaluation of the world – and also the idiosyncrasy of their perceptions – their distinctness and particularity to themselves – amount to what may be termed an individual tropology or technology. It is the individuality of our shaping of the external world, our providing ourselves with personal contexts of action, that I shall treat more specifically in this final part of the chapter.

'Tropology' and 'technology' convey an understanding of the ubiquitous process of externalising and objectifying the experiences of the human body: constructing the outside world as an image of our perceptions of things, parts, relations, functions, complexities and contradictions internal to ourselves. Through these representations, one attains to knowledge and control; by objectifying oneself one comes to know oneself, also to see oneself in a context of self-control. It is through externalisation and the contexts of significance this provides that individuals come to consciousness.

This also points up the inherent diversity of processes of externalisation, and the inherent subjectivity of the objectifications it gives onto.

For the external object is not the internal perception, as Bateson would say; while the transformation from the one to the other might hope to retain a connecting pattern of differences, still they remain different logical types. Moreover, what is lost in the transformation is the process of determination of perceptual meaning, the recovery of which can never be anything but indeterminate. It is for this reason that Bateson describes all human phenomena as appearances, dependent upon individual perception and mapping, upon guessing at wholes from parts. Since there can be no direct communication between logical levels or types (between experience and its objectification), individuals are 'free' to perceive, and act on perceptions, independently of others even while seemingly in interaction with them. Moreover, Bateson insists upon what he called the 'non-responsiveness' of human perception and its evolution. Both the objective form and the subjective content of representation derived *a priori* from individual externalisation rather than exterior determination or environmental demand.

Finally, then, when Bateson explains that the unit of evolution is man-environment rather than man or environment *per se*[9] – a mind immanent in 'pathways and messages' both inside the body and outside (1972: 436) – we can appreciate, paradoxically as it may seem, not just the absoluteness of human individuality but also the ultimate reality of such individuality in human being. Man-environment – the map of perceptions in which the human individual continues to place himself and in whose terms he continues to act (independent of any ineffable thingness of the environment) – is the individual foundation upon which all else rests.

This also includes context. Context comes to be understood as something particular and personal, more private to the individual than publicly shared and inherent in an interactional setting. For, context concerns the ways in which individuals continue to imbue tropes and techniques with meaning, cognitively relating to them, and relating particular tropes and techniques to others. Hence, the same context may pertain in any number of externally different settings —and the converse: the 'same' moment of interaction may be made cognitively significant in any number of different ways. Individuals may inhabit any number of very different contexts, at once or over time, depending on their particular and personal processes of externalisation. Context is something which individuals bring to their interactions with others and deploy in their actions and interpretations.

This is not to say that there cannot be regularity or consistency between contextual definition and external setting, but that the decision of this relation is an internal one, not forced upon the individual by supposed structural immanencies of the situation or by partners in the interaction. It is the individual who decides upon the lineaments, meaning and identity of particular settings, their links to other habitual settings, and the behaviours appropriate to himself, and to others, in each. This does not preclude the possibility of contextualisation and meaning becoming shared, however. If interactions represent situations where individual contexts are deployed and expressed, then there is the possibility, as Fernandez put it, of an empathetic meeting: of individuals at least sharing a sense of what it is 'like' in the context of another's life even if not within the latter sensorium as such. This is part-and-parcel of the extended negotiation between individuals in which we have found Doris and Fred partaking.

To recall, once more, the Russellian notion of logical types and levels which Bateson sees as marking at once the differentiation and the interrelation of the world, one might say that there can be different levels of context. In disinterring the logic behind and meaning within Doris's and Fred's words, then, we moved among a number of domains of significance: from the broader to the more proximate, the more private to the more potentially shared. Context begins as an individual representation, originating in individual processes of externalisation, but inasmuch as interactions between individuals give onto levels of routine social organisation of more inclusive (if less meaningful, less meaning-rich) kinds, one might identify different levels of context, of greater and lesser simplicity and ambiguity, in which the primary contexts of greater or lesser numbers of individuals formally meet (cf. Rapport 1994). Through negotiation, through empathy and through chance it is possible for the contextual representations made by different individuals (as with the same individual at different times) to overlap.

In short, there are a number of possible levels in terms of which social interaction can be read, as Dilley puts it (1991: 32), from the more private to the more public, the more latent to the more manifest. One can record the diversity of contextualisation which pertains to one individual, at one time and over time, and one can record the diversity which pertains among individuals as they interact and negotiate ongoing social relations. What is to be remembered is that context remains first and foremost a domain of significance of personal provenance.[10]

Notes

1. The root of the word, Cooper explains, is *tuche*, meaning chance, fate or that which lies beyond human control. *Techne* is therefore what turns chance to human advantage (1993: 279).
2. In part, Ingold project's (1992: passim) is comparable. What the Greek word *techne* should alert us to, Ingold suggests, is the artistry, the expressiveness and the aestheticism, inherent in crafting a world, and the bodily skills of practising within it. Instead, we fetishise the process of objectification as such; what the seventeenth-

century compound word *technology* has led us to emphasise is that technological application entails an objective system of rational principles and rules: we make an object out of our making of objects. Properly, however, a 'technologist' is a being wholly immersed in the rational nexus of an instrumental coping-in-the-world – while we have come to see merely the mechanical application of technological rules.

3. Or again: cell to tissue to organ to organism to society; individual human being to human society to ecosystem (Bateson 1972: 433, 415).

4. Berkeley's error was in confusing logical types. 'The falling tree that no-one hears makes no sound' is a correct conclusion inasmuch as 'tree', 'sound' and 'fall' exist as such only as part of a human system of classification and communication; (the quotation marks are basic to their nature). But admitting this truth says nothing at all about the ineffable world of thingness where latent differences – standing and falling trees – do not become human information (Bateson 1980: 108).

5. Death, conversely, Bateson defines as the breaking up of recursive circuits (1980: 142).

6. The effect is nevertheless a real one for Bateson, and highly significant. It is sufficient to differentiate, for instance, the mind, a system of interacting parts, from other such systems. Galaxies, sand dunes, toy cars are similarly wholes of parts, then, but they do not amount to 'thinking systems' themselves. For some reason, the recursive process in these interacting systems does not lead to circuitry of higher logical levels, to meta-levels, so that there is here no perceiving of their own perceptions, no consciousness. The ontology of the specialness of the mind is one of 'the great untouched questions', Bateson concludes (1980: 226).

7. Bateson derives a definition of stress from his notion of the normal creativity of the individual as energy source (1980: 245). 'Stress', then, is: 'the lack of alternative pathways engendered in and by an organism, all of them being in current use. Here is a lack of flexibility resulting from excessive demands having previously been placed upon the thinking system.

8. It is for this reason, Bateson elaborates, that history is unpredictable and does not lend itself to the teleology of a Marxian (or otherwise deterministic) analysis. Since the evolution of individuals' world-views is unpredictable, individuals are not interchangeable in the process of cultural invention and social change; history cannot be written (any more than culture and society) in denial or ignorance of individual specificity for it is of the utmost significance which individual does what. Individual uniqueness means that individuals, acting as individuals, are never party to 'convergent' or tautological social processes (1980: 51-52), while such concepts as Group Mind and a Collective Unconscious become meaningless (1936: 176).

9. Bateson (1972: 423, 426): 'organism plus environment'; 'organism-in-its-environment.' For the unit of evolution always includes a completed pathway of messages surrounding the protoplasmic aggregate. Hence: DNA-in-the-cell, cell-in-the-body, body-in-the-environment.

10. I am very grateful to Deborah Wickering, Bob Cooper, Nick Lee, Jannis Kallinikos and David Knights for their critical commentary on versions of this essay.

Bibliography

Bateson, G. 1936. *Naven*. Cambridge: Cambridge University Press.

———. 1958. 'Language and psychotherapy', *Psychiatry* 21: 96-100.

———. 1959. 'Anthropological theories'. *Science* 129: 294-98.

———. 1972. *Steps to an ecology of mind*. London: Paladin.

———. 1980. *Mind and nature: a necessary unity*. Glasgow: Fontana.

———— and D. Jackson, J. Haley, and J. Weakland. 1974. 'Towards a theory of schizophrenia'. In D. Jackson (ed.), *Communication, family and marriage.* 32-49. Palo Alto: Science and Behaviour Books.

———— and J. Reusch. 1951. *Communication.* New York: Norton.

Berger, P. 1969. *The sacred canopy.* New York: Doubleday.

Berger, P. and T. Luckmann. 1966. *The social construction of reality.* New York: Doubleday.

Cooper, R. 1993. 'Technologies of representation'. In P. Ahonen (ed.), *Tracing the semiotic boundaries of politics.* 279-312. Berlin: Mouton de Gruyter.

Dilley, R. 1991. 'Interpreting Tukolor oral literature: the myth of origin of the nine Mabube clan names'. In P. Baxter and R. Fardon (eds), 'Voice, genre, text: anthropological essays in Africa and beyond'. *Bulletin of John Rylands University Library of Manchester* 73(3): 25-36.

Fernandez, J. 1977. 'Poetry in motion: being moved by amusement, by mockery and by mortality in the Asturian countryside'. *New Literary History* VIII:3: 459-83.

————. 1982. *Bwiti.* Princeton: Princeton University Press.

————. 1986. 'Persuasions and Performances: of the beast in every body... and the metaphors of everyman'. In his *Persuasions and performances.* 3-27. Bloomington: Indiana University Press.

————. 1992. 'What it is like to be a Banzie: on sharing the experience of an equatorial microcosm'. In J. Gort, H. Vroom, R. Fernhout and A. Wessels (eds), *On sharing religious experience.* 125-35. Amsterdam: Rodopi.

Foucault, M. 1977. *Language, counter-memory, practice.* Ithaca: Cornell University Press.

Gadamer, H-G. 1976. *Philosophical hermeneutics.* Berkeley: University of California Press.

Ingold, T. 1992. 'Technology, language, intelligence: a reconsideration of basic concepts'. In K. Gibson and T. Ingold (eds), *Tools, language and cognition in human evolution.* 337-45. Cambridge: Cambridge University Press.

Rapport, N.J. 1993. *Diverse world-views in an English village.* Edinburgh: Edinburgh University Press.

————. 1994. '"Busted for hash": common catchwords and individual identities in a Canadian city'. In V. Amit-Talai and H. Lustiger-Thaler (eds), *Urban lives.* 129-57. Toronto: McClelland and Stewart.

————. 1995. 'Migrant selves and stereotypes: personal context in a postmodern world'. In S. Pile and N. Thrift (eds) *Mapping the subject.* 267-82. London: Routledge.

Sapir, E. 1956. *Culture, language and personality.* Berkeley: University of California Press.

Wagner, R. 1991. 'Poetics and the recentering of anthropology'. In I. Brady (ed.), *Anthropological poetics.* 37-46. Savage: Rowman Littlefield.

Wallace, A.F.C. 1961. 'The psychic unity of human groups'. In B. Kaplan (ed.), *Studying personality cross-culturally.* 129-58. New York: Harper and Row.

Chapter 9

CULTURE AND CONTEXT

THE EFFECTS OF VISIBILITY

Penelope Harvey

Context and the Cultural Construct

Context and interpretation have a problematic status in contemporary cultural analysis. Theories of knowledge, concepts of truth and authenticity, modes of description and interpretation have been shaken by the critiques of certain forms of modernist scholarship, particularly those that advocate the general application of abstracted theoretical entities. In some disciplines such as history and sociology this challenge to the flattening effect of generalised theoretical context has been met by the (re)introduction of the concept of culture, above all to explain the differing outcomes of modernisation and account for its subjective, interpretative aspects.[1] This 'cultural turn' introduced a consideration of the dynamics of everyday life and operated as a force to reformulate traditional disciplinary concerns (Robertson 1992).

With regard to culture, anthropologists have a somewhat different trajectory behind them. In this field there is a concern that the concept of culture has become a liability, over-homogenising, too static – an effect of description rather than its precondition. Nevertheless it is a concept which seems hard to dispose of, lying as it does at the heart of the anthropological endeavour.

Culture is construed as a repository of information, explicit in the techniques of ethnomethodologists whose entry into another culture is through acquiring the tools of 'knowing how' to operate within its categories. The

goal is to uncover ground rules, templates, codes, structures as informa-
tion-bearing devices. The concept of culture thus demarcates the distinctiveness of the kind of information needed to be a member of a particular
group, enclave, institution. ... All societies thus 'have' culture, and the 'how
to' rules and practices by which people conduct their lives afford an unwitting reservoir of information for the outsider. It is because we think that all
societies have cultures, that we can play one off against another, engage in
comparison, and ultimately use one's own culture as a foil for understanding others. (Strathern 1987a: 30)

It is a commonplace of anthropological discourse to understand the
objectification of social knowledge in rules and norms, as cultural
constructs. Constructs are by their very nature partial and the
knowledge required to make sense of them is contextual. There is
always something else that can be revealed from another perspective.
In this sense forms are never complete but can always be added to
through thicker and thicker description, increasing the layers of contextualisation.

This awareness of culture as construct provoked reflection on the
constructed nature of anthropologists' own cultural products, the
processes through which ethnographic knowledge emerges as such[2]
and the ways in which contextual knowledge entails its own power, a
power which can imply a degree of control by the knower over the
known.[3] Anthropologists now have to deal with the awareness that
the objectifications of ethnographic monographs are at best partial, at
worst erroneous and misleading representations. Furthermore, as the
authorised knowledge of experts, particular interpretations might
have real material effects. Indeed, those who criticise the interven-
tionist nature of such practice, seek merely to move the site of the
effect from the researched to the researching community. The consistent feature, integral to all academic practice, is that new knowledge is
established in relation to, and often refutation of, previous expertise
(Bourdieu 1984). Thus radicals and reactionaries fight in similar ways
over foundational assumptions, interpretative possibilities, and issues
of adequate contextualisation. Nor are these processes particular to
the production and exchange of academic knowledge. Processes of
contextualisation and recontextualisation are themselves aspects of
communicative activity more generally and such interactions can
always be imbued with the effects of power. Thus, for the partial construct to operate as knowledge, authorisation and the establishment of
expertise is required.

The construct has another implication. People study the cultural
construction of sexuality, of childhood, of death, of economy, kinship,
etc. Such formulations assume an inherent point of comparison as the
analyst examines how a stable entity takes a particular form. Thus,

cultural constructionism posits cultural difference but not incommensurability. This aspect of the concept of culture as construct bears an uncanny resemblance to the outcomes of commodification processes, the worlds of advertising and entertainment where difference proliferates but there is no hint of incommensurability.[4] As culture becomes ubiquitous so does context, and as culture becomes increasingly reflexive, so too the context implodes.

Thirdly, the notion of culture as construct carries a connotation of intentionality and has often been linked to the assumption that cultural practices, and particularly cultural artefacts, are intrinsically communicative and that the task of the cultural analyst is to recover these meanings through interpretation. An alternative approach is to look at what cultural practice does, to study situated effects rather than attempting to recover cognitive schemas.[5] These positions emerge from decades of debate on the relationship between system and practice, representation and experience, but the issue is not trivial and returns us to the necessity of some kind of appeal to context. For as soon as we engage in the description of cultural effects, inevitably interpretative, provisional and partial, we call forth the necessity of contextualisation, the need to explain the cultural and social preconditions for such effects. Anthropological practice thus requires contextualisation. However, the practices which anthropologists describe are not necessarily adequately represented in these terms. Thus we find a further effect of partiality a concern with the nature of the gaps and spaces that descriptions produce.

One such gap, which is the subject of recent writings by Strathern, is that which emerges from the comparison between Melanesian and Euro-American ways of knowing. Collective activities such as clan engagements or initiation rituals are effective to the extent that they take pre-existing social relations apart (Strathern 1992b). Cultural practices are directed to eliciting particular partial forms, through processes of deconstruction or decomposition. Persons and social 'bodies' are ontologically whole, and effective cultural practice involves producing particular versions of that whole in social interactions. Thus fragmentation of the body/person/clan is an explicit aim of particular kinds of exchange. For these (remarkably Lacanian) subjects cultural work is about deconstructing merged/total unreproductive entities, about creating difference rather than achieving social unity.[6] Euro-Americans place the emphasis elsewhere. Here, it is the connections, not the separations, which are achieved, in cultural practice. Separation and fragmentation is deemed problematic.

My argument has come full circle in an attempt to show that contemporary problems with context and interpretation are intimately related to the notion of culture as construct. It is modernist notions of the construct, of the idea that knowledge emerges through progressive accumulation, and of a particular relationship between representation and truth, which has created the conditions for its own collapse. Strathern's distinction between Melanesian and Western forms of sociality, thus indicate an important contrast between approaches which posit ontological wholeness and see cultural practice as directed to fragmentation ('Melanesian'), and those which posit ontological fragmentation and see cultural practice as directed to building, construction, and accumulation ('Western'). In recent discussions of the ways in which distinctions are drawn within and between social entities, Strathern (1991b) and Wagner (1991) have addressed the partiality of *this* particular construct. They stress that the contrast also operates within what have been bounded as Melanesian or Western domains. Such arguments on the effects of scale in relation to the kinds of knowledge we produce as anthropologists echo Latour's claim that the West has never been modern (Latour 1993). He argues that it is the ability to invoke this paradigm situationally that has sustained western political and scientific dominance. It is in this spirit that I have explored the distinctions between 'Western' and 'Melanesian' understandings of culture and context as a means of revealing the centrality of the construct for anthropological practice, and of discussing the implicit dimensions of power in the relationship between interpretation and knowledge.

In the following sections of this chapter these issues are discussed in relation to two quite distinct research projects, whose differences both replicate and mediate the contrast between the Western and Melanesian cultural models described above. The first of these projects concerned Andean bilinguals and led me to reconsider the dynamic between preconditions and emergent effects in the communicative practices of these speakers.[7] The second centred on a World Fair, the Expo '92 held in Seville in 1992, and looked at the current relationship between three modernist institutions – the nation-state, the universal exhibition and the discipline of social anthropology.[8] This latter study raised interesting questions about anthropological method, particularly about how to locate/limit 'context' and about what kind of knowledge interpretation affords. In many ways the Expo '92 research exemplifies why 'context' is a problem for contemporary social theory, and perhaps particularly for social anthropology, and thus throws light on the earlier, more orthodox study. In both cases the heuristic role of both context and interpretation for the generation of anthropological knowledge will be considered. A guiding concern is to illustrate the difference between (i) the idea that knowledge/understanding is achieved via contextualisation, a process in which additional information is brought to bear from outside and beyond the interaction itself, and (ii) the idea that knowledge/understanding is achieved via interaction and concrete situated practice, that things are known in terms of their consequences and cultural entities are always in process.

Bilingualism in Contemporary Southern Peru

In the mid-1980s I lived in a bilingual community of Spanish/Quechua speakers in the southern Peruvian Andes and studied the use of bilingualism as a political resource, and the role of language in the establishment and maintenance of hierarchical social relations (Harvey 1987, 1991). Following Bourdieu (1977) and Bloch (1975), I was particularly interested in the relationship between power and symbolic practice. My initial naive intention had been to provide what many writers within sociolinguistics, pragmatics, the ethnography of speaking and critical linguistics were calling for – a more systematic account of the non-linguistic knowledge, the immediate social context, of linguistic interaction.[9] I would look at who said what to whom, when and where in order to account for the ways in which language carries meaning. However, 'context' is indeed the snake oil of sociolinguistics; it did not make everything better despite the claims.[10]

Who people were, what was said, and in which language, even the nature of the occasion itself, were clearly outcomes not starting points. In the first place there is the problem of how to distinguish and differentiate languages. The only constant I came up with here was the way in which the languages were symbolically discrete in the sense that one implicitly stood as context for the other. Thus to say something in Spanish was not the semantic equivalent of the utterance of the same propositional content in Quechua. To speak in one language was always implicitly not to speak in the other. Speaker identities were equally problematic and often contested in the very exchanges that I sought to describe. To further complicate matters language and identity were inextricably linked. The model of linguistic interaction as a reflection of social context with its related understanding of stable categories of persons, actions and events was not working.

The following examples are narratives of linguistic confrontation in which the links between ethnic identity and language use are explicitly addressed.

The Judge's Office

The event occurred in the judge's office in Ocongate, a small town in southern Peru. A woman had come to complain to the judge that she had been beaten and insulted by her husband. She told her story first, in Quechua, while the husband was made to wait outside. He was then called in to give his account of events. He started to explain in Spanish that he could not confirm or deny what his wife had said as he had been drunk and had subsequently forgotten everything. The judge cut him short annoyed that he was speaking in Spanish. *'Manachu runasimita yachanki? Eres misti o qué cosa? '* (Don't you know Quechua? Are you a misti or what?) The man repeated his short account in Quechua. The woman then spoke again in Quechua, crying and telling the judge of what had happened to her and how her husband mistreated her and her children. Having heard both sides of the story the judge intervened. Speaking in Quechua he started by stating that drunkenness was no excuse for the man's behaviour. He expressed particular concern over the mistreatment of the children and tried to explain to the man that children have a distinct psychology. At this point he started moving between Quechua and Spanish as he found difficulty in expressing some of the concepts he was trying to communicate in Quechua. The increasing use of Spanish also coincided with a softening attitude towards the husband. The judge finally ordered that the man be detained in the police post for 24 hours but explained to me afterwards that not everyone accepted their punishment as quietly as this man had: *'otros contestan gritando, pero este hombre es buena persona bien razonable'* (others answer back shouting, but this man is a good man, very reasonable). He respected the man for in turn respecting his authority, a respect that could have been communicated by the use of Spanish.

To contextualise this example, I would need to explain some of the complex connotations that lie behind the linguistic manoeuvres, and consider particularly the ethnic tensions that these exchanges reveal.

The couple had travelled to visit the judge from the hinterland of Ocongate, the district capital in which state services such as the schools, the police, the town hall and the judges are concentrated. In relation to the couple, the judge is a paternal figure, authorised by powers beyond the village at the provincial and departmental level. A judge seeks to apply both local knowledge and external authority in the exercise of his office. Dynamics of gender and ethnicity were clearly in play from the start of the interaction and were manifest in distinctions of dress, posture, and language. The woman was a monolingual Quechua speaker, both the men were bilingual.

Why did the man try to speak in Spanish when the conversation had already commenced in Quechua, the common language for all participants? One effect of his use of Spanish was to distinguish himself from his wife and simultaneously associate himself with the judge. It is also possible that by extension he hoped to evoke a parallel sense of authority to that of the judge whose position is clearly bolstered by an appeal to literacy, manifest in the extreme bureaucracy attending all his dealings. However, what the man actually said stood in contrast to this use of Spanish. He immediately appealed to his drunkenness. This appeal evoked a justification in terms of a particular 'Indian' sociality in which persons are commonly deemed not responsible for their actions while drunk and indeed it is quite usual for people to forget everything they said and did when drunk (Harvey 1991). However it would have been problematic to state this defence in Quechua. To do so might have the effect of distancing judge from defendant, and furthermore reveal that distance as one of ethnic difference. To make the claim in Spanish would muddle this distinction. However, the judge was not having it, and interpreting, even exaggerating this implicit claim to ethnic identity (as *misti*) he challenged the man over his language use. The judge implied that to speak Spanish in his office you had to be a *misti*. This category was produced *as if* it were self-evident, and as if it were also self-evident that the defendant could not claim that status.

The term *misti* operates locally in opposition to the category Indian – more usually euphemistically replaced by the term *campesino*. In the example given here, the judge uses the term *misti* to denote the non-Indian, the respected citizen, one who holds authority backed by knowledge and experience from a world beyond the village, a paternal figure.[11]

Having heard both sides of the argument the judge distances himself from the ('Indian') convention of memory loss through drunkenness. He also further distinguishes himself from the man by appealing to knowledge of child psychology, information that so clearly derives from outside the local area that it became impossible to speak about in Quechua. The man meanwhile did not challenge the judge's authority in any way. He allowed the judge to categorise, to establish the parameters of difference.

It is clear from this example that it was not equivalent for the parties to this interaction to speak in Spanish or Quechua. Spanish carried a particular moral status in this case, not uncontested, but because the judge was in a position to impose his interpretation and to prevent challenge, he was able to establish the context in which his point of view could be validated.

What interests me about this example is that despite the fact that we have an apparently very clear cut case, one that I might not have had difficulties in saying who said what to whom and in which language, the dynamics of the situation would have been lost in an approach which took the relative status of participants for granted. The judge had to prevent the man from speaking Spanish in order to assert his authority, he could only show himself as *misti* by creating the distance between himself and the man. Once he had established his authority through an appeal to that possibility and once he was sure that he was not being challenged that kind of absolute distinction became less important. He could then carry on an interaction that was more ambiguous in terms of these 'identities'. In fact by the end of the interchange the similarities between the two men in terms of gender and moral uprightness were more to the fore. By the end of the meeting the woman's complaint had been put to one side as the judge pointed out to me what a nice and reasonable man he had been dealing with.

Ascension Day

The occasion was the Ascension Day festival, which is the initial stage of the huge Corpus Christi procession to the shrine of the Señor de Qoyllorrit'i. The shrine is situated on the slopes of Mount Sinakara and linked in both mythology and close geographical location to the powerful mountain spirit of Ausangate that dominates the landscape of the Ocongate region. The miraculous Christ figure, whose form appears etched on a rock around which the high mountain chapel has been built, attracts about 20,000 pilgrims to the annual festival.[12] Antonio, a man from Chakachimpa had received the junior of two ritual responsibilities (*cargos*) for the coming year. From the outside Chakachimpa tends to be thought of as part of the town of Ocongate, although internally the relationship between the two is ambiguous, the people of Chakachimpa claiming a degree of autonomy in response to a sense of superiority common among Ocongate residents. Antonio had taken the image of the Christ from the Church in Ocongate, across the river to his house. Here a vigil would be kept until the Privosti, the senior *cargo* holder from Ocongate, came to fetch it. During the vigil, groups of dancers came to the house to pay their respects to the image. Two men from Ocongate, representatives of the Brotherhood that manages the Qoyllorrit'i shrine and known in this capacity as *celadores*, were also present. Their function was to ensure that the vigil was carried out correctly and with respect. Alcohol and coca were passed round. Before long, a fight broke out between the leader of one of the dance groups (the Ch'unchos) and the *celadores*. The dancer had failed to leave his whip on the altar, and the *celadores* decided to impose their authority. Their approach was somewhat heavy-handed and insults began to fly. Both sides used Quechua to hurl abuses at each other, but each used it in different ways.

The dancer added the Quechua diminutive suffixes to the *celadores'* Christian names while the *celadores* addressed the dancer in Quechua, and called him an Indian, adding that the term had positive connotations in comparison to the brute he was.

Several hours later, another argument broke out. The Privosti's wife arrived saying that her husband was drunk and unable to come and collect the image that should be handed over to her brother who was accompanying her. Antonio refused, saying in Quechua that he could only hand it over to the Privosti himself. He said that the village authorities had given him this *cargo* as a responsible and respected member of the community and he therefore had to carry out his responsibilities to the letter.

The captain of another dance group (the Qollas) tried to intervene with a suggestion in Spanish and was promptly told by Antonio to speak in Quechua.

In terms of the contextualisation of this narrative it is important to point out that the problem was not directly connected to the fact that people were drinking. Despite the best efforts of the Catholic authorities, the cult of this miraculous Christ is enacted in ways that stress indigenous forms of sociality, and commensality is an important principle.[13] During a vigil the host will ply guests with alcohol and coca. This means of establishing connections on an equal basis with all who visit the image and simultaneously drawing in those forces that animate the landscape, through libations to the Earth and the hill spirits, is seen as totally appropriate behaviour.

The confrontations were about contested authority. The *celadores* represented external institutional control and the contested hierarchical relationship between Ocongate and Chakachimpa. Despite its regional importance and semi-integration into the Catholic Church, the power of this shrine locally derives as strongly from its association with the hill spirits and the special relationship between the miraculous Christ, the dancers, and the people of the town as it does with the Church, which the cult manages effectively to by-pass. The attempts by the *celadores* to actually impose their standards of propriety were therefore clearly going to be inflammatory. Language played a crucial role in the dynamics of the conflict as it was through language, and in particular the contrasting uses of Quechua or Spanish that people tried to categorise and simultaneously demean each other.

The first exchange was in Quechua. In a ritual context such as this, the use of Quechua could have been entirely appropriate, respectful and affectionate – acknowledging a common local identity and attachment to the Quechua speaking forces of the landscape. Potential ambiguities were rife however. The dancer's use of Quechua could easily be interpreted as an attempt to undermine the external authority of the *celadores* by appealing to the alternative authority of local community. Such a suspicion would have been strengthened by the dancer's use of diminutive suffixes that were particularly mocking as they work as modes of endearment in Spanish but as demeaning insults in Quechua. The *celadores* were quite explicitly using Quechua to demean, and referred directly to Quechua as the language of the *indio bruto*. Similar forms with potentially contradictory connotations were juxtaposed in this exchange. On the one hand, Quechua, which carries the possibility of the language of local community, and can invoke an inclusive moral consensus which draws together the human and the spirit world, also enacted in the consumption of alcohol and coca; on the other hand, Quechua as the language of the Indian, the subordinate to *misti* authority and civilisation validated from the outside by institutions associated with wider knowledge and more encompassing morality – here most concretely manifest in the wider institution of the Catholic Church.

Things calmed down until the Privosti's wife arrived. Antonio was anxious to avoid another confrontation with the *celadores* which had shown so clearly that their outside authority was not welcome locally, but which had also produced their powerful response, the insult to local indigenous identity, the source of Antonio's own authority in this event. He attempted to re-establish this authority as *cargo* holder and recover the connotation of respect and affection appropriate to that indigenous identity. If he could sustain the use of Quechua he might be able to emphasise the sense in which Ocongate and Chakachimpa constitute a single local religious community and pre-empt the alternative more divisive and exclusionary interpretations of identity claims which stress the difference between Spanish and Quechua speakers.

When the captain of the Qollas, a university student home for the vacation, tried to support him in Spanish, Antonio turned on him. It was obviously important to Antonio that the conversation remain in Quechua. He had been speaking extensively in this language, defending his authority as *cargo* holder, and he was not going to have this position undermined by being ranked as a Quechua speaker in opposition to the Spanish speakers present. He could maintain his position by not allowing the language switch. Drunk, he dared to stand up to the Spanish speakers by declaring Quechua as the language of authority.

These two examples reflect a particular concern on my part to look at the workings of power and interest. The analysis aims to show how identities are never stable and always require recognition from others to be rendered effective. Identities are thus intersubjective and embedded in social relations. Language is one of the symbolic activities which acts as a medium for such relations, and which carries the complexities and indeterminacies of meaning that are precisely the stuff from which human interactions produce the mirages of stability.

This interpretation can be further contextualised in terms of theoretical debates about identity in the Andes and beyond, and can thus take on the more specific form of anthropological knowledge. In my opinion the ethnicity debates in Andean studies have been seriously hampered by the cultural construct model which focuses on the *mestizo* and the indian as distinct coherent and singular (even if complex) identities, categories to which particular groups of people can be more or less happily assigned, with a vague blurred middle zone where terminology gets more confused and we find the *cholo*, or 'problems' of upward or downward mobility. However I also think that the Andes provides a very particular challenge to anthropological theories of identity which those working in, for example, Melanesia do not have to face in quite the same way. As writers such as Wagner (1991) and Strathern (1991b) have pointed out, western theories of identity, and the cultural constructionist approach, take as their starting point the distinction between individual and society – a distinction which is seen as most inappropriate and external to Melanesian understandings of sociality. Writers on Western sociality note the historical specificity of this concept (Handler 1994) and the ways in which a focus on identity obscures understandings of the relationships that sustain the plausibility of autonomous entities in social life. However in the Andean region, with 500 years of co-existence with Western thought it is not surprising that many local institutions and discourses resonate, even reproduce the categories of Western jurisprudence and political ideologies, not to mention the social and spiritual concerns filtered through the teachings of the Catholic Church. Andean cultural practice can never exist apart from these ideas (in the ways that the practices of Melanesia can be said to do so)[14] for they have been forged in relationship to them and thus must incorporate them, even in strategies of radical rejection.

Thus I can state, following Wagner, that it is important to recognise that it is the cultural construct model and the links between identity and coherence that makes a problem for social theorists and associated policy makers, out of what I take to be a common Andean desire to be simultaneously mestizo and indian, and to embrace thereby both individualist and collectivist socialities. If however we look simply at people in relationships it is possible to see that the simultaneity of *mestizo* and indian sociality is an effect of interaction. And here the parallel with the Melanesian analyses is more visible: 'a fractal person is never a unit standing in relation to an aggregate, or an aggregate standing in relation to a unit, but always an entity with relationship integrally implied' (Wagner, 1991: 163).

These examples thus present two kinds of knowledge. The anthropological knowledge is that achieved via both ethnographic and theoretical contextualisation. While acknowledgedly partial and particular it also constitutes a certain claim to expertise that then awaits refutation or confirmation from other experts. However my presentation also seeks to show that for those involved what really matters are the immediate effects of the exchanges. They are engaged in particular confrontations and are attending to the consequences of previous interactions. There are constructs and contextual features which participants manage to render salient in the process of social interaction but there is no enduring objectification. The problem with the metaphor of the construct is that it renders this process static.

A provisional contrast could thus be drawn between a move from interpretation to anthropological knowledge via a process of legitimation which appeals explicitly to contextualising practice, and the embodied knowledge of social actors which is brought to bear in their engagement with the immediate circumstances of everyday life. However the contextualising practices which these actors employ suggest that such distinctions are far from absolute.

Expo '92 – Excessive Contextualisation

The Expo study produced and mediated this contrast in a rather different way. Indeed the Expo '92 seems to have generated par excellence the kind of model of itself that Strathern is seeking to combat or at least draw attention to in her critique of the ubiquity of the cultural construct in anthropological accounts. This might be because the Expo was so clearly located within particular Western cultural and political practices, simultaneously highly modernist yet also hyper-aware of itself as such and of the artifice of its own forms and practices.

One hundred and twelve nations participated in the Expo together with multinational companies such as Siemens and Fujitsu. Over 40 million visits were made to the site during the six months, from April to October 1992, that the fair occupied the Island of La Cartuja in Seville. It is important to appreciate the extent to which the Expo was produced for public consumption and how much of what was going on there was therefore highly accessible. There were press packs, daily bulletins, reams of printed information, videos, postcards, guidebooks, maps and even architects drawings. There was also a continual running commentary in the national and international media. In other words the event was produced textually, you did not actually have to go to Seville to find out a great deal about the Expo.

As a Universal Exhibition, Expo '92 was in many ways a typical instance of this highly modernist institution and as such it reproduced many of the forms and intentions of the universal fairs of the 19th century. Nation-states displayed cultural artefacts and technological expertise in their individual pavilions, seeking to educate and entertain the visiting public. The obligations of the organisers of a fair with universal status are less concerned with the actual bringing together of exhibitors from all over the globe than with enacting a theme that simultaneously promotes the unity of mankind and the uniqueness of individual societies. The theme for Expo '92 was 'The Age of Discoveries'.

Yet in its late 20th-century guise this universal fair distinguished itself from the fairs of the previous century in the degree to which it exhibited an awareness of itself, of its own history and its own artifice. The exhibitors mused on the nature of modernity and explicitly addressed the central issues in sociological debates about globalisation such as: multiculturalism and the plural nature of society, the links between the global and the local, the temporal and the universal, the ironic play with similarity and difference, the familiar and the strange, the traditional and the modern, uniqueness and wholeness, discontinuity and continuity.

The integrating effects of electronic technologies, global capital and the shared simultaneity of televisual media were also addressed in the exhibits. The Expo itself was in many ways constituted through these possibilities. The histories of technological innovation were displayed, although not all nations chose to promote the same version of modernity. In most general terms there was a clear distinction between those nations who sought to display the development of resources, the production of wealth and the promotion of health and education, and those who played with the possibilities of hyper-reality afforded by the most recent innovations in communications technologies and the commodification inherent in capitalism. These distinctions clearly illustrated the tensions between production and consumption as possible foci in contemporary considerations of the nature of modernity.

Familiar questions of identity were also highlighted. Thus while the Expo marketed the nation-state, sought to display national cultures and promote them as commodities to be consumed by tourists and business investors, some exhibitors were also raising quite explicitly the question of 'what is a nation'? The exhibits were in many ways providing the visitor with contextual information for 'knowing' about the particular nations and contemporary society more generally. They gave information on sources, influences and points of origin but they did not pretend to be in any way exhaustive.

An explicit guiding principle for many of the national pavilions was the desire to disrupt stereotypes. Peru for example had very little Inka material in an attempt to show that they could trace their history back twenty-seven centuries beyond the Inkas. Japan concentrated on tradition rather than technology and Britain took the reverse tactic, working against an image of isolationist tradition-bound nation of Beefeaters, Welsh ladies, Scottish kilts and Morris dancers. Late 20th-century Britain is the nation that constructed The Channel Tunnel, and is thus linked to Europe with the latest communications technologies, a vibrant economic force in the contemporary world.

Other challenges to the stereotype were more radical and worked against the concept of the nation altogether. Switzerland for example greeted pavilion visitors with a Ben Vautier artwork from 1935 consisting of the message: 'Switzerland does not exist'. The accompanying explanation pointed out that there was no common culture or language in Switzerland. This starting point of their exhibition, the challenge posed by the lack of a common linguistic and cultural foundation for their national identity was dealt with in their exhibit that suggested a solution in communicative multiplicity, summed up in the slogan *'je pense donc je suisse'*.

Another very radical exhibit was that of Czechoslovakia – a pavilion that housed a glass sculpture displayed through a show of light and sound. The Czechoslovakians had deposed a Communist government during the planning stages of the Expo and the new organisers had held a competition for the design of the interior of the pavilion. This abstract modern sculpture had won by nine votes to seven. The judges had liked it because they believed that it would produce a memorable experience for those who visited. They thought that the experience of engaging with the exhibit, of using it to explore one's own fantasies and associations, was a worthwhile memory of the Expo. They said that other displays of culture and history would soon be forgotten. Furthermore they had wanted to distance themselves from the content of their recent past. The Commissioner with whom I spoke had been on the selection panel and had himself favoured an exhibit which consisted just of a space of grass, a flag pole and the Czech flag – no past just a new future.

The Expo, so clearly located within particular Western cultural and political practices, thus seems to provide an example of the effects of cultural constructionism that Strathern associated with a particular form of Western representational practice. It provides a concrete instance of the nightmare of endless replication, a cultural artefact built as if to demonstrate the possibilities and limitations of an entirely consumerist world. Thus there is the appearance of choice, of multiple perspectives, yet the cultural forms on show are nevertheless clearly reformulations and repetitions of each other. Sameness and familiarity undermine the promise of difference.[15]

As suggested above it is not just proliferation but also implosion that accompanies the notion of the construct. How should we approach the relationship between interpretation and context in an institution which itself is already reflexively utilising the techniques and knowledges that social scientists are still grappling to comprehend and transform into metaphorical idioms for the purposes of description?

The Siemens exhibit evoked an image of the relationship between tradition and innovation in which innovation is simply tradition transformed – a point illustrated by the auditorium seats circling around the same spaces whose contents were transformed and recontextualised as you reapproached them. The message they conveyed was that transformations in communications technologies developed until isolated systems reached their limits. Then came the most recent transformation, the evolution of networks and the merging of systems. A film that was also about the evolution of networks had a philosophy credit. My sense of anthropology as a rather pale reflection of the cultural idioms of our time was growing. Anthropologists were not the only ones moving from identities to relationships, we were simply using metaphors that had lives and uses well ahead of our appropriation.

I have suggested that the Expo is about the public production of image and discourse. In this sense it is perhaps the archetypal form for those cultural theorists who treat culture as text, as construct, as fodder for hermeneutics. Like it or not, the event is vastly over-interpreted on every front, and that over-interpretation is part of what constitutes the event. Cultural forms are interpreted quite promiscuously in the promotional literature. Meaning is attributed to objects as required for the wider argument. As a textually produced event, it was also impossible not to pre-interpret. Before I went I already knew a lot about the history, politics and the economics of this institution and its particular occurrence in Seville. However at another level this process of interminable interpretation was a quite inappropriate response to this event.

My initial response to finding myself on the Expo site was that overwhelming sense of alienation that I associate with being a tourist. There was a huge amount going on but it was very hard to work out what. For example I suddenly came across an Indonesian procession – people began to line the walkway to watch and they dispersed again when it had passed by. As might be expected at the start of fieldwork, you do not quite know what is going on locally, although you sense that you could find out if only you knew how. Then something else happens which grabs your attention and that of other people, a crowd forms, an event occurs although you are not quite sure what it is, as it passes you by, and then people get on with what they were doing before. The activity is something you watch, something that is happening outside of you, you do not know where it comes from, where it is going to, what it is for or what it is about – it is just there.

It is important for me to address these first impressions because my subsequent understanding of what was happening was one of the ways in which my experience at Expo must have differed from that of many visitors. But I also want to point out that much of my early confusion resulted from my ambition to understand. Unpractised in the ways of living Western leisure parks, I was of course behaving in a totally inappropriate way. Experiences were being laid before me for me to enjoy.[16]

What did it mean then to do anthropology of this event? Whose knowledge would I be attempting to approximate/translate? The event was obviously highly complex, but the problem was not simply one of how to handle a multiplicity of perspectives, although it is true that I could envisage no obvious point of identification through which to produce a generalisable ethnographic subject, which would not simultaneously prevent me from understanding the wider event. The problem was not to do with the complexity of the event but with the challenge it offered to our conceptions of ethnographic knowledge, and our abilities to present such knowledge.

Anthropologists might normally expect to produce this knowledge through a detailed observation of their relationships with those with whom they are living and working. We look at how people react to us, and how they react to others in our presence. We seek to identify the various ways in which we might be participating in a particular event. Furthermore because we are looking at cultural 'others' it is sufficient to understand the relationship between us to know something about how those we study live their relationships. At the Expo my anthropological insights were clearly idiosyncratic. Expo was designed for rapid consumption, for fleeting visits, people queued for hours to get into most pavilions. Most visitors see relatively little of the whole and what they did see they tended to see quickly. To study these fleeting experiences would have taken me away from the event into the huge diversity of the lives of the visitors. I took another route, equally problematic. Working with a press pass, I could see more, and see it more easily. I could stay longer, I had a chance to go back and to get different kinds of explanatory materials. However, the fact of being there did not mean that I was participating.

How does this differ from the standard experience of anthropological fieldwork? Traditional ethnographers sit in the village. Lack of understanding is like that of a child, and we attempt to catch up on a learning experience. It could be argued, as Clifford has done (1992), that the site of anthropological knowledge is no longer the village or the house, but is more comparable to the motel or the hotel lobby, a space through which people move. His point is that the world is not static and anthropology is having difficulty in maintaining the fiction of a stable context for the social relations we describe. But this image of movement does not quite capture my problem. I became increasingly aware that there was not necessarily any particular knowledge to be recovered in the sense of patiently piecing together the implicit knowledge of those around me. In a very short time, I knew more about what was going on than most visitors, yet at the same time I did not know, and could not find out from sitting there, how the visitors were contextualising these experiences for themselves. When I asked two British visitors what they thought about the UK pavilion, they said that it was better than the Welsh Garden Festival but not as good as

Disney. Their evaluation entailed a contextualisation in terms that were not available to me through participant observation of the event itself. What does that say about the notion of context that anthropologists implicitly work with? Putting things into their social context implies the attempt to make explicit the connections that are made by people as they live their relations to other people and to things (Strathern 1995). An understanding of the process of contextualisation has always implied looking beyond the immediate, available interactions, but we have also maintained the notion that those experiences would become available through the period of extended participant observation, indeed this is the rationale for our extended periods of fieldwork. In a situation such as Expo that is quite patently not the case.

Furthermore it cannot be argued that I was basically trying to recover the experience of those with whom I was interacting. This British couple who were highly suspicious of me approaching them, thinking that I was probably trying to sell them a time-share, did a deal to talk with me in order to swap information. They would tell me what they thought about the British pavilion, if I would tell them what I knew about what was going on and what they should go and see. Thus by studying Expo I was in effect cutting myself off from the experience of those around me. This again is an aspect of all ethnographic research as illustrated by the Peru examples. However, in the Expo it had a twist. Basically, by doing anthropology at Expo, by trying to articulate for myself something of the way in which it was operating as a cultural event, by constantly trying to contextualise what I saw and heard, I would inevitably get involved in a kind of grotesque parody of the event itself.

The Expo, as cultural event, played with the idea of context, showed it to be both about accumulating and adding knowledge, enabling links between nations, uniting them in various evolutionary histories from 1492-1992 and beyond. The event was explicitly constructed to convey certain meanings and contexts were required to interpret these modernist messages and to reveal the processes through which nations and multinationals were or were not successfully produced as viable social entities which could then be brought into relationships. But the contexts were not implicit, they were on display and their display produced a parallel, but different set of effects. Culture was everywhere, each nation had some. It appeared in multiple guises, as high art, civilisation, history, identity, daily life, and evolutionary process. The pluralism was presented as a series of options. Culture, visible as a construct, is simply a matter of choice or image to be consumed, effective if it played into particular emotional responses and provoked pleasure or stimulated desire for further consumption. The cultural constructionism of Western representational practice now appears integral to the embodied knowledge of social actors, and the problem for anthropology is that this process appears to undermine both the expertise of academic knowledge and the authenticity of the subjects concerned.

Conclusions

The Expo and the Peruvian examples can be used to draw out a contrast between concepts of culture, understandings of context and kinds of knowledge that are produced through the interpretative process. My concern in the conclusion is to consider the relationship between (i) knowledge as representation and (ii) knowledge as effect[17], and between the Western and Melanesian models discussed in the introduction. Knowledge as representation indicates a process in which a particular state of affairs, the context, is held to be foundational, and at least in this perspective, stable and enduring. In the second case it is the instability and contingency of what is known that is foregrounded. Now context is itself emergent, not prior, and understanding of what might momentarily be deemed stable and foundational is achieved via interaction and through attention to social effects. These two approaches can themselves be taken as two alternative perspectives but they do not operate as choices that can be brought together in the way that the Expo ranged cultural choice for the consumer. Contexts cannot be simultaneously generative and emergent. To thus confuse effect with cause makes it impossible to account for the cultural specificity of how certain conditions come to operate as more foundational than others. The advantage of juxtaposing these two positions is to highlight the ways in which a consideration of context is in itself a consideration of social relations and the workings of creative and/or coercive power. The Expo '92 study is used here to recontextualise the Peru study and to direct attention to the ways in which these two possibilities, knowledge as representation and knowledge as effect do, nevertheless, feed into each other. Perhaps the problem for contemporary anthropology is the awareness that these (and presumably other) perspectival options do not necessarily amount to knowing more or knowing 'better' because to focus on effect is to efface the preconditions and reconfigure the terms of interaction.

If we return to the examples of linguistic interaction in the Andes it is clear that we can interpret the interactions both through an appeal to foundational preconditions (context) and through the recognition of particular effects (the processes of recontextualisation). The conversations I described were shown to be dependent on interpretative outcomes, themselves situated within parameters of possibility, which are entirely cultural/contingent despite their self-evidence to the parties concerned. It is precisely this link between the contingent and the naturalised which can be explored through a focus on the relationship between context and interpretation. If the implication of this approach is, as Sperber seems to suggest that anthropologists can only interpret rather than describe, it also implies that the ways in which description and interpretation are made to differ are themselves crucial. My interest in this field is in how certain aspects of social interaction come to hold the status of the self-evident, how interpretations come to take on the status of descriptions. Sperber and Wilson's (1986) account of ostensive-inferential communication, for example, seeks to establish a certain stability or descriptive account which transcends the vagaries of interpretation and enables them to explain how it is that people do manage to communicate despite the unpredictability of contextual effects. The principle they invoke is that of 'relevance'.[18] However, it is interesting, that this descriptive possibility itself requires a very restricted definition of communication, ostensive-inferential communication, in which communication is only deemed to have occurred if the communicative intent of the speaker is recovered. Descriptive adequacy in this model can thus only be achieved at the expense of any account of the kinds of examples which I gave above, examples which demonstrated the ways in which people ignore, misconstrue, confuse and deny the intentions of others.

Thus for Sperber and Wilson, as much as for the Andean speakers, attempts to fix certain assumptions as foundational, are, when looked at in terms of effects, about making certain possibilities visible at the expense of others. In the Peru study this raised questions about relative power, questions which we can now bring to bear on the production of anthropological (or philosophical) knowledge. In the Peru study I, as anthropologist, was seeking to identify the foundational assumptions which were implicit in the workings of the dialogues, the patterns and expectations which were activated in the interactions. In the Expo study, by contrast, I was forced to watch myself doing this, as the Expo fascinated visitors by its displays of effects, producing contexts and constructs for visitors to consume, as both representations and as the vehicles for straight sensation. Strathern (1991a) has emphasised the difficulty of using the concept of perspective (context) once awareness of it is brought into play. When distinct perspectives are set alongside each other, as choices for viewers, we experience the 'multiplier effect of innumerable perspectives', the idea that no context or perspective can ever provide an adequate account. The term 'post-pluralism' acknowledges the recognition that increased diversity entails loss. Analytic attention is thus redirected to the lack which perspective entails rather than the possibilities of totalising vistas which perspective might have entailed in a pluralist framework. In a post-plural cultural environment, the notions of context and culture thus lose explanatory force and the focus on effects emerges as a more appropriate analytical language.

However, there is a twist. As the Expo study makes clear, it is not just anthropological theory that had become aware of the partial nature of the connections that our concepts of context and culture afford. The social and cultural processes through which these possibilities emerged also generated other cultural forms, such as the Expo itself. Here we find that the kind of 'culture' which is displayed, is one that can achieve the effect of highly commensurable difference, a commodified object not far removed from our familiar Western social scientific concept of the construct. The notion of the cultural construct is one that celebrates multiplicity, perspectives can always be added and the model is thus highly productive in an environment in which both specificity and connectedness are valued. Expo '92 reveals that the cultural construct is a late 20th-century artefact that can now endlessly reproduce itself, continually opening new perspectives that effectively undermine the possibilities for producing that generalised knowledge of power and interest on which critical scholarship has traditionally depended. It is this dilemma which sustains, even generates concern over the tension between knowledge as representation and knowledge as effect.

How then might we conduct a critical anthropology at the turn of the century? Context will remain an important concept but one to be used attentively. The Expo study demonstrates why it is important to try and understand the contexts of our own cultural production, for these contexts produce both the commodified pluralism of the Expo '92 and the possibilities for critical analysis. If contextualisation gives us the possibility of talking about relationships, about scale, about comparison and allows us to observe the exercise of power, it also 'fits' our cultural conceit that knowing where something came from will tell you what it is. What I have tried to show in this chapter, is that such knowledge, the ways in which we hold things stable in order to explain, should become the focus of our analytical attention. It is the conditions that sustain particular ways of knowing that we should be attentive to if we are to sustain a critically useful sense of 'context'.

Notes

1. Thanks to Nikos Papastergiadis and Patrick Joyce for their extremely interesting discussion of these points.
2. *See* for example: Clifford and Marcus 1986, Clifford 1988, Fardon 1990, Strathern 1987a, b and 1991, Ullin 1991.
3. *See* for example: Asad 1986, Clifford 1988, Foucault 1980, Said 1989, Stocking 1983.

4. Strathern (1992a) has made the point that the cultural construct is not an exclusively anthropological formulation. It is one that is shared by many cultural analysts and implicitly lies behind the critical project of deconstruction which seeks to denaturalise, reveal and rewrite.

5. This is an agenda which Sperber has been seeking to establish for anthropology since his 1985 publication *On Anthropological Knowledge* in which he criticises the general application of the linguistic or communicative model in anthropological analysis. More recently Ingold (1993) has challenged Sperber's cognitivist approach while maintaining the importance of the study of cognition for contemporary anthropology.

6. James F. Wiener will notice the effects of our conversations here.

7. The initial stages of this research (1983-85) were funded by the ESRC for a Ph.D. in social anthropology, *see* Harvey 1987. Two subsequent research visits were also made in 1987, funded by the British Academy and in 1988, funded by the Nuffield Foundation (Harvey 1994a, b, c).

8. Research on the Expo carried out in 1992 was initially conceived together with Laura Rival and was funded by British Academy.

9. *See* for example Gumperz 1982, Hymes 1974, Levinson 1983.

10. My thanks to Peter Gow for drawing this metaphor to my attention.

11. Women are not *mistis*.

12. For detailed discussion of the pilgrimage to this shrine see Sallnow (1987).

13. This aspect is less visible at the shrine itself where the Brotherhood have strong control and where commercial interests make the communal meals and integration of the dance troops less easy to see.

14. I should point out that much of Strathern's work challenges the idea that all cultural understandings can be rendered analogous through comparison. Her rich discussion of the specifics of incommensurability, argued through the ethnography of Melanesia, is not dealt with here except implicitly in discussion of contrasting notions of identity and origin.

15. See Strathern (1992a) for a parallel discussion of new reproductive technologies.

16. This distinction is acknowlegedly problematic as much enjoyment itself depended on at least a recognition of the intrinsic inter-textuality of the event and thus on interpretative practice. It is thus not interpretation *per se* which causes problems but the links between interpretation and a more encompassing knowledge of the event. I am grateful to the graduate students of the Anthropology Board, University of California at Santa Cruz for bringing this point up for discussion.

17. See Fabian chapter 4 for a similar distinction between knowledge as representation and knowledge as practice.

18. The principle of relevance appears to be a philosophical equivalent to the 'principle of charity' on which Pascal Engels elaborated at the conference in St Andrews.

Bibliography

Asad, T. 1986. 'The concept of cultural translation in British social anthropology'. In J. Clifford and G. Marcus (eds), *Writing culture*: 146-64. Berkeley: University of California Press.

Bloch, M. (ed.). 1975. *Political language and oratory in traditional society*. London: Academic Press.

Bourdieu, P. 1977. 'The economics of linguistic exchange'. *Social Science Information*, SVI:6: 645-68.

————— .1984. *Homo academicus*. Oxford: Polity Press.

Clifford, J. 1988. *The predicament of culture: twentieth century ethnography, literature and art*. Cambridge, M.A.: Harvard University Press

—————. 1992. 'Traveling cultures', in L. Grossberg, C. Nelson and P. Treichler (eds), *Cultural studies*: 96-116. New York: Routledge.

—————. and George Marcus. 1986. *Writing culture*. Berkeley: University of California Press

Fardon, R. (ed.). 1990. *Localizing strategies: regional traditions of ethnographic writing*. Edinburgh: University Press; Washington: Smithsonian Institution Press.

Foucault, M. 1980. *Power/knowledge: selected interviews and other writings 1972-77*. C. Gordon (ed.). Brighton: Harvester.

Gumperz, J. 1982. *Discourse strategies*. Cambridge: Cambridge University Press.

Handler, R. 1994. 'Is "identity" a useful cross-cultural concept?'. In J. Gillis (ed.), *Commemorations: the politics of national identity*. Princeton: Princeton University Press.

Harvey, P. 1987. *Language and the power of history: the discourse of bilinguals in Ocongate (southern Peru)*. Ph.D. dissertation: London School of Economics.

—————. 1991. 'Drunken speech and the construction of meaning – bilingual competence in the southern Peruvian Andes'. *Language in Society* 20:1: 1-36.

—————. 1994a. 'Gender, community and confrontation: power relations in drunkenness in Ocongate (southern Peru)'. In M. McDonald (ed.), *Gender, drink and drugs*: 209-33. Oxford: Berg.

—————. 1994b. 'The presence and absence of speech in the communication of gender'. In P. Burton, K. Dyson and S. Ardener (eds), *Bilingual women: anthropological approaches to second langauge use*: 44-64. Oxford: Berg.

—————. 1994c. 'Domestic violence in the Peruvian Andes'. In P. Harvey and P. Gow (eds), *Sex and violence: issues in representation and experience*. London: Routledge

Hymes, D. 1974. *Foundations in sociolinguistics: an ethnographic approach*. Philadelphia: University of Pennsylvania Press.

Ingold, T. 1993. Technology, language, intelligence: a reconsideration of basic concepts. In K. Gibson and T. Ingold (eds), *Tools, language and cognition in human evolution*. Cambridge: Cambridge University Press.

Latour, B. 1993. *We have never been modern*. Trans. C. Porter. Cambridge M.A.: Harvard University Press.

Levinson, S. 1983. *Pragmatics*. Cambridge: Cambridge University Press.

Robertson, R. 1992. *Globalization: social theory and global culture*. London: Sage.

Said, E. 1989. 'Representing the colonized: anthropology's interlocutors'. *Critical Inquiry* 15(2): 205-25.

Sallnow, M. 1987. *Pilgrims of the Andes: regional cults in Cusco*. Washington DC: Smithsonian Institution Press.

Sperber, D. 1985. *On anthropological knowledge*. Cambridge: Cambridge University Press.

Sperber, D. and D. Wilson. 1986. *Relevance: communication and cognition*. Oxford: Basil Blackwell.

Stocking, G. (ed.). 1983. *Observers observed: essays on ethnographic fieldwork.* Madison: University of Wisconsin Press.

Strathern, M. 1987a. 'The limits of auto-anthropology'. In A. Jackson (ed.), *Anthropology at home.* London: Tavistock Publications.

————.1987b. 'Out of context: the persuasive fictions of anthropology'. *Current anthropology* 28(3): 251-81.

————.1991a. *Partial connections.* Lanham, M.D..: Rowman & Littlefield Publishers Inc.

————. 1991b. 'Introduction'. In M. Godelier and M. Strathern (eds), *Big men and great men: personifications of power in Melanesia.* Cambridge: Cambridge University Press.

————. 1992a. *Reproducing the future: anthropology, kinship and the new reproductive technologies.* Manchester: Manchester University Press.

————. 1992b. 'The decomposition of an event' *Cultural anthropology* 7(2): 244-54.

————. 1995. *Shifting contexts: Transformations of anthropological knowledge.* London: Routledge.

Ullin, R. 1991. 'Critical anthropology twenty years later: modernism and postmodernism in anthropology'. *Critique of anthropology* II(1): 63-89.

Wagner, R. 1991. 'The fractal person'. In M. Godelier and M. Strathern (eds), *Big men and great men: personifications of power in Melanesia.* Cambridge: Cambridge University Press.

INDEX